www.wadsworth.com

www.wadsworth.com is the World Wide Web site for Wadsworth and is your direct source to dozens of online resources.

At *www.wadsworth.com* you can find out about supplements, demonstration software, and student resources. You can also send email to many of our authors and preview new publications and exciting new technologies.

www.wadsworth.com
Changing the way the world learns®

THE CONTEMPORARY CONGRESS

Fourth Edition

Burdett A. Loomis
UNIVERSITY OF KANSAS

Wendy J. Schiller
BROWN UNIVERSITY

THOMSON

WADSWORTH

Australia • Canada • Mexico • Singapore • Spain
United Kingdom • United States

THOMSON

WADSWORTH

Publisher: *Clark Baxter*
Executive Editor: *David Tatom*
Assistant Editor: *Rebecca Green*
Editorial Assistant: *Reena Thomas*
Technology Project Manager:
Melinda Newfarmer
Marketing Manager: *Janise Fry*
Marketing Assistant: *Mary Ho*
Advertising Project Manager:
Nathaniel Bergson-Michelson
Project Manager, Editorial Production:
Catherine Morris

Print/Media Buyer: *Jessica Reed*
Permissions Editor: *Kiely Sexton*
Production Service:
Stratford Publishing Services
Copy Editor: *Leslie Connor*
Cover Designer: *Brian Salisbury*
Cover Image: *AP Photo/Beth Keiser*
Text and Cover Printer: *Webcom*
Compositor: *Stratford Publishing Services*

For more information about our products,
contact us at:

**Thomson Learning
Academic Resource Center
1-800-423-0563**

For permission to use material from
this text, contact us by:

Phone: 1-800-730-2214
Fax: 1-800-730-2215
Web: http://www.thomsonrights.com

Library of Congress Control Number: 2003108607

ISBN 0-534-17330-6

Wadsworth/Thomson Learning
10 Davis Drive
Belmont, CA 94002-3098
USA

Asia
Thomson Learning
5 Shenton Way #01-01
UIC Building
Singapore 068808

Australia/New Zealand
Thomson Learning
102 Dodds Street
Southbank, Victoria 3006
Australia

Canada
Nelson
1120 Birchmount Road
Toronto, Ontario M1K 5G4
Canada

Europe/Middle East/Africa
Thomson Learning
High Holborn House
50/51 Bedford Row
London WC1R 4LR
United Kingdom

Latin America
Thomson Learning
Seneca, 53
Colonia Polanco
11560 Mexico D.F.
Mexico

Spain/Portugal
Paraninfo
Calle/Magallanes, 25
28015 Madrid, Spain

Contents

Preface

After taking a two-year hiatus, *The Contemporary Congress* returns to its two-year cycle of providing a brief, readable text on Congress. The fourth edition offers all the usual updates, including the most recent information on the 108th Congress, elected in November 2002. Among various changes in this edition, the most important by far is the addition of Professor Wendy Schiller, from Brown University, as a coauthor. With her expertise on the Senate and on distributive politics, along with her practical experience on Capitol Hill, Wendy brings a wealth of enthusiasm and academic stature to the project.

In terms of substance, we provide a much richer context for the continuing ascendancy of Republicans on Capitol Hill. Our sense of the Republican era is more nuanced as we reconsider a Congress that, since 1995, has remained almost exclusively in GOP hands. Indeed, save for the partisan defection of Republican Senator James Jeffords (Vt.) in 2001, which temporarily left the Senate under Democratic control, Republicans would have held control of both chambers for the entire decade following their historic 1994 election sweep. At the same time, GOP majorities have remained narrow and problematic. With the onset of unified Republican party government in 2003, Republican leaders are now experiencing some of the same difficulties in enacting their president's agenda that their Democratic predecessors encountered during the first two years of the Clinton presidency.

Some broad trends have continued apace. For example, congressional committees have consistently lost ground in the battle for power with party leaders. And party leaders have added to their strength by increasing their control over the flow of campaign funds within their caucuses. Moreover, even safe-seat lawmakers have become persistent solicitors of campaign funds, which they then funnel to their partisan colleagues or challengers who are running in competitive races.

We have changed some elements of *The Contemporary Congress*, while retaining its identity as a broad, accessible, and reasonably comprehensive book. We still emphasize the individual legislator's "enterprise" while increasing our focus on congressional parties, which have grown steadily more important during the past twenty-five years. We have also added some recent examples, while not forsaking those past narratives (e.g., Representative Margolies-Mezvinsly's crucial vote on the first Clinton budget in 1993) that help define the nature of the choices in congressional life.

All in all, we remain committed to providing an introduction to the U.S. Congress that integrates academic studies, both classic and recent, with the actual politics of Capitol Hill. Building on our academic research and our past experiences on the Hill, we hope that our continued fascination with Congress—both as real-life institution and object of scholarly inquiry—comes through in this text.

Burdett Loomis
Lawrence, Kansas

Wendy Schiller
Providence, Rhode Island

About the Authors

Burdett A. Loomis is a professor of political science at the University of Kansas. He received his Ph.D. from the University of Wisconsin, Madison, in 1974; served as an American Political Science Congressional Fellow in 1975–1976; and has taught at the University of Kansas since 1979.

He has written on a variety of topics, including Congress, interest groups, state legislatures, and public policy. Among his books are *The New American Politician* (Basic, 1988); *Time, Politics, and Policy: A Legislative Year* (University Press of Kansas, 1994); and *The Sound of Money*, with Darrell West (Norton, 1999). He edited *Esteemed Colleagues: Civility and Deliberation in the United States Senate* (Brookings, 2000) and recently was a coauthor of *Republic on Trial* (CQ Press, 2002), a defense of representative democracy. In addition, he has co-edited six editions of *Interest Group Politics* (CQ Press). At present he is at work on a major project that examines the "industry of politics."

In 1984, Professor Loomis directed the Congressional Management Project, which produced the first of many editions of *Setting Course: A Congressional Management Guide,* a book that helps newly elected legislators in organizing their offices and activities on Capitol Hill. Aside from teaching courses on congressional politics, interest groups, and policy making, since 1983 Professor Loomis has directed public internship programs in Washington and Topeka. He won a Kemper Teaching Award in 1996, in part for his work in establishing the University of Kansas' Washington Semester Program. He lives in Lawrence, Kansas, with his wife Michel and son Dakota.

Wendy J. Schiller is associate professor of political science and public policy at Brown University. She received her Ph.D from the University of Rochester in 1994, was a visiting scholar at Princeton University in 1993–1994, and has been at Brown University since 1994. Prior to getting her doctorate, Professor Schiller was a legislative staff assistant to Senator Daniel P. Moynihan (D-NY) from 1986 to 1988 and a lobbyist for the New York State Office of Federal Affairs under Governor Mario M. Cuomo from 1988 to 1989.

She has published work on bill sponsorship, the dynamics of Senate delegations, and interest group lobbying on trade politics. Her book *Partners and*

Rivals: Representation in U.S. Senate Delegations was published by Princeton University Press (2000). She is currently working on a book that examines the effects of political geography and bicameralism on interest group lobbying in trade, environmental, and agricultural policy.

At Brown, Dr. Schiller teaches courses on parties and interest groups, Congress and public policy, and introductory statistics. She lives in Providence, Rhode Island.

One
THE DRAMA OF
REPRESENTATION

T he U.S. Congress is, to be sure, a national political institution. But its roots are planted in 435 constituencies, each of which engages in its own biennial electoral drama. Every two years, in 435 congressional districts, candidates conduct locally based campaigns to determine who will make national policy decisions. Portuguese-speaking fishermen from the Massachusetts coast, Chicago suburbanites, and rural Oregonians, among others, must sort out who can represent their interests and those of the nation. Our examination of the Congress begins with one district where the politics of the 1990s has played out in a series of dramatic episodes.

NATIONAL POLITICS COMES HOME:
PENNSYLVANIA'S THIRTEENTH DISTRICT, 1992–2002

Although this Philadelphia-area congressional district does include some pockets of black voters, its core population is "overwhelmingly white and Republican" — with many residents living along the historic and affluent "Main Line" corridor.[1] Despite its traditional Republicanism, the district has proven unpredictable in recent elections; for example, its voters supported George Bush for president in 1988 by a twenty-point margin, yet it narrowly opted for Bill Clinton four years later. For the past twenty years, neither major party could take the allegiance of the Thirteenth District's electorate for granted, and the congressional elections over this period have demonstrated how national and local forces combine to produce a complex and sometimes contradictory representational linkage between legislator and constituency.

Act I

August 5, 1993. The vote was at hand on the most important proposal of President Bill Clinton's initial year in office — a five-year, $492-billion deficit reduction package. The top House Democratic leaders and the party's extensive whip organization had worked relentlessly to round up every available vote in support of the deficit reduction proposals that had resulted from endless hours of negotiations in House–Senate conference committee meetings. Almost every representative had come to the floor, eager to witness the concluding scene of this extended struggle. For those who remained undecided, there was no place to run, no place to hide.

As the fifteen minutes[2] formally allowed for voting expired, almost all members had cast their ballots, but the electronic tally board showed the result was still in doubt. President Clinton's fellow Democrats would have to provide the margin of victory; no Republican had broken party ranks. Unanimously, the 174 minority-party legislators had voted against the Clinton package, with its combination of spending cuts and tax increases. Four Democratic members remained in the well of the House, waiting to cast their votes. Representative David Minge, a conservative first-term Minnesotan, wanted considerably more in spending cuts. Representative David Thornton, from the president's own state of Arkansas, and Representative Pat Williams, from Montana's wide-open spaces and ordinarily a staunch party loyalist, objected to the 4.3-cent gas tax increase. The president called Williams and pleaded, "I can't win this without you. My presidency is at stake."[3] Williams agreed to support the package, despite his desire to cast a No vote that would please his constituents, who often drove long distances across Big Sky Country.

Representatives Thornton and Minge refused to budge, and both voted against the Clinton budget. For Thornton, to oppose his fellow Arkansan was an especially difficult decision. In the end, however, he observed, "My job is to represent the people of the Second Congressional District."[4]

That left the House's verdict on the Clinton budget proposal in the hands of first-term Representative Marjorie Margolies-Mezvinsky (D-Pa.), who had previously announced her opposition to the plan and had steadfastly resisted all tax increases. Although Bill Clinton had received 46 percent of the vote — a bit above his average across the nation — in her upscale, suburban Philadelphia district, Margolies-Mezvinsky won her seat, held by Republicans for the previous seventy-six years, by the extremely narrow margin of 1,373 votes out of 254,000 cast. She had triumphed, she argued, because of her stand "on two basic principles: deficit reduction and holding the line on taxes."[5] True to her word, in May, during the initial House consideration of the 1994 budget, she had voted against the Clinton package. But now the president and the Democratic leadership turned up the heat. Three months earlier, her support had not been needed, and she could cast her ballot in line with her constituents' clear preferences. By August, however, the House's backing for the budget bill had waned, and her vote had become essential for passage. The pressure on Representative Margolies-Mezvinsky was immense.

As she recounted, "The Speaker requested that I come down to the well [of the House chamber] and cast my vote. The scoreboard showed the vote was 216-216. Pat Williams (D-Mont.) and I stood in the well, surrounded by our Democratic peers. Barbara Kennelly, one of those encircling us, leaned over and said, 'You can't let the president down.' I stood there for a moment, and then I heard someone whisper in my ear, 'We need your vote.' 'You've got it,' I replied."[6] With that, she joined Representative Williams and signaled her Yes vote in support of the measure. As she walked down the aisle of the House, "one Democrat after another hugged her, patted her on the back and touched her as if she were Joan of Arc. Her Democratic colleagues cheered as the Republicans jeered 'Goodbye, Marjorie.'"[7] Her vote, crucial for her president and her party leadership, had placed her very reelection in jeopardy. Could she explain her actions to her constituents? The question would hang in the air until November 1994.

For Representative Margolies-Mezvinsky, there may have been no way to avoid extensive publicity, but there would be many more opportunities to play to her legions of constituents, supporters, fellow partisans, and prospective opponents. Moreover, her price for voting with the president was his guarantee to appear at a conference on entitlement spending that she would hold in the fall. Clinton did participate in the Philadelphia event, which was nationally televised on C-SPAN, but Margolies-Mezvinsky's constituents were not appeased. She entered the 1994 campaign season badly trailing her prospective Republican opponents.

Act II

On November 9, 1994, voters across the country rose up to defeat thirty-six congressional incumbents — thirty-four in the House, two in the Senate, and every one of them a Democrat. By a margin of 8,000 votes, Representative Margolies-Mezvinsky's constituents chose her Republican challenger, Jon Fox, in a rematch of the 1992 election.

In the end, the continuing focus on Margolies-Mezvinsky's budget vote was exceptional; the vote was important, but it was only one of a thousand or so recorded votes she cast before submitting herself to the electorate in November 1994. Rarely does a single vote spell doom for a legislator, but the visibility of her action made it difficult to overcome. Indeed, retribution from one's constituents is nothing new. In a previous era, for example, Representative Brooks Hays (D-Ark.) cast a highly visible and unpopular vote in favor of a 1957 civil rights bill; he lost the next election despite a national Democratic landslide. Hays's defeat functioned as a beacon of caution for a generation of legislators who wondered if the next vote might be the one against which their constituents might react.

In January 1995, the 104th Congress convened with fifty-two additional Republicans in the House, giving them a majority for the first time in forty years. The nine-seat GOP gain in the Senate meant that Republican majorities would organize both chambers. Representative Newt Gingrich (R-Ga.) and Senator Bob Dole (R-Kans.) became Speaker and majority leader, respectively, their majorities bolstered by seventy-three new Republican representatives and eleven first-term Republican senators. Remarkably, not one sitting Republican lost his or her seat in 1994. In suburban Philadelphia and across the nation, the voters repudiated the Democratic Congress. Within five months of Election Day, as they had promised, Republican leaders had brought to a vote in the House all ten items in their widely publicized Contract with America, and nine of the ten had won approval.

Act III

November 5, 1996. Representative Jon Fox faced his first reelection verdict with much the same vulnerability that had plagued Representative Margolies-Mezvinsky two years earlier. As one of the seventy-three freshmen Republican stalwarts in the 104th Congress, he had recorded a 97 percent support score on legislation drawn from the Contract with America, and he backed the GOP position on 85 percent of the partisan votes in 1995, a level of support that placed him among the most independent first-term Republicans. Still, on the vast majority of votes, he had supported a party and, especially, a leader (Speaker Newt Gingrich) whom the public had grown to view as extreme. In 1996, the pull of his moderate district had begun to move Representative Fox even further from a lockstep party voting record. As the election neared, his 1996 party support score slipped to 77 percent, and he cast votes against the party on the highly visible effort to repeal the assault weapons ban as well as on increasing the minimum wage.

Given the modest margin of his well-publicized 1994 victory, Representative Fox found himself a prime target for both Democrats and organized interests in 1996. He won the dubious distinction of being placed on the AFL-CIO's hit list for 1996, and so-called independent expenditures from labor poured into the district in the form of advertising that linked Fox to alleged Republican extremism, especially on Medicare and education issues. Although former Representative Margolies-Mezvinsky did not seek to regain her seat, the Democrats nominated Joseph Hoeffel, a well-qualified, well-funded candidate. The question at hand was whether Representative Fox could win enough local support to offset the apparent distaste of many of his constituents for the style and substance of the Republican House in the 104th Congress. With moderation on environmental issues and a willingness to oppose his own leaders, the congressman hoped to convey his desire to respond to local concerns on broad national issues.

In the end, Jon Fox retained his seat by fewer than one hundred votes, a margin that symbolized the national competitiveness of the 1996 elections. Representative Fox would head into the 105th Congress with a very different message from his constituents than he received two years earlier. His attempt to distance himself from some elements of the Republican Congress had succeeded, but just barely. At least in Pennsylvania's Thirteenth District, the 1994 and 1996 elections demonstrated that attentive constituents can insist that their representatives be responsive or face the real threat of enforced retirement. Looking forward to the election of 1998, Representative Fox could hardly take his support for granted.

Epilogue

The drama of Pennsylvania's Thirteenth District continued apace in 1997–1998. Representative Jon Fox had scarcely a moment's rest after the 1996 election. Seeking to position himself as a moderate, Fox remained under attack from both the right wing of his own party and the impending opposition of Democrat Joe Hoeffel in the general election. Fox compiled a reasonably moderate voting record over the course of the 105th Congress (he was among the twenty-five most moderate Republicans in the *National Journal*'s rankings for 1997–1998), but this did little to ward off strong challengers in either the Republican primary or the general election. Not only did Hoeffel challenge him again, this time with better funding, but the incumbent was also forced to defeat three challengers in the Republican primary.

Hoeffel built on his 1996 base, raising $1.27 million in 1998 as opposed to $704,000 two years earlier. Fox also raised more money ($2 million, up from $1.4 million in 1996), but his primary election campaign expenses reduced the amount he could spend against Hoeffel. More generally, Fox found himself pulled by much the same forces that brought down Representative Margolies-Mezvinsky four years earlier. The congressional Republican remained to the right of the moderate voters in Pennsylvania's Thirteenth District. Fox found himself caught between factions of the Republican Party in the primary and then had to face a well-prepared, well-financed moderate Democrat in the general election. The ultimate result was not a complete surprise; Fox lost by more than 9,000 votes out of 175,000 cast. The Thirteenth District remained a battleground — defined both by local and national forces.

In the 2000 and 2002 contests, Representative Hoeffel retained his seat, but Republicans continued to run vigorous races in the Thirteenth District, which remained highly competitive in the wake of the 2002 redistricting. In 2000, Hoeffel won with 53 percent of the vote, spending almost $1.8 million on his campaign. Two years later, his GOP opponent outspent him, $1.8 million to $1.55 million, and Hoeffel's vote total dropped to 51 percent. As a loyal and relatively liberal Democrat in a highly competitive district, Representative Hoeffel remains near the top of the Republican list of targets; he has continued to keep his seat, but not without a tough fight every two years.

THE CENTRIFUGAL CONGRESS

Each year 435 separate House electorates and 33 or 34 state electorates (only a third of the Senate seats are contested in any given election) make their separate decisions and create a new Congress. Following the Framers' outline, the Congress brings together a remarkable variety of legislators, especially in an era of increasing representation of minorities and women. Party leaders and presidents consistently face difficulties in building coherent majorities that can pass legislation. Why is this so?

For the Congress, at least, the answer seems deceptively simple. In responding to 50 state electorates, 435 separate House constituencies, and thousands of distinct interests, the institution has organized itself in decentralized ways that impede the building of consistent majorities that can pass coherent legislation on difficult issues. This is not a recent phenomenon. Congress has traditionally been the "slow institution," emphasizing representation of interests rather than rapid, perhaps overly hasty, responses.[8]

Although members of Congress adopt party labels, express their support or opposition to presidential policies, and seek to solve difficult societal problems, they must ultimately answer to 435 distinct constituencies in the House and 50 separate state electorates in the Senate. For the most part, American legislators are on their own as they seek election and reelection. They must raise the funds to finance their own campaigns, although parties and presidents will offer some assistance. Moreover, they must often survive primary elections within their own party, just to claim the Democratic or Republican label that they will carry into the November general election.[9]

Coming to Capitol Hill, legislators will seek the help of party leaders and the president, especially if they share a party affiliation, but they will also react to the pressures of interest groups, the pull of the committees to which they have been assigned, the pleas of the bureaucracy that provides seemingly limitless information, and, of course, the often-inconsistent communications from their own constituents. They will be, as were Representatives Fox and Margolies-Mezvinsky, pushed and pulled from all directions. This struggle is both mystifying and off-putting to those who seek to understand congressional politics. But Congress is not entirely without order as it seeks to represent constituents and make coherent national policies.

Indeed, the Republicans' success in capturing the Congress in 1994, pressing forward with a highly partisan agenda in 1995, and retaining control of both houses for the next decade (save for the Senate for eighteen months in 2001–2002) has shown that a reasonably homogeneous party can overcome many of the decentralizing tendencies of Capitol Hill politics. Republican House members have accorded substantial authority to their elected party leaders; most notably, the GOP membership has chosen to embrace the order imposed by a centralized party leadership, as opposed to that of a strong committee system. In the Senate, Republicans have presided over a closely divided though increasingly partisan body. But the individualistic Senate has remained far more resistant to strong party leadership. Moreover, as congressional Republicans have sought to govern across the broad landscape of American politics, they have discovered some merits within the decentralized framework of the committee system, in which expertise may temper ideology in the policy process. Still, in the 108th Congress (2003–2004), with the ascension of veteran GOP Whip Tom DeLay to House Majority Leader, the Republican leadership has imposed increasingly stringent party loyalty standards on those who become committee chairs.[10] In the House, at least, centripetal forces continue to restrain the fragmentation of the legislative process.

REPRESENTATION AND COLLECTIVE CHOICE

The U.S. Congress is a representative institution comprising two bodies that must make a series of collective, authoritative decisions — laws.[11] Ordinarily, this occurs by majority vote or, more accurately, a series of majority votes. Representatives and senators, although sporting party labels and owing much to their respective leaders within the Congress, are still beholden to their own distinct district and statewide electorates. Political scientists Roger Davidson and Walter Oleszek distinguish between two different, if overlapping, visions of the U.S. Congress. On one hand, the legislators constitute a "Congress of Ambassadors," which congregates in Washington to pursue the interests of the individual states and districts. On the other hand, they meet together as a single "deliberative assembly" to address issues and reach accords that roughly serve the broad, collective interest of the nation as a whole.[12]

This sounds straightforward, but from its founding, the United States has embraced an independent, powerful legislature that has often been at odds with the two other branches of government — the presidency and the judiciary. Without direct, formal ties to the executive (in contrast to a parliamentary system[13] in which cabinet ministers are drawn from the legislature), the individual lawmakers have prospered by representing their own constituents, districts, states, regions, and specific interests, often at the expense of ill-defined or chimerical national interests. Legislative structures and practices have evolved that facilitate this tendency toward representation of particular interests, thereby making it difficult to construct majorities. The rules of the Senate, for example, have long protected the rights of minorities, most notably by requiring supermajorities (usually sixty votes, but sometimes two-thirds of the members) to shut off debate on a bill. Indeed, extended debate — the filibuster — may be the most distinctive feature of the highly individualistic U.S. Senate.[14]

Although protecting the rights of individual legislators has forged the nature of the U.S. Senate, it is the decentralization of the committee system that has historically marked the operation of the House of Representatives. With its large membership, the chamber has used committees to conduct much of its legislative business. Writing in 1885, Woodrow Wilson observed that the entire House "sits, not for serious discussion, but to sanction the conclusions of its committees as rapidly as possible."[15] Even in 1885 this statement was hyperbole, but it does convey the House's organizational tendency toward decentralization through subunits, as opposed to a highly centralized party structure (as, for example, in the British Parliament). Although the relative power of committees has varied since 1789, it is the standing committee system, as much as any other characteristic, that has defined the operation of the House of Representatives.

Representation as Responsiveness

Legislators take representation very seriously. Although one common, negative view of the Congress depicts it as frequently immobilized by its ties to individual constituencies and interests, such a perspective may largely reflect the highly representative nature of the institution. Political theorist Hannah Pitkin has argued that political representation means "acting in the interest of the represented, in a manner responsive to them."[16] But knowing the wishes of one's constituents across a wide range of complex issues is difficult at best, given most citizens' low levels of knowledge and interest in most policy controversies. Nonetheless, motivated by their desire to win reelection, members of Congress seek to represent their constituents as best they can, often trying to anticipate their desires.[17] In this context, representation may be best viewed as a set of overlapping attempts to respond to "a number of targets" within a legislator's environment.[18]

Indeed, Heinz Eulau and Paul Karps advance our understanding of representation by pushing beyond simple agreement on policy preferences between legislators and their constituents. Rather, they outline four kinds of responsiveness that, taken together, constitute representation. These are, respectively, service responsiveness, allocation responsiveness, symbolic responsiveness, and policy responsiveness.[19] That is, legislators seek to respond to specific constituent problems, such as a lost Social Security check (service); they seek to obtain funding for district-based programs (allocation); they reassure constituents by their actions and words (symbolic); and they seek to pass programs that will broadly help the nation as a whole, which by definition includes their constituents (policy).

Put in slightly different terms, on some issues representatives act as the *delegates* of their constituents, especially when their interests and preferences are clear.[20] Conversely, on other issues, such as the budget, they act more like *trustees* who have to sort through complex policy options and decide what is most "in the interest of the represented," to use Pitkin's language. After making such a policy choice, they then have to explain their actions to their constituents. This after-the-fact explanatory behavior is central to representation in that it allows constituents to assess their legislators' broad policy decisions, which are often made with only a vague sense of district opinion. Members of Congress must anticipate their constituents' reactions and subsequently educate them in terms of the merits of a vote or policy position. If a legislator has acted responsively on the dimensions of service, allocation, and symbolism, he or she may well have more latitude in convincing district constituents to accept the less popular policy choices made on their behalf.[21]

Deliberation

The focus on individual legislators and their attention to their own districts has often obscured the role of the Congress as a deliberative body capable of engaging in productive debates on policy issues, large and small.[22] Such discussions do not always occur. For example, the 1993–1994 congressional consideration of President Clinton's health care reform proposals produced little reasoned give-and-take. Rather, deliberation simply disappeared under a deluge of highly publicized claims, counterclaims, and appeals to emotion.[23] More generally, meaningful deliberation is often missing in congressional debates.[24] As David Vogler and Sidney Waldman point out, reaching decisions on difficult issues is more than simply producing a majority that carries the day. They conclude that the democratic legitimacy of Congress rests on both the legislative process and the resulting policies. The value of unitary democracy (which emphasizes face-to-face deliberation) is found not simply in widespread agreement or consensus but in the creative nature of the process itself.[25]

The potential for creative solutions to difficult problems continues to reside within the Congress, and there is ample opportunity for deliberation, although much more so in committees, within informal task forces, and perhaps in the House gym than on the floor of either chamber. Only rarely can one tune in to C-SPAN and observe substantive deliberation among legislators who are seeking to exercise their creative powers. Rather, the viewer is treated to legislative posturing par excellence, in which almost all senators and representatives represent some specific point of view. Effective deliberation, to the extent that it occurs at all, takes place offstage, where legislators need not worry that their constituents and campaign contributors are watching intently.

Ironically, when Congress does rise to the occasion and acts either as a decisive policy-making body or as a deliberative assembly, the normally skeptical, even cynical, public embraces the congressional actions. The Congress that worked with Lyndon Johnson to enact his expansive Great Society programs achieved widespread popularity among the public; twenty-five years later, another Congress won accolades for its cogent deliberations over the merits of a war in the Persian Gulf. But public support dipped to new lows for the Congress that cobbled together a highly symbolic crime bill in 1994 and found itself unable to engage in much useful debate over health care reform. As a rule, individual legislators can act in their *own* interests, but Congress as a collective finds it most difficult to act for the *whole*.

Making Decisions, Choosing Policies

The Congress, both as a whole and as a pair of separate chambers, operates as a decision-making machine. That is, the House and Senate continually make decisions that affect major segments of the American public. Both in committee and on the floor of the House or Senate, legislators must choose between policy alternatives, day in, day out. Over the course of a full two-year Congress, a legislator will vote more than a thousand times on the floor and at least as many times in committees and subcommittees. In addition, lawmakers must make decisions on what specific legislation they will sponsor or cosponsor.[26]

Just because the Congress makes a great many decisions on an almost routine basis does not mean that congressional decision making is either efficient or effective. Rather, Congress's choices are frequently constrained — by the president's agenda, by the economy, or simply by the requirement of finding a majority of votes to pass a specific proposal. All the while, the members of Congress seek to be responsive to their constituents and to the electorate as a whole.

What, then, are we to make of the rush of legislation that the House of Representatives passed in the wake of the 1994 elections? The Republicans followed their historic electoral sweep with a legislative whirlwind in the House that was without parallel in this century. Speaker Gingrich and the House GOP captured the agenda and brought the ten Contract with America items to a vote. An initial analysis would give them high marks for responsiveness and, perhaps, representation and low scores for deliberation. By effectively nationalizing the 1994 congressional elections, using the Contract as a legislative agenda, and setting up their individual House offices, Republicans demonstrated all four kinds of responsiveness:

1. By refusing to cut back on office staff, they retained the ability to provide high levels of service to their constituents.
2. By supporting a tax cut, they sought to allocate funds back to their constituents.
3. By passing the balanced budget constitutional amendment, they adopted a policy that was backed by the public at large.
4. By voting in favor of a term-limits amendment, but by less than the required two-thirds majority, they proved themselves symbolically responsive to a popular public position without endangering their own seats.

More generally, the Contract allowed House Republicans to claim that they were acting in response to an overall mandate from the electorate, even if the Contract was at best a minor element of their triumph.

At the same time, the initial months of Speaker Gingrich's tenure in the House proved almost completely devoid of deliberation. Proposed constitutional amendments were pushed through committees in a few days, as were tax cuts. When the first one hundred days came to a close, the Senate found itself with a huge backlog of major policy initiatives that had been passed with little or no deliberation in the House. Indeed, many House Republicans assumed, even hoped, that the Senate's slower, deliberative style would temper the energy and partisanship of the House actions. And in large measure, the Senate did its job, although many of the Contract items did become law, albeit in modified form.

Almost a decade later, Republican House leaders, backed by their members, have systematically embraced the idea that they can use their majority to push legislative items such as tax cuts or post–9/11 restrictions on civil liberties. At the same time, their Republican majority counterparts in the Senate do not have the same power to force the passage of legislation. The Senate, although more partisan than a decade ago, remains a chamber where moderation and compromise are required to pass most legislation. Overall, party-based centralization has become the defining characteristic of the House, while individual deal-making remains an important facet of legislating in an increasingly partisan Senate.

THE CONTEMPORARY CONGRESS

This book addresses the tension between the constituency-oriented, individualistic Congress that emphasizes the representation of particular interests and the Congress that can, on occasion, act coherently to pursue some broader representative goals, perhaps achieving this through creative deliberation. Much of this tension is expressed in organizational terms, with overall tendencies toward decentralization and individualism being countered by the centralizing forces of party and presidential leadership. Even the most centrifugal of forces, such as locally oriented congressional elections, sometimes reflect the unifying pull of national trends, as demonstrated by the elections of 1964, 1974, 1980, and, most recently, 1994.

This book provides a series of related pictures of the Congress that builds on the three aspects of legislative life:

1. The strong element of fragmentation, or decentralization, which reflects centrifugal forces on the Congress. These forces result from the pull of district constituencies, congressional committees, reelection campaigns, individual member offices, and the effects of interests outside the institution.

2. The corresponding centralizing (or centripetal) forces, such as the party leadership, the president, and, on occasion, landmark elections, clear trends in public opinion, national crises, and broad coalitions of interests.

3. The continuing tensions between centrifugal and centripetal forces within the Congress. Even in the extremely decentralized, fragmented period of the late 1970s, there were many forces pushing the Congress toward greater centralization.

It is the interplay between these forces that presents the most interesting elements of Congress, as was the case when Representative Margolies-Mezvinsky's wrenching vote choice placed her squarely between her loyalty to Democratic party leaders and her constituents. In the decade since that vote, the struggle to balance party allegiance, committee loyalty, and responsiveness to constituents continues to define the legislative process, especially in the House.

The next chapter traces the evolution of the modern Congress across two centuries of representation. Chapter 3 focuses on the congressional context, especially the growth of organized interests and the explosion of national policy, which create hundreds upon hundreds of new constituencies for members to represent. At the same time, the Congress is increasingly made up of relatively young and conservative Republicans who express skepticism toward many federal programs but may well discover virtues in those that benefit their districts.

Chapters 4, 5, 8, and 9 emphasize the foundations of congressional policy making: elections, parties, committees, and the "enterprises" that surround each senator and representative.[27] Individual legislators mount their own campaigns, with a party label and ideology, then come to Congress and operate within the specialized environments of committees and control substantial resources that afford them great flexibility of action.

Chapter 7 focuses on the formal and informal elements of congressional decision making. The formal rules and procedures of the Congress can determine the outcomes of legislative initiatives and may allow party leaders to dominate the proceedings, especially in the House. At the same time, informal rules of the game, or "folkways," provide an interpersonal context for legislative actions, as lawmakers observe (or don't) norms that encourage civil behavior even as they disagree. The increase in partisanship on Capitol Hill has challenged the civility of congressional behavior and created chasms between members in the House and Senate that did not exist a decade ago.

Chapter 6 offer insights into the usual channels of coordination and centralization on Capitol Hill, direction from congressional party leaders and the president. The 1992 election of Bill Clinton brought with it the promise of single-party control of the executive and legislative branches for the first time in twelve years, yet President Clinton found it difficult to muster party-based majorities, especially in light of Senate-delaying tactics that often required sixty votes to overcome. Given Republican majorities in both houses in 2003, President George W. Bush governs with single-party control but, as in the case of President Clinton, narrow partisan margins in the House and the individualism of the Senate offer considerable obstacles to his ability to enact his policy agenda.

Chapter 10 offers three case studies: (1) the impeachment trial of President Clinton, (2) the passage of President Bush's education reforms, and (3) the fiscal year 2003 appropriations process. These case studies are designed to illustrate the interaction of partisanship, policy, and distributive politics in Congress discussed throughout this book. More broadly, they demonstrate the constant tug-of-war between centrifugal and centripetal forces on Capitol Hill — a struggle well anticipated by the Framers and thoroughly incorporated into our political life by the Constitution and more than two hundred years of legislative practice.

CHAPTER BIBLIOGRAPHY

Mayhew, David. *America's Congress.* New Haven, CT: Yale University Press, 2000.

Price, David E. *The Congressional Experience,* 2nd ed. Boulder, CO: Westview Press, 2000.

Stewart, Charles, III. *Analyzing Congress.* New York: Norton, 2001.

Wolfensberger, Donald R. *Congress and the People: Deliberative Democracy on Trial.* Washington, D.C., and Baltimore: Woodrow Wilson Center Press/Johns Hopkins University Press, 2001.

NOTES

1. Philip B. Duncan and Christine C. Lawrence, eds., *Politics in America, 1996* (Washington, DC: Congressional Quarterly, 1995), p. 1146. The "Main Line" refers to a railroad line that has long served its upscale commuters.

2. At present, members get seventeen minutes.

3. Clifford Krauss, "Whips Use Soft Touch to Succeed," *New York Times,* August 7, 1993, p. 29.

4. Ibid.

5. Richard E. Cohen, "Baptism by Fire for House Newcomers," *National Journal,* June 5, 1993, p. 1366.

6. Marjorie Margolies-Mezvinsky, *A Woman's Place . . .* (New York: Crown, 1994), p. 202.

7. Krauss, "Whips Use Soft Touch."

8. Richard F. Fenno, Jr., "Strengthening a Congressional Strength," in Norman J. Ornstein, ed., *Congress in Change* (New York: Praeger, 1975).

9. Alaska, Washington, and Louisiana hold blanket primaries: If no candidate wins a majority, the top two vote-getters, regardless of party, face each other in a runoff.

10. Jim VandeHei and Juliet Eilperin, "GOP Leaders Tighten Hold in the House," *Washington Post,* January 13, 2003, p. A1. Also see Derek Willis, "Republicans Mix It Up When Assigning House Chairmen for the 108th," *CQ Weekly,* January 11, 2003, pp. 89–94.

11. David Vogler, *The Politics of Congress,* 6th ed. (Madison, WI: Brown & Benchmark, 1993).

12. Roger Davidson and Walter Oleszek, *Congress and Its Members,* 6th ed. (Washington, DC: CQ Press, 1998).

13. In parliamentary systems, the executive (e.g., the prime minister) is often the leader of the majority party (or coalition among parties) *within* the chamber. The distinction between legislature and executive is thus blurred, especially when compared with the United States's separation of powers.

14. Sarah A. Binder and Steven S. Smith, *Politics or Principle?* (Washington, DC: Brookings Institution, 1997).

15. Woodrow Wilson, *Congressional Government* (Boston: Houghton Mifflin, 1885).

16. Hannah Pitkin, *The Concept of Representation* (Berkeley: University of California Press, 1967), p. 209.

17. See Douglas Arnold, *The Logic of Congressional Action* (New Haven, CT: Yale University Press, 1990).

18. Heinz Eulau and Paul D. Karps, "The Puzzle of Representation: Specifying Components of Responsiveness," *Legislative Studies Quarterly* 2 (August 1977): p. 241. Much of the following relies on the line of argument in this article.

19. Eulau and Karps, "The Puzzle of Representation."

20. The trustee–delegate distinction between representative styles has its roots in Edmund Burke's speech to his Bristol parliamentary constituents in the eighteenth century. The modern discussion derives from Warren E. Miller and Donald E. Stokes, "Constituency Influence in Congress," *American Political Science Review* 57 (March 1963): pp. 45–57.

21. For more extensive development of this theme, see Richard F. Fenno, Jr., *Home Style* (Boston: Little, Brown, 1978), and Arnold, *The Logic of Congressional Action.*

22. Joseph M. Bessette has produced the most cogent examination of congressional deliberation in *The Mild Voice of Reason* (Chicago: University of Chicago Press, 1994).

23. See, for example, James Fallows, "A Triumph of Misinformation," *The Atlantic* 275 (January 1995): pp. 26–37.

24. See, for example, the arguments put forth by Representative Gerald Soloman (R-N.Y.) and Donald R. Wolfensberger, "The Decline of Deliberative Democracy in the House and Proposals for Change," *Harvard Journal of Legislation* 31 (1993): pp. 320–370.

25. David J. Vogler and Sidney R. Waldman, *Congress and Democracy* (Washington, DC: CQ Press, 1984), p. 166. More generally on deliberation, see Bessette, *The Mild Voice of Reason*.

26. For a discussion of bill sponsorship, see Wendy J. Schiller, "Senators as Political Entrepreneurs: Bill Sponsorship in the U.S. Senate." *American Journal of Political Science* 39, no. 1 (1995): pp. 186–203.

27. Robert Salisbury and Kenneth Shepsle, "The U.S. Congressman as Enterprise," *Legislative Studies Quarterly* 6 (November 1981): pp. 559–576.

Two
CONGRESSIONAL DECENTRALIZATION IN DESIGN AND EVOLUTION

T he Framers of the Constitution faced a dilemma: how to create a strong national government that would not use its powers in arbitrary or anti-democratic ways. Within the republican construct of federalism and a separation of powers, the powers of the Congress were spelled out in far more detail than were those of the executive or judicial branches. The contradictory concerns of how to concentrate power and simultaneously limit it led the Framers to design a potentially powerful Congress that is capable of acting quickly and decisively but is ordinarily slow and cautious in struggling to represent the disparate interests of its widely varied constituencies. The Framers might have a difficult time recognizing the size and scope of the modern presidency or the policy reach of the Supreme Court (for example, the *Roe v. Wade* abortion decision based on the "right to privacy," which is nowhere detailed in the Constitution), but most would have been at home in the 2000 congressional debate on granting Permanent Normal Trade Relations status to China (China Free Trade), in which national benefits (increased exports through lower tariffs) were juxtaposed against potential local costs (the loss of jobs to cheaper foreign labor).

THE FRAMERS CONSTRUCT A CONGRESS

Although they recognized the need for a strong, effective central government, the Framers worried greatly over the potential for abuse that comes with any concentration of power. After all, they had fought a revolution to rid themselves of the British monarchy. By providing the Congress with large grants of well-defined authority, most notably the powers to tax and spend, they placed the largest share of national power in legislative hands. At the same time, "the Framers regarded [the Congress as likely] to succeed in deceiving and dominating the people."[1] They thus engineered a number of design features into the Constitution to reduce the possibility of systematic abuse by willful congressional majorities. Its three basic elements were:

1. The representation of "a multiplicity of interests" within an "extended republic."[2]

2. The separation of powers at the national level into the legislative, judicial, and executive branches.

3. The creation of a bicameral (two-chamber) legislative body.

These provisions defined a decentralized congressional structure in three distinct ways. First, the representational nature of the legislature would work against the concentration of power. The Framers knew from firsthand experience how difficult it was to build majority positions from the diverse views harbored by legislators with differing state and regional backgrounds. Even so, vigorous representation of various interests and constituencies was scarcely enough to check a determined congressional majority. Curbing the potential for tyranny required permanent structural barriers to legislative dominance. This was accomplished by constructing both external and internal limitations on the congressional majorities — the separation of powers and bicameralism, respectively.

Thus, the separation of powers provides both independence for each of the three branches and the capacity for each branch to retain that independence by checking the actions of the others.[3] This elemental decentralizing feature of American government has produced legendary intragovernmental confrontations ranging from the congressional censure of President Andrew Jackson in 1834 to the Supreme Court's unanimous 1974 decision requiring President Richard Nixon to hand over the Watergate tapes to the Congress. The 1998–1999 impeachment and acquittal of President Clinton only reemphasized the potential for destructive confrontation.[4]

At the same time, interbranch cooperation is crucial, especially between the executive and legislative branches, for the power of the national government to be effectively mustered. Thus, presidents must continually act to promote their legislative agendas, while the Congress presses its own oversight of the executive branch and government bureaucracy. In addition, the judicial branch imposes serious constraints on congressional actions, given its powers to rule laws unconstitutional and to interpret their applications. A substantial amount of legislative activity results from Congress's responses to judicial decisions (for example, abortion policy in the wake of *Roe v. Wade* and subsequent cases).

Finally, not content to rely on external checks on the Congress, the Framers created formidable internal restraints as well. Most of these derive from the adoption of a bicameral structure with distinctive bases of power for each legislative chamber. Given the tendency of legislative authority to dominate in a representative government, James Madison concluded that "the remedy for this inconvenience is, to divide the legislature into different branches; and to render them, by different modes of election, and different principles of action, as little connected with each other, as the nature of their common functions and their common dependence on society, will admit."[5]

The Constitutional Convention's fundamental compromise was to create a two-chamber structure in which only members of the lower body, the House of Representatives, would be elected directly by the people. Senators would be selected by state legislatures, and each state would be represented by two senators, regardless of its population.[6] Senate terms would stretch for six years, as opposed to the two years given representatives. The Senate would be accorded the power to ratify treaties and confirm executive branch appointments, and the House would be granted the sole authority to originate revenue bills.

Among their myriad accomplishments, the Framers of the Constitution succeeded in laying the groundwork for a strong national government. This potential for centralized power — realized in fits and starts over the past two hundred years — was simultaneously checked by representation of diverse interests, the separation of powers, and a bicameralism that roughly balanced the strengths of the two chambers. Even before the first Congress met or before George Washington assumed the presidency, the stage had been set for the tensions between centrifugal and centripetal forces that have characterized American legislative politics since 1789.

What follows is in no way a complete history, even in outline form, of the U.S. Congress. Rather, laying out a succession of congressional eras offers a series of sketches on how the legislature has developed since its inception and how the initial tensions over representation and structural experiments, such as bicameralism, have shaped the nature of the institution. Indeed, even as Republicans won control of both houses of Congress in 1994 for the first time in forty years, Speaker Gingrich and his unified band of 230 GOP representatives were forced to contend with a Senate that was slow to act, especially in passing a House-generated agenda, and a Democratic president who exercised his constitutional powers, both by actually vetoing legislation and, more often, by threatening further vetoes.

THE EARLY CONGRESS: ORGANIZATION AND TENSIONS

Despite defining congressional powers more clearly, and at much greater length, than the other national branches of government, the Constitution did little to dictate how the two houses would be organized.[7] No mention is ever made of committees or political parties; only the offices of Speaker, president of the Senate (the vice president), and the Senate's president pro tempore are noted, although without any demarcation of their duties. The larger size of the House (65 members in 1789 and 181 by 1813, in contrast to 26 and 36 senators for the same years, respectively) led to the development of a more complex structure to conduct its business. To take advantage of its numbers, the House soon developed the decentralized standing committee system that remains an organizational hallmark of the body. Concurrently, however, the House's size also fostered the growth of political parties that served to pull together the diverse interests of their members, who had begun to feel the centrifugal pull of their committees as well as that of their constituencies.

For the first ten Congresses, most committees operated as ad hoc bodies to "perfect" the work done by the Committee of the Whole House,[8] but gradually — especially after 1825 — standing committees, which continued from one Congress to the next, took on the major tasks of writing and revising legislation.[9] Reliance on growing numbers of committees illustrates the increased decentralization of the House. This organizational style benefited the average representative by allowing each committee to become expert in its own policy area and to share that knowledge with the rest of the members.[10] Moreover, by facilitating a division of labor, the House could take advantage of the very condition — its large number of members — that rendered it most unwieldy.

As committees were beginning to develop the specialized expertise essential to address particular issues, the House also needed some way to build consistent majorities. As with committees, congressional leaders turned to a structural answer. American politicians of the 1790s to 1830s gradually invented a new organization designed for a republican form of government — the political party.[11] Although scholars disagree about the extent of partisanship and party organization in the first two decades of constitutional government, there were distinct factions that opposed each other in elections and within the legislature. As early as the Second Congress (1791), even though parties had not become formalized, "common ideas and concerns were fast binding men together, and when Congress met, many individuals in both houses became more or less firmly aligned into two voting groups — Federalists on one side and Republican-minded [a Madison–Jefferson faction] on the other."[12]

The central figure in establishing strong parties and leadership in the House was Representative Henry Clay of Kentucky, who energized the Speakership during his three periods of service in that chamber. By 1814, Clay and his colleagues "had succeeded in erecting a new system, based on the party caucus, in which legislative leadership was now the prerogative of a group of prominent men in the House of Representatives."[13]

Party divisions and organizational strength would vary over the next four decades, but by 1825 the beginnings of a stable party system with regular leaders and consistent voting patterns had taken firm hold as a centralizing force within the House. Indeed, by this time, both committees and parties were established to the point that a scholar could write in 1917, "so far as its organization was concerned, the House of Representatives had assumed its present form."[14] This is a significant observation for contemporary legislative politics because the House of the 1825 and 1917 eras contained both strong committee systems and powerful party leaderships, much like that of the Democratic House of Speaker Jim Wright (1987–1989) and the Republican chamber under Speaker Newt Gingrich (1995–1999).

Through the early 1820s the House, with its emerging structure and growing numbers, was accorded more weight than the Senate, largely because of the direct election of its members.[15] The Senate, however, was also changing, if more through evolution than through the impatient leadership of Clay. By 1830, the Senate had moved from being an elitist imitation of the English House of Lords to a strongly American institution. Commenting on the evolution of the chamber, Elaine Swift observes that the Senate began to respond more to citizen voters than to the state legislatures that formally elected its members, and it became increasingly active in developing its own legislation. The Senate thus "came to be more like the House . . . [and] the executive could no longer bank on its all-but-certain support."[16]

SENATE INDIVIDUALISM AND HOUSE FRAGMENTATION: 1830–1860

By the beginning of the Jackson administration in 1829, the Senate had begun to attract the most formidable leaders of the day, such as Kentucky's Henry Clay. Clay had instituted vigorous party leadership in the House before serving as secretary of state and continued his illustrious, meandering career by returning to Congress in 1831 as a Whig senator. There he would join such notables as Daniel Webster (Whig-Mass.), John Calhoun (D-S.C.), and Thomas Hart Benton (D-Mo.) in a chamber composed of the most notable men of the era. The French observer Alexis de Tocqueville contrasted the "vulgarity" he found in the House with the Senate, which he described as being filled with "eloquent advocates, distinguished generals, wise magistrates, and statesmen of note."[17]

Although many senators operated skillfully behind the scenes, this was a time of great individual oratory and sweeping attempts to hold the Union together. Setting the stage for the era's politics was the legendary Webster–Hayne debate of 1829, which defined the slavery issue in terms of the survival of the Union as a whole. Several other subthemes also ran through the Senate of the 1830s, most of them revolving around the roles of the states and the national government, slavery, the populistic aims of Jackson and the Democratic Party, and the sectional split within the Democrats' ranks between New York's Martin Van Buren and John Calhoun.[18] The freedom of individual action within the still-small Senate (forty-eight members in 1831) meant that coalitions could form and reform as these able legislators jockeyed for advantage over a wide range of issues. All the while, they understood that their fundamental division over slavery might destroy the very system of government that allowed them to flourish.

In contrast, the House found it difficult to organize itself coherently in the 1830–1860 period. With a larger, less stable membership than the Senate, the House could not rely as easily on the leadership of strong individual legislators. Nor could it count on its party factions and sectional interests to provide the organizational coherence demanded by the fractious body. Extended, bitter contests for the Speakership became commonplace. In 1849, for example, five major groupings vied for control, and a Speaker was finally elected on the sixty-third ballot after the members agreed that the office could be awarded to the candidate who won a plurality, not a majority, of the votes. In 1855, a mix of Whigs, Republicans (a newly formed party), Democrats, and various minor parties went 133 ballots before selecting (again by plurality) antislavery Representative Nathaniel Banks (Mass.) of the nativist American (Know-Nothing) Party.

Finally, in the Thirty-sixth Congress (1859–1861), which again harbored no clear party majority, forty-four ballots over three months were required to elect the most unlikely of Speakers: William Pennington (R-N.J.), who was serving his first (and last!) term in the House. His election to this post matched Henry Clay's 1811 victory as a first-term representative, but Clay had won the Speakership because of his strong personality and forceful leadership qualities; conversely, Pennington was the lowest common denominator in a highly fragmented chamber of a nation that was about to burst apart.

THE RISE OF THE MODERN CONGRESS: 1860–1920

Between the Civil War years and the end of World War I, the U.S. Congress underwent a series of organizational restructurings that culminated in what can be called its modern form by about 1920. The combination of a growing national industrial base and an increasing U.S. role in world affairs required the legislative branch to adapt to a very different environment than that of the pre-1860 United States, in which an agrarian nation had wrestled with the fundamental, highly divisive slavery issue.

Over the 1860–1920 period, the Congress experimented with strong party leadership in both chambers, created and then limited a separate committee for appropriations, first dominated a series of weak presidents and later looked to the president for coherent leadership initiatives, and eventually moved toward the mixture of standing committee decentralization and oligarchy that would characterize the institution until the mid-1960s. Why such a flurry of activity? As a representative body, the Congress adapts to its environment. New members enter the body, new issues come before it, and new party alignments arise. In the course of adapting to broad societal changes, such as industrialization in the late 1800s and early 1900s, the Congress has often restructured itself internally to consolidate power and regularize procedure.[19]

The House

For more than a quarter-century after the Civil War, Congress stood astride national politics and policy making, but battles raged over the control of both chambers. Standing committees dominated the legislative process, especially after the House stripped the upstart Appropriations Committee (established in 1865) of much of its authority. At the same time, a number of strong Speakers increased the power of their office; in particular, the Speaker could appoint all committee members and could aggressively employ his power to recognize members who wished to speak. Still, Roger Davidson and Walter Oleszek conclude that in the 1880s, "despite growth in the Speaker's prerogatives, centrifugal forces in the House remained strong, even dominant."[20] Although committees contributed to this dominance, even more significant was the almost total inability of House majorities to work their will, largely because of delaying tactics that allowed any member to slow actions of the chamber to a crawl.

Enter Speaker Thomas Brackett Reed (R-Maine), elected to lead the House in 1889. In his first three months as Speaker he rewrote the House rules from his position as chair of the Rules Committee and as presiding officer revised the rules for recognition of a quorum (a majority of all members). Since the 1830s the House had operated under the odd but powerful precedent of not recognizing the presence of those who sat mute in the chamber, refusing to answer a quorum call.[21] As Representative Benjamin Butterworth (R-Ohio) put it, a member may, "while present, arise in his place and assert that he is absent, and we must take his word for it. What an absurdity on the face of it. . . . It is the weapon of anarchy."[22] A unanimous, if slender, Republican majority upheld Reed's decision that all members physically present would be counted as present in constituting a quorum. This ruling was reconfirmed by the Democrats when they took control of the House in the early 1890s.

Reed's quorum ruling and other rules that consolidated organizational power opened the way for twenty years of great centralization in the House.[23] Speakers Reed, Charles Crisp (D-Ga.), and, most notably, Joseph Cannon (R-Ill.) increasingly employed the formidable weapons that the position had accumulated. From 1903 to 1909, "Uncle Joe" Cannon steadily became more dictatorial (the word is not too strong) in his command of the House.[24] Finally, in 1910 a coalition of minority Democrats and insurgent Republican reformers (many from the Midwest) broke the Speaker's hold over the combination of power levers that permitted him to dominate the process and outcomes of House decision making. As we shall see later in more detail, Cannon had lost control of the majority that allowed him to function as an autocrat. The support of his fellow Republicans, which was crucial to his dominance, had crumbled. Cannon remained as Speaker for the rest of the term, but both his personal power and that of the office were greatly diminished.

For a few years, the Democratic Party caucus and the presidential leadership of Woodrow Wilson combined to retain some relatively strong centripetal momentum in the House, but this dissipated with increasing disagreement over international policies surrounding World War I.[25] By 1920, strong party leadership had given way to a decentralized committee system as the principal means of organizing the House — a condition that was not to change for more than half a century.

The Senate

In his classic account of the nineteenth-century Senate, historian David Rothman concludes that:

> the Senate of 1869 was very much like its predecessors; by 1901 it had come to resemble its successors. . . . Senators in the 1870s . . . were free to go about their business more or less as they pleased. By 1900 all this had changed. The

party caucus and its chieftains determined who would sit on which committees and looked after the business calendar in detail. Members were forced to seek their favors or remain without influence in the chamber. At the same time, both organizations imposed unprecedented discipline on roll calls.[26]

Though the House could consolidate power around the constitutional office of the Speaker, the Senate had no similar touchstone. Ironically, strong political parties at the state and local levels formed the context from which centripetal forces flowed into the Senate, where party ties rose in importance through the 1880s and 1890s. Most members of this now-sizeable body (ninety lawmakers in 1901) functioned as party loyalists, who provided the votes for the policy positions endorsed by the leadership-dominated party caucus.[27]

Occupying the central positions within the Republican caucus of the 1890s were the chair, Iowa's William Allison, and Rhode Island's Nelson Aldrich, perhaps the most talented and influential member of the chamber. They dominated Senate policy making through a combination of formal and informal linkages. The Allison–Aldrich faction gained control of overlapping party committees and standing committee positions to dominate the chamber's agenda and its policy outcomes. For example, controlling the Republican Steering Committee "confirmed the power of the Allison–Aldrich faction over the Senate business. Arranging the legislative schedule in detail, week by week, the committee extended the party leaders' authority unimpaired from the caucus to the chamber. Senators knew they had to consult the committee before attempting to raise even minor matters."[28]

Remnants of the traditional Senate individualism remained, but those Republicans who refused to cooperate with the Allison–Aldrich group found themselves without influence. As Rothman notes, "Anyone could use the chamber as a forum and address the nation. Senators willing to abandon the opportunity to increase their own authority could act freely, following their own inclinations. . . . But barring a takeover of the party offices, they could hardly affect the exercise of power. The country might honor their names, but the Senate barely felt their presence."[29]

Given the underlying differences among senators, based on region, party, interests, and ideology, the Senate's centralization could not hold for long, and the Republican caucus's domination eroded over the 1901–1912 period. The individualistic, centrifugal forces of the chamber came to the fore in caucus challenges to Aldrich, the growing strength of Progressive senators (often supported by President Theodore Roosevelt), and the election of a Democratic Senate to complement the presidential victory of Democrat Woodrow Wilson in the 1912 election. In addition to the partisan turnover of 1912 came the 1913 adoption of the Seventeenth Amendment to the Constitution, which provided for the direct election of senators. No longer would state legislatures and state party machines formally dominate the selection process, although by the time of the amendment's ratification, most states already selected Senate candidates through the primary election process.[30]

Finally, the Senate did change one further fundamental element of its procedure. From its inception, the Senate had allowed unlimited debate on any subject. The filibuster — or its threat — had proved a powerful tool for many Senate giants of the past. This was one of the strongest decentralizing elements within the entire legislative process. An individual senator (or, more likely, a band of legislators with similar, intense feelings) could indefinitely delay consideration of a crucial bill. This occurred in 1917, when, in President Wilson's words, "a little group of willful men" blocked his armed neutrality bill, which had the public support of seventy-five of ninety-six senators.[31]

In the aftermath of this inability to act, the Senate adopted cloture, the first measure that provided a mechanism to shut off debate; cloture could be imposed by a two-thirds vote of those present and voting. Although this procedure was employed in 1919 to end a filibuster on ratification of the Versailles Treaty, until the late 1970s the Senate rarely approved cloture, save in extraordinary cases such as the 1964 civil rights bill. The filibuster remained a potent weapon, both in its occasional implementation and in its frequent use as threat.[32]

The Drift toward Decentralization

Allied with the Republican presidencies of William McKinley (1897–1901) and Theodore Roosevelt (1901–1908), the House's strong Speakership and the Senate's dominant Allison–Aldrich faction served to concentrate legislative power in the congressional parties at the turn of the century. The ability of legislative party leaders to set the nation's policy agenda became increasingly important in that the industrializing U.S. society was demanding more of the federal government.[33] In the Fortieth Congress (1867–1869), lawmakers introduced a total of 3,003 bills; by the Fifty-second Congress (1891–1893) that number had grown to 14,518, and the Sixtieth Congress (1907–1909) witnessed the introduction of almost 38,000 bills, more than a twelve-fold increase in forty years.[34] This volume of legislation eventually benefited those restive representatives and senators who desired to reduce the power of their party leaders.

Some mechanism was needed to handle this immense flow of prospective legislation. The committee system offered the most obvious organizational response for the Congress. In fact, the number of standing committees had proliferated in both chambers, to the point that in 1918 the House had sixty such units and the Senate a staggering seventy-four. The sheer number of committees might imply the development of a highly decentralized Congress, but through 1910 party leaders combined their leadership roles with those of key committees to produce strongly centralized operations in both chambers.[35] With Speaker Cannon's defeat, the subsequent waning of Democratic caucus unity in the House after 1914, and the Senate's growing fragmentation in the period from 1901 to 1919, congressional party organizations could no longer move bills through the legislative process in a predictable, timely manner. Relying on committees would be essential for the sake of coherence. Such reliance dictated that both chambers reform their committee systems, which they did in 1919 and again, more meaningfully, in 1946.

THE DEVELOPMENT AND DECLINE OF THE TEXTBOOK CONGRESS: 1920–1970

Although Woodrow Wilson could celebrate the work of congressional committees in the 1880s, their great ascendancy did not come until fifty years later and lasted well into the 1960s. Gradually, over the 1920s, 1930s, and 1940s, committee strength grew, and members almost universally advanced on the basis of their seniority — the length of their consecutive tenure on a given committee. The 1946 Legislative Reorganization Act sharply reduced the number of committees in both chambers and thus sharply increased the value of the remaining standing committee chairmanships — nineteen in the House, fifteen in the Senate.

The committee-dominated Congress of the 1950s coincided with the first systematic analysis of the Congress by political scientists trained in behavioral methods.[36] Scholars and students received a much fuller picture of the Congress of the period from the late 1950s to 1970 than of any previous era. The Congress of this time was relatively stable, which allowed for well-documented, detailed analyses to capture the essence of an increasingly complex institution. There is no question that this generation of congressional scholars "got it right." The strength of their analyses produced a cumulative picture, circa 1970, which was so clear and detailed that it dominated conventional views of the Congress long after the institution changed profoundly in the 1970s and 1980s.

With his term *the textbook Congress,* political scientist Kenneth Shepsle has captured the extent to which the studies made up a received wisdom that still shapes many perceptions of legislative politics.[37] In representing their constituencies and making national policy, legislators confront tensions that "derive from three competing imperatives — geographical, jurisdictional, and partisan. . . . Congress is [thus] an arena for constituencies, committees, and [party-based] coalitions. The textbook Congress of the 1950s represented an equilibrium among these imperatives involving an institutional bargain that gave prominence to committees."[38] Although legendary party leaders such as Speaker Sam Rayburn (D-Tex.) and Senate Majority Leader Lyndon Johnson (D-Tex.) wielded substantial personal power in the 1950s, the Congress of these years emphasized the work of autonomous committees as directed by a set of senior chairmen.[39] The textbook Congress was both decentralized and oligarchic: decentralized in that committee chairs dominated their own policy domains; oligarchic in that top party leaders, committee chairs, and chairs of the thirteen Appropriations Committee subcommittees in each chamber all benefited from their joint control of the domestic policy agenda. Although the House relied more heavily on committee work than did the Senate, the same general committee-based equilibrium existed in both chambers.

The organizationally stable Congress of the 1950s did not bend easily to the winds of change. Popular pressure for more educational spending fell victim to procedural wrangling. In the face of filibusters and a hostile bloc of southern senators, civil rights legislation proceeded slowly in the aftermath of the Supreme Court's 1954 *Brown v. Board of Education* school desegregation ruling. Nor was medical care for the elderly allowed to wend its way through the legislative process. The committee-dominated system proved superb at slowing the pace of policy change in a narrowly Democratic Congress that faced the moderate-to-conservative Republican presidency of Dwight Eisenhower.[40] Indeed, the title of Robert Bendiner's study of educational policy making *Obstacle Course on Capitol Hill* would have been equally apt in describing the limited progress of many other policy initiatives.[41]

The congressional equilibrium began to change with the Democratic landslide in the 1958 congressional elections, which greatly increased the size of the party's majorities in both chambers. More important, many of the newly elected legislators were relatively liberal and committed to policy changes. Six years later another surge of Democratic legislators ascended Capitol Hill, brought there in part by Lyndon Johnson's sweeping presidential victory over Senator Barry Goldwater (R-Ariz.). Despite coming in disproportionate numbers from Republican districts, these rank-and-file Democratic legislators proved crucial to the passage of several of Johnson's ambitious domestic programs.[42] Liberal voting records denied many first-termers a chance for reelection; those who survived, however, felt entitled to a real voice within the legislative process. The major outlet for this voice came in positions taken by the Democratic Study Group, a body of House Democrats that formed after the 1958 elections.[43] This unofficial but well-organized group consistently pressed for a reform agenda, which included reducing the power of committee chairmen.

The standing committee oligarchy was thus ripe for challenge by the late 1960s. Party leaders had begun to chip away at the chairs' powers, while reformist junior members hungered for responsibility within the committee structure. Both leaders and backbenchers stood to gain from reining in the chairs; change was inevitable, but with it came great disruption that lasted for a decade.

REFORMING THE CONGRESS: THE 1970s

> *It is the members who run Congress. And we will get pretty much the kind of Congress they want. We shall get a different kind of Congress when we elect different kinds of congressmen.*
>
> Richard E. Fenno, Jr.

Beginning in 1958, continuing through the 1960s, and culminating in the 1974 and 1976 elections for Democrats and the 1978 and 1980 elections for Republicans, we did get different kinds of new members. Subsequently, we got a different kind of Congress. Fenno's deceptively simple statement captures the essential ability of lawmakers to determine the nature of their institution.[44] More indirectly, voters can roughly determine the direction and extent of change, even if they are unaware of the specific mechanics.

In general, the newly elected legislators were impatient, eager to use their expertise, and unconcerned if they ruffled some senior members' feathers.[45] In the House, subcommittees gained a measure of independent authority; members sought and received many more resources for their offices; most votes on the floor were recorded and thus open to public scrutiny; and the Democratic Caucus provided enhanced powers for the Speaker and the top party leaders. Shepsle summarizes:

> The revolt of the 1970s thus strengthened four power centers. It liberated *members and subcommittees,* restored to the *Speakership* an authority it had not known since the days of Joe Cannon, and invigorated the *party caucus.* Some of the reforms had a decentralizing effect, some a recentralizing effect. Standing committees and their chairs were caught in the middle. Geography and party benefited; the division-of-labor jurisdictions were its victims.[46]

The powerful but relatively brief reform era of the late 1960s–1970s produced a highly unstable political environment on Capitol Hill, especially in the House. Even though they held the presidency under Jimmy Carter and enjoyed comfortable numerical advantages over the Republicans in both chambers, Democrats could not generate consistent congressional majorities to pass major policy initiatives. Leaders and backbenchers alike struggled to understand what their reforms had wrought.[47]

THE DEMOCRATIC POSTREFORM CONGRESS: 1980–1994

Many analyses of the Congress of the late 1970s emphasized, with good reason, the proliferation of subcommittees, the growth of individual members' resources, and the apparent weakness of both the Carter presidency and the Democratic legislative leadership. In 1980, Republicans ran a pointed national campaign advertisement that depicted Democratic Speaker Tip O'Neill as unresponsive and woefully out of touch on important, pressing issues.[48] Building on substantial public dissatisfaction, Republican candidates performed well in 1980, capturing the Senate and narrowing the Democrats' majority in the House to the point that President Reagan's initial tax and budget proposals won speedy congressional approval as conservative Democrats joined with Republicans to provide majority support.

Speaker O'Neill and his fellow House Democrats were not quite dead, however. Their rejuvenation over the next few years derived in part from the Speaker's winning personality; by the time he retired from the House in 1986, he could point to popularity levels that had surpassed those of Ronald Reagan. O'Neill, a great listener, could find grounds to bring together the different strands of the legislative party. Equally important, however, were the aggressive use of party-strengthening reforms adopted in the 1970s and the consistent reduction of ideological disagreements among House Democrats.[49] Thus, the personally popular O'Neill could lead an increasingly homogeneous group of partisans with a combination of carrots, such as including many members within the leadership, and sticks, such as controlling the process of appointing members to committee seats.

By the 1980s, majority party members, most of whom had been elected in 1974 or later, decided that they wanted, in Fenno's words, a "different kind of Congress." When these members judged, finally, that the "legislative process was no longer producing the legislation they needed, the costs of maintaining the legislative status quo [embodied in the committee-dominated 'textbook Congress'] became very high." At the same time, continues congressional scholar Barbara Sinclair, "the costs of change in the direction of stronger party leadership declined," as House Democrats grew more similar in their ideologies.[50]

If the reforms of the House produced large-scale changes in the 1970s and 1980s, with fragmentation giving way to Speaker Jim Wright's consolidation of leadership powers in 1987–1988, the Senate of the same period underwent a less striking, more evolutionary transformation.[51] By 1989, both Senate parties had strong, partisan floor leaders in place (Senators Bob Dole [R-Kans.] and George Mitchell [D-Maine]), but the chamber continued to respect the almost sacred status of the individual member. A lone senator could often tie the institution in knots, as the whole deferred to the "rights" of a single willful legislator. Senators like Jesse Helms (R-N.C.) and Howard Metzenbaum (D-Ohio) gained notoriety and power as they proved willing, time and again, to bring Senate business to a halt if their desires were not accommodated.[52]

THE REPUBLICAN ERA, 1994–

After forty years of Democratic control of the House (the longest continuous stretch of partisan control in the American experience), Republicans won a majority of seats in 1994 and have retained a narrow majority since then. Indeed, the Republican House majority for the 108th Congress (2003–2004), 229 out of 435, is exactly the same margin as they had in 1995. Democrats also lost control of the Senate in 1994, by a 53–47 margin, and have continued as the minority in that chamber save for the May 2001–December 2002 period in which they held a one-vote majority after Vermont's James Jeffords abandoned the Republicans to become an Independent and caucus with the fifty Democratic senators.

The results of the 1998, 2000, and 2002 elections demonstrated the tenuous nature of party control in the Republican era. For example, in 1998, at the prodding of Majority Whip Tom DeLay, Republicans pushed through impeachment of President Clinton on a series of party-line votes in the House. But in the Senate, where moderation more often prevails, some Republicans refused to toe the party line and voted to acquit the president. Voters' responses to the impeachment proceedings in the House were negative, and the Republican majority lost seats as a result. Ironically, the first victim of the Republicans' reduced majority was Speaker Newt Gingrich, who was the individual most responsible for creating his party's triumph in 1994. Indeed, Gingrich was pushed out of the Speakership when six Republican representatives announced in December 1998 that they would not vote for him as Speaker when the House organized itself in January 1999.

Narrow margins offer the potential for disproportionate power to groupings of even a few members, especially on the majority side. Republicans thus sought a leader who would represent the conservatism of their members without alienating more moderate, more institutionally oriented legislators. Strangely enough, they had to make this choice twice — first selecting Appropriations Committee chair Robert Livingston (R-La.), only to have him resign in the wake of an impeachment-related admission of extramarital affairs. Subsequently, the party turned to little-known Representative Dennis Hastert (R-Ill.), a widely respected conservative who had maintained cordial relations with all wings of his own party, as well as with many Democrats. In an early speech Hastert proclaimed, "I will meet you [Democrats] halfway, maybe more so on occasion. I expect you to meet me halfway, too."[53] The Hastert Speakership has proven somewhat kinder and gentler than that of Gingrich, but Hastert has presided over a House that remains contentious and partisan.

With a thin majority in the House and increasingly assertive committee chairmen, the Republican leadership did allow centrifugal forces some leeway, but in 2003 Speaker Hastert and Majority Leader DeLay demonstrated that they could constrain the committee chairs when push came to shove; moreover, they were perfectly willing to punish members who had opposed them in the past. Thus, Representative Chris Shays (R-Ct.), sponsor of the Shays–Meehan campaign reform legislation that was enacted in 2002, was passed over in his bid to become chair of the Government Reform Committee. But the leadership's retribution against Shays paled before its actions in promoting Representative Richard Pombo (R-Calif.), a DeLay protégé and ardent foe of environmental regulations, to chair the Resources Committee, a move that hurdled him over several colleagues with greater seniority.[54]

In addition, Republican committee chairmen have remained subject to six-year term limits on their positions, while the Republican conference lifted the eight-year limitation on the Speaker's tenure. All in all, the post-1994 Republican era in the House has witnessed a systematic and highly successful centralization of party leadership power.

Less dramatically, but at least equally important, the Senate has also grown more partisan under Republican control. Beginning in 1994, a slow change occurred in the Senate whereby party unity grew stronger and indulgence of individual senators' tactics decreased. As the parties began to engage in "message politics," in which each party would try to frame every policy and major vote as a partisan campaign issue, pressure on senators to vote with the party increased.[55] The 1990s saw a marked rise in levels of party voting in the Senate.[56] Still, despite the increase in partisanship, the Senate has taken few formal organizational steps or made changes in the rules that substantially limit individual senators' powers. One major reason for the lack of substantive Senate rules changes is that members from both parties know that with a mere one- or two-seat majority, the next election can bring a shift back to the minority. Consequently, all senators have real incentives to preserve their individual powers.

THE CONGRESS OVER TIME

Regardless of which party holds the House and Senate majorities on Capitol Hill, the postreform Congress has evolved from the constitutional and organizational institution of previous eras. The Congress remains highly responsive to constituency interests, even when it addresses national issues such as health care, homeland security, and education. The separation of powers continues to affect its operations. Committees and party leaders remain central to congressional organization. Henry Clay and John C. Calhoun would recognize the ins and outs of politics on Capitol Hill 150 years after their salad days.

At the same time, there have been great changes, both within the Congress and in its relations with its environment. This chapter has traced some continuities and changes on Capitol Hill. Before considering these in more detail, we will examine some external forces that affect the capacity of Congress to act. In particular, we will look at the growth of advocacy groups and organized interests and the related expansion in the role of government. Clay and Calhoun may have faced the slavery question, the single most divisive issue in the American experience, but they did not have to parcel out a $2.4 trillion annual budget and respond to tens of thousands of special interests and lobbyists seeking to influence thousands of separate federal programs. In many ways, the seeds of fragmentation and individualism on Capitol Hill are sown by interests from across the country (and beyond) whose lobbyists congregate in committee rooms and whose fax messages pile high on 535 legislators' desks. The politics of Congress remains a politics of representation.

CHAPTER BIBLIOGRAPHY

MacNeil, Neil. *Forge of Democracy: The House of Representatives*. New York: David McKay, 1963.

Schickler, Eric. *Disjointed Pluralism: Institutional Innovation and the Development of the U.S. Congress*. Princeton, NJ: Princeton University Press, 2001.

Swift, Elaine. *The Making of an American Senate*. Ann Arbor: University of Michigan Press, 1996.

Notes

1. For an extended discussion, see Martin Diamond, Winston M. Fish, and Herbert Garfinkle, *The Democratic Republic* (Chicago: Rand McNally, 1966), pp. 75ff.

2. Ibid.

3. See Louis Fisher, *The Politics of Shared Power,* 2nd ed. (Washington, DC: CQ Press, 1987), pp. 4ff.

4. On the Jackson episode, see Senator Robert C. Byrd, "The Senate Censures Andrew Jackson," in his *The Senate 1789–1989: Addresses on the History of the United States Senate* (Washington, DC: Government Printing Office, 1988), pp. 127–141. Among many sources on Nixon and the White House tapes, see Louis Fisher, *Constitutional Conflicts between Congress and the President* (Princeton, NJ: Princeton University Press, 1985), pp. 213ff.

5. From *Federalist,* No. 51.

6. This practice was ended by the 1913 ratification of the Seventeenth Amendment, which provided for the popular election of senators, although such elections had been adopted widely, if informally, in many states.

7. Elaine Swift argues that the Senate, in particular, consumed much of the Framers' attention. See her *The Making of an American Senate* (Ann Arbor: University of Michigan Press, 1997).

8. George Galloway, *History of the House of Representatives* (New York: Thomas Crowell, 1961), p. 70. The Committee of the Whole House is the organizational format in which the House conducts almost all of its business. Rules are somewhat more permissive in this circumstance, and the legislative process is expedited. See Walter Oleszek, *Congressional Procedures and the Policy Process,* 3rd ed. (Washington, DC: CQ Press, 1989), pp. 144ff.

9. Joseph Cooper, perhaps the leading scholar of congressional organization, concludes that a standing committee system was established by Jackson's presidency. See his *Origins of the Standing Committees and the Development of the Modern House* (Houston, TX: Rice University Press, 1970). Galloway, *History of the House,* puts the date at 1816, although he notes that "by 1825, with the appointment of their chairmen by the Speaker . . . so far as its organization was concerned the House of Representatives had assumed its present form," p. 99.

10. The contribution of committees to both particularism and the beneficial sharing of expertise is explored at some length in Chapter 8.

11. The scholarship here is extensive. In relation to Congress, see, for example, James S. Young, *The Washington Community: 1800–1828* (New York: Columbia University Press, 1966); Allan G. Bogue and Mark Marlaire, "Of Mess and Men: The Boardinghouse and Congressional Voting, 1821–1842," *American Journal of Political Science* 19 (May 1975): pp. 207–230; and John F. Hoadley, *Origins of American Political Parties* (Lexington: University of Kentucky Press, 1986).

12. Alvin M. Josephy, Jr., *On the Hill* (New York: Touchstone, 1979), p. 79.

13. Galloway, *History of the House,* p. 99.

14. Ralph V. Harlow, *The History of Legislative Methods in the Period before 1825* (New Haven, CT: Yale University Press, 1917), pp. 176–177.

15. Ross K. Baker, *House and Senate,* 2nd ed. (New York: Norton, 1995), pp. 37–38.

16. Swift, *The Making of an American Senate,* p. 140.

17. From *Democracy in America,* quoted in *Origins and Development of Congress,* 2nd ed. (Washington, DC: Congressional Quarterly, Inc., 1982), p. 215.

18. Byrd, *The Senate: 1789–1989,* p. 107.

19. See Roger Davidson and Walter Oleszek, "Adaptation and Consolidation: Structured Innovation in the U.S. House of Representatives," *Legislature Studies Quarterly* 1 (1977): pp. 37ff.

20. Ibid., p. 23.

21. Davidson and Oleszek note that the "disappearing quorum appears to have originated with [former President] John Quincy Adams, . . . who served with distinction in the House after leaving the White House." Adams refused to vote on a proslavery measure in 1832, and enough fellow members joined him so that a quorum was not present. The House could not conduct business absent a quorum (a majority of its members). "Armed with this precedent, obstructionist minorities for more than fifty years could bring the work of the House to a halt." *Congress against Itself* (Bloomington: University of Indiana Press, 1977), p. 23.

22. Quoted in Samuel W. McCall, *The Life of Thomas Brackett Reed* (Boston: Houghton Mifflin, 1914), p. 170.

23. Randall Strahan, "Thomas Brackett Reed and the Rise of Party Government," in Roger H. Davidson, Susan Webb Hammond, and Raymond W. Smock, eds., *Masters of the House* (Boulder, CO: Westview Press, 1998), pp. 33–62.

24. A compact summary of Cannon's actions can be found in Davidson and Oleszek, *Congress against Itself,* pp. 25ff. See also Ronald Peters, *The American*

Speakership (Washington, DC: CQ Press, 1990).

25. James S. Fleming, "Oscar W. Underwood: The First Modern House Leader, 1911–1915," in *Masters of the House,* pp. 91–118.

26. David J. Rothman, *Politics and Power* (New York: Atheneum, 1969), p. 4. Some of the arguments in the following paragraphs are drawn from Rothman's work.

27. Over the years Republicans have often called their caucus the Republican Conference. The term *caucus* is used here as a generic description of all the members of one party in one legislative chamber.

28. Rothman, *Politics and Power,* pp. 58–59.

29. Ibid., p. 60.

30. Congressional Quarterly's *Origins and Development of Congress,* 2nd ed., cites congressional scholar George Galloway, who notes "that more than half [the senators] chosen by legislative caucuses [in the states] were subsequently approved [through reelection to their office] by the people."

31. Ibid., p. 244.

32. Sarah A. Binder and Steven S. Smith, *Politics or Principle?* (Washington, DC: Brookings Institution, 1997), pp. 114–115.

33. See Stephen Skowronek, *Building the New American State* (New York: Cambridge University Press, 1982).

34. Roger Davidson and Walter Oleszek, *Congress and Its Members,* 3rd ed. (Washington, DC: CQ Press, 1990), p. 30.

35. Steven S. Smith and Christopher J. Deering, *Committees in Congress,* 2nd ed. (Washington, DC: CQ Press, 1990), p. 34.

36. Although many careful scholars had described and analyzed the Congress prior to the 1950s, never before was there such a systematic examination of the institution. The American Political Science Association's Study of Congress project sponsored much of the work by such scholars as Richard F. Fenno, Jr., Robert Peabody, John Manley, and Charles Jones.

37. Kenneth A. Shepsle, "The Changing Textbook Congress," in John E. Chubb and Paul E. Peterson, eds., *Can the Government Govern?* (Washington, DC: Brookings Institution, 1989), pp. 238–266.

38. Shepsle, "The Changing Textbook Congress," p. 239.

39. In the 1950s, with the exception of Representative Leonor Sullivan (D-Mo.), chair of the Merchant Marine and Fisheries Committee, committee chairs were men, and Congress was a bastion of white, middle-aged (and older) men. On Johnson, among many others, see Ralph Huitt, "Democratic Party Leadership in the Senate," *American Political Science Review* 60 (1961): pp. 331–344; on Rayburn, see D. B. Hardeman and Donald C. Bacon, *Rayburn* (Lanham, MD: Madison Books, 1987).

40. James Sundquist's *Politics and Policy* (Washington, DC: Brookings Institution, 1968) provides an excellent guide to the obstructionism of the 1950s as well as the policy changes of the 1960s.

41. Robert Bendiner, *Obstacle Course on Capitol Hill* (New York: McGraw-Hill, 1964).

42. See, in particular, Jeff Fishel, *Party and Opposition* (New York: David McKay, 1973), pp. 161ff.

43. Arthur G. Stevens, Jr., Arthur H. Miller, and Thomas E. Mann, "Mobilization of Liberal Strength in the House,

1955–1970: The Democratic Study Group," *American Political Science Review* 68 (1974): pp. 667–681.

44. Richard F. Fenno, Jr., "If, as Ralph Nader Says, Congress Is the 'Broken Branch,' How Come We Love Our Congressmen So Much?" in Norman J. Ornstein, ed., *Congress in Change* (New York: Praeger, 1975), p. 287.

45. See Burdett Loomis, *The New American Politician* (New York: Basic Books, 1988), chap. 1.

46. Shepsle, "The Changing Textbook Congress," p. 256.

47. A good collection of articles by leading scholars that captures the difficulties of the reform era can be found in Frank Mackaman, ed., *Understanding Congressional Leadership* (Washington, DC: CQ Press, 1981).

48. The commercial portrayed O'Neill as driving a car and ignoring the pleas of a young aide, who warned him that they were running out of gas. Although effective, the ad focused great attention on the Speaker, increased his stature as a national figure, and encouraged him to take a more aggressive stance toward the Reagan programs in 1981 and beyond.

49. These issues will be considered at greater length later in this book (in Chapter 5, especially). A minimal list of key sources includes David Rohde, *Parties and Leaders in the Postreform House* (Chicago: University of Chicago Press, 1991); Barbara Sinclair, *Legislators, Leaders, and Lawmaking* (Baltimore: Johns Hopkins University Press, 1995); and Roger H. Davidson, ed., *The Postreform Congress* (New York: St. Martin's, 1992).

50. Sinclair, *Legislators, Leaders, and Lawmaking*, p. 301. See also Sinclair, "Tip O'Neill and Contemporary House

Leadership," in *Masters of the House,* pp. 289–318.

51. See especially, Barbara Sinclair, *The Transformation of the U.S. Senate* (Baltimore: Johns Hopkins University Press, 1989).

52. Why this is so requires some detailed untangling; see Chapter 9.

53. Richard E. Cohen and Marilyn Werber Serafini, "In the Eye of the House Hurricane," *National Journal,* January 2 and 9, 1999, p. 49.

54. Michael Doyle, "Pombo Wins Key Leadership Post," *Modesto Bee,* January 9, 2003, p. A1.

55. C. Lawrence Evans. "Committees, Leaders, and Message Politics," in Lawrence C. Dodd and Bruce Oppenheimer, eds. *Congress Reconsidered* (Washington DC: CQ Press, 2001); also see Patrick Sellers, "Strategy and Background in Congressional Campaigns," *American Political Science Review* 92 (1998): 159–171.

56. For 2001–2002 figures, see Chapter 5.

Three

THE CHANGING
ENVIRONMENT OF
CONGRESSIONAL POLITICS

M any of the centrifugal forces affecting Congress originate outside the institution. Indeed, as a representative body, Congress was designed to offer easy access to those interests and individuals who sought influence over policy. To a greater or lesser extent, it has always fulfilled this goal. Until the mid-twentieth century, save in extraordinary circumstances (war, the Great Depression), Congress met for about half the year. From July through January, members would live at home, among their constituents. With the New Deal, World War II, and the growth of government, to say nothing of the widespread installation of air conditioning in Washington, congressional sessions have come to run virtually year-round. At the same time, air travel has afforded almost all members the opportunity to live in their districts and join the "Tuesday through Thursday" club of those who spend three days a week in Washington. Although many recently elected legislators have made this choice, the sight of California lawmakers stumbling into committee hearings after returning on the Tuesday morning red-eye flight scarcely offers the promise of serious legislating. In addition, large increases in staff allotments, the growth of district offices, and advances in communication mean that almost all members are well informed about their districts, regardless of their formal place of residence. Indeed, for all the talk of legislators being out of touch with their constituents, a strong case exists that they know altogether too much about the preferences of their most vocal and visible local district interests.

CONGRESS: THE PERMEABLE BRANCH

In Washington, members of Congress can almost always carve out a few minutes from their busy schedules to chat with visitors from their districts. Moreover, responding to constituent communications (increasingly electronic) receives priority attention from legislative offices. After all, it is the home folks who have sent the representatives to Capitol Hill. But access to Congress is scarcely limited to members' constituents. Traditionally, interest groups have found lawmakers hospitable to their requests for time and attention.

The ease of obtaining a legislative audience contrasts markedly with the lengthy process of winning a hearing in the judiciary or the difficulty of gaining an audience with top-level executive-branch officials. During its 2001–2002 session, for example, the Supreme Court agreed to hear a mere seventy-eight oral arguments from among the thousands of appeals filed. Likewise, the presidency and the top rungs of the bureaucracy are highly insulated from most citizens, electronic mail and town hall–style meetings notwithstanding. In contrast, the Congress — especially the House — has always opened its doors to complaints and requests from citizens and organized interests.[1] Over the years, as the national government has grown larger and made increasingly important decisions, the demands on Congress have risen in number and intensity, but even before the policy explosions of the New Deal and the Great Society there were many instances of intense, sophisticated, and frequently successful lobbying efforts by organized interests.

As industry expanded and flourished in the 1870s, interests swarmed around Congress, often directly and corruptly influencing individual legislators. For example, in the years following World War I, the farm lobby, led by the American Farm Bureau Federation (AFBF) demonstrated its worth — in terms of information and support — for dozens of legislators, who repaid the agriculture interests with increasing access to the process of lawmaking.[2] More subtle than most interests from the pre-1900 era, the farm lobby often worked through farmers back in the legislators' home districts. The political and policy information that farm groups provided to members of Congress gave them good reason to listen to these organizations. Legislators have always faced great uncertainties in understanding both the policy and political effects of their actions; well-informed groups such as the AFBF could offer information that would make members a bit less uncertain, especially in terms of their constituents' opinions and the positions of the farm community. Providing regular access to the Farm Bureau thus benefited both the lawmakers and the interest group.

The "textbook Congress" that emerged by the 1950s dictated a committee orientation for interests in search of access. In the 1950s many committees served as one corner of close-knit triangular relationships, variously labeled "cozy" or "iron" triangles, that linked them to key outside interests and, as the third corner, to particular agencies within the federal bureaucracy.[3] For example, sugar interests worked with the appropriate Agriculture Committee subcommittees in the House and Senate and the relevant U.S. Department of Agriculture officials to maintain domestic sugar prices that were consistently several times higher than those in world markets. By the 1960s, various interests began to challenge the tidy, profitable sugar subsystem. Consumer and environmental groups, among others, began to influence agriculture policies. In 1974, the sugar triangle broke apart, as the subcommittee could not maintain control over the price support policies.[4] Subsequently, however, sugar interests succeeded in lobbying a broad mix of legislators to reconstruct a similar marketing system that continues to fix U.S. prices at a considerably higher level than elsewhere in the world.

More generally, while the Congress changed greatly from 1960 into the 1980s, so too did its environment. In parallel, related developments, more interest groups became politically active as more governmental policies prompted them to action.[5] Environmental groups, for example, possessed almost no political clout in the 1950s; either they emphasized traditional conservation issues or they remained outside the policy debate. By 1970, both traditional and newly formed environmental organizations had become major players in policy making on issues that ranged from pesticide levels to air quality standards to toxic waste disposal. As a result, many old policy assumptions, such as maximizing returns for domestic sugar producers, were successfully challenged.[6]

Not only did interest groups serve as effective advocates on behalf of specific programs, but new policies engendered new agencies, even whole new departments such as Energy and Education, each with its own turf to protect. As the federal budget rose from $100 billion in 1969 to $2.4 trillion in 2004, many interests had become entrenched within government as well as outside it. Legislative consideration of issues thus has proceeded within a complicated, dense environment of complex policies and numerous organized interests.[7]

Equally important, in the 1960s presidents like John F. Kennedy and Lyndon Johnson could promise new programs for particular constituencies, such as the poor and the elderly, which would largely distribute new benefits.[8] Indeed, the impulse to distribute benefits to specific constituents and interests operates as a key centrifugal force within the Congress.[9] Lawmakers seek to deliver concentrated benefits (such as a dam or farm support payments) paid for by widely dispersed costs (a cent or two from every tax dollar). But as both federal programs and budget deficits have grown, distributive politics has proven an increasingly difficult game to play.

From the 1990s on, budget rules have generally decreed that for every policy winner there must be a policy loser. Large budget deficits meant that new programs have to compete against established policies. Moreover, so-called entitlement programs, such as Medicaid or farm price support payments, often require more funds, and the expenditures must increase the deficit or come from some other program. But where? Such redistributive questions continually bedevil members of Congress, who cannot endlessly distribute benefits when the government consistently spends more than it takes in. Redistributive policies — which reallocate funds from one sector of society to another, as in welfare — ordinarily produce sharp conflicts on Capitol Hill.[10] The contentious partisan battles over budgets in the 1980s and 1990s did little to increase public confidence in the Congress, largely because individual legislators have continued to seek to funnel benefits to their constituencies and their favored interests.

At the same time, the Congress has placed restrictive caps on overall spending, which pose difficulties in responding to new priorities, such as increased defense allocations, even when there is a federal budget surplus. The post–9/11 expansion of costs for homeland security and national defense demonstrate one way to increase spending. Few senators or representatives want to be seen as unsupportive of measures designed to enhance our security. Indeed, the budget surpluses of 1999–2001 quickly disappeared by 2002–2003, as the effects of the Bush tax cut interacted with the costs of fighting terrorism at home and abroad, the dramatic slowdown in the economy, and the preparations for war with Iraq. Still, most pressures on federal spending have not come from military threats; rather, they have flowed from domestic concerns, often at the behest of organized interests.

This chapter explores four major changes in the congressional environment: the advocacy explosion, as the number and specialization of interests have grown steadily since the 1960s; the policy explosion and the impact of sixty years of an activist federal government; the overwhelming attention given to budgetary considerations since the early 1980s — the so-called *fiscalization* of policy making; and relatively low levels of respect for Congress. The growing numbers of interests and policies have exerted significant decentralizing pressures on the Congress, whereas the fiscalization of policy has operated to centralize congressional actions, as budgetary concerns dominate decision making. And the low public standing of Congress may make it all the more difficult for its members to address divisive, and potentially unpopular, policies.

Related to these developments, several other external changes also have occurred; these range from the gradual weakening (and then strengthening) of political parties to the growing political sophistication of business interests to major transformations in the media and in information technology. In short, the Congress of the 1950s did its work in a very different context than does the Congress of the twenty-first century. Overall, the contemporary Congress has grown both highly responsive to particular interests and remarkably insular within the highly competitive, highly partisan environment of Washington policy making and Capitol Hill politics.

The Advocacy Explosion

Although organized interests have a long and storied history of making their case on Capitol Hill, and many contemporary lobbying techniques had their origin near the turn of the twentieth century, current patterns of legislative advocacy derive from the growth of interest groups since the 1960s.[11] In the early 1960s political scientists, if not journalists, often discounted the impact of interest groups on most policy making. Lobbyists plied their trade, of course, but many interests lacked the resources and sophistication to wield much influence.[12] Between 1960 and 1990, the number of active organized interests and their use of a wide range of techniques for influencing policymakers rose sharply. Simply put, more lobbyists have been working for more interests and have been employing more tactics to affect policy outcomes. Although much popular attention has been directed toward the tremendous post-1974 growth of political action committees (from 608 PACs in 1974 to 4,009 in 1984, with a slight rise to 4,328 for the 2001–2002 electoral cycle),[13] organized interests have expanded their actions across the board. The number of Washington-based interest representatives grew from 4,000 in 1977 to about 17,000 in 2002; registered lobbyists rose in numbers from around 1,000 in the 1960s to almost 6,000 in 1981 and to an astonishing 20,000 in 2002; trade associations relocated their offices to Washington in great numbers during the 1980s; and between 1973 and 1983, the District of Columbia Bar increased its membership from around 11,000 lawyers to more than 37,000.[14] As of the mid-1990s, the best estimate of the number of individuals who earn their living from Washington-based attempts to influence policies stood at an astounding 91,000.[15] Among these are more than 19,000 "governmental affairs experts" who represent an almost limitless number of interests.[16]

The advocacy explosion has not affected all sectors of the Washington community with equal force. Most notable, perhaps, have been the declining role of labor unions, the growing presence of corporate and professional interests, and the increasing importance of large-scale citizens groups, ranging from Common Cause to the Sierra Club to the American Association of Retired Persons and its 33 million members.[17] And many of these membership groups have become less and less tied to dues collected from their members.[18] In addition, American states, cities, and other governmental units came to Washington in droves during the 1970s era of revenue sharing, stayed to press their cases during the leaner years of the Reagan administration, and have remained to lobby against unfunded federal mandates.[19] In addition, foreign governments and private interests, often acting through sophisticated Washington lobbying and public relations firms, have become important players in the complex politics of trade, foreign aid, and international business.[20]

From the 1960s through 2000, the thousands of interests actively seeking to influence congressional decisions multiplied several times over. Equally important, however, has been the wide variety of strategies and tactics that organized interests have employed in their efforts to gain advantage. By the end of the 1980s a majority of Washington-based organizations reported using more than twenty different techniques for exercising influence; these ranged from testifying at legislative hearings to joining coalitions to mounting grassroots lobbying efforts.[21] At the same time, these groups have used most of these techniques considerably more often than they had in the past. For example, two-thirds of the organizations noted that they paid increased attention to press relations, worked harder at building coalitions, and spent more time contacting governmental officials.[22]

By the 1990s more and more interests were finding ways to use the Internet for building support, identifying contributors, organizing grassroots operations, and constructing issue-specific coalitions.[23] And these advances represented just the beginning of a wave of technological changes that will affect the ability of advocates to target their messages to legislators, staffers, key supporters, and policy elites, among others.

In the end, the advocacy explosion encompasses at least three distinct elements. First, there are more groups and interests in the fray. Second, there are many new techniques available to all interests; computers and enhanced communication capacities allow groups to serve as linking agents between the public — or specific sectors of the public — and legislators. Third, both well-established groups and new entries are employing a more extensive range of techniques to influence policy decisions.[24] As a result, more messages from more interests than ever before are aimed at legislators in more timely ways. Whether they hear those messages remains an open question.

Lobbying: Information, Access, and Influence

Despite their personal staffs, committee staffs, and a host of support agencies, members of Congress often find it difficult to inform themselves adequately on a wide range of policies. There is a great deal to know, and time pressures are often intense. This does not mean that they do not have enough information on most issues. Quite the contrary. Capitol Hill is awash in information: from congressional staff (see Chapter 9), from think tanks, from the media, and, of course, from organized interests and lobbyists. But truly useful information is often in short supply. Legislators operate under highly uncertain conditions much of the time, and they must frequently act with less than perfect information on a given subject.

Useful information comes in three general types: (1) political intelligence that lays out the reelection consequences of members' actions, (2) process-oriented details that allow for assessing the chances that a bill will make it through the legislative process, and (3) policy data that spell out the impact of a proposal.[25] As one insider account puts it:

> Lobbyists see it as their job to persuade legislators that voters are on the lobbyists' side. . . . [They] know that the best way to guarantee that their point of view will be heard is to take the constituents with them when they go to speak to members of Congress. Lobbyists also function as unpaid staff to the decision-makers . . . [and] provide information about both policy and process that [legislators] cannot get. . . .[26]

Thus, from an informational perspective, lobbyists are providing a kind of subsidy to lawmakers. The lingering question remains, what do they expect from such subsidies?[27]

Although lobbyists are important sources of information, they must first gather bits and pieces of relevant data that will be of use to legislators, and then they must have access to those they desire to influence. Thus, much of lobbying resides in accumulating useful (that is, not widely known) information and finding ways to get the material to relevant legislators. Lobbyists gain access in various ways, including socializing (subject to some restrictions in the wake of 1995 reforms[28]), making campaign contributions, and developing reputations for providing accurate and useful information.

Once access has been obtained, however, two questions remain: Whom does one seek to lobby? And under what conditions does access allow for influence? Despite the intriguing first steps of some congressional scholars, there is no clear answer concerning who becomes the target of lobbying.[29] Although hard-boiled foes are rarely sought out, both allies and the undecided (and even nondogmatic opponents) are frequently the objects of attention. As for influence, lobbying most often succeeds when it focuses on low-profile issues and legislation, as opposed to matters that stir the public's interest. It is no accident that highly complex issues such as telecommunications reform and tax law generate tremendous amounts of lobbying in that the complexities of both policies and procedures offer great opportunities for advocates to turn access into influence as they shape arguments that favor their causes, often on an obscure procedural point or some dense wording, buried deep inside a comprehensive piece of legislation.

Public Lobbying: International Trade, 1993–2002

Even when conflict over legislation becomes highly publicized, organized interests can still affect decisions on Capitol Hill. The continuing struggles over U.S. trade policy illustrate how the interest group environment can shape congressional actions. In the early 1990s, the Congress was faced with implementing the North American Free Trade Agreement (NAFTA) and ratifying the General Agreement on Tariffs and Trade (GATT). Given that both agreements enjoyed the strong support of Presidents Reagan, Bush, and Clinton, the Congress represented the logical venue for opponents to mount their attacks, which emphasized the loss of American jobs (with NAFTA) and national sovereignty (with GATT), in that international tribunals could rule against some practices of U.S. businesses.

Opponents of NAFTA included an unlikely coalition of organized labor, including textile and apparel workers, consumer advocates (particularly Ralph Nader), some environmental groups, and, perhaps most importantly, 1992 Reform Party presidential candidate Ross Perot. Perot brought both his own constituents and his highly public tactics to the battle. Indeed, Nader, the environmentalists, and Perot combined to produce an effective outside attack on the trade accord; they could direct their own supporters to lobby hundreds of members of Congress while they simultaneously advertised extensively against the pact. Only late in the day did NAFTA backers, many prompted by President Clinton, counter the public arguments of Perot, Nader, and their allies.

NAFTA opponents did not have to rely solely on sophisticated grassroots lobbying techniques, clever public relations, and considerable paid advertising to gain ground in the House; they enjoyed the support of key Democratic legislators near the core of the party leadership. House Democratic Whip David Bonior (D-Mich.) proved inexhaustible in his coordination of opposing forces within the House. Less public, to reduce the embarrassment for his own party's president, was the firm opposition of House Majority Leader Richard Gephardt (D-Mo.). As a highly representative body (both Bonior's and Gephardt's districts included large numbers of union members), the House encourages interests to seek out powerful champions to provide inside leadership on key issues.[30] NAFTA foes could scarcely have done better than to enlist two of the three top leaders in the House. Only after the Clinton White House made some eleventh-hour pleas, agreed to a few modest concessions, and issued several specific policy clarifications did NAFTA win House approval. The opponents had set the terms of the debate, mounted impressive grassroots campaigns by constituents, and benefited from advertising purchased by Perot and others.

Many of the same interests came together to oppose GATT's approval in late 1994. Obscured by the debate over health care reform, GATT provides a somewhat different illustration of the ways in which organized groups and the Congress can serve each other's needs. Although some business interests opposed NAFTA, virtually all major corporate bodies expressed strong support for the lower tariffs promised by GATT.[31] GATT induced considerably less public opposition than did NAFTA. Nonetheless, congressional consideration of the treaty offered an attractive opportunity for foes of the trade pact. In the Senate, which is usually free trade oriented, opponents had a champion in Senator Ernest Hollings (D-S.C.), whose state's textile industry desired protection from the competition of cheap foreign labor. Using his individual power as a senator, Hollings succeeded in holding up a vote on GATT for forty-five days — from early October until after the 1994 congressional elections. Opponents hoped that this delay would allow them to mount a vigorous and public challenge to GATT, with Ross Perot again playing a major role. In the case of GATT, constituents' concerns were expressed through one senator's active support, coupled with the House's overall sensitivity to district concerns, thus providing an opening for groups to delay or defeat trade legislation.

Helped by generally supportive Republican leaders, the Clinton administration won approval for the treaty, but only after vigorous debate. Given a design that usually discourages speedy or efficient decision making, Congress offered organized interests, with their increased numbers and capacities to mobilize key constituents, an inviting opportunity to take advantage of the very openness that defines the institution.[32]

In 1998, the protectionist coalition forces prevailed when the House decisively defeated (243-180) a bill that would have granted President Clinton the same "fast track" authority that every president since Gerald Ford had enjoyed.[33] Such authority is crucial to passing a trade bill through the Congress in that it allows a single up-or-down vote on the legislation. By denying Clinton fast track power, the House essentially killed trade legislation by opening it up to dozens, even hundreds, of special interest provisions. Members of the House and Senate were reacting to the negative effects of NAFTA and GATT on local industries in their districts and states, and some members who had previously supported free trade changed their votes.[34]

In 2000, Bill Clinton waged a rugged battle against the same set of forces to extend "permanent normalized trading relations" with China, and in 2002 George W. Bush narrowly regained the right to negotiate on a fast track basis, overcoming the opposition of labor unions and environmentalists to gain a House majority (215-212). To obtain this bargaining authority, Bush agreed to a Senate compromise, put forward by Majority Leader Tom Daschle (D-S.D.), that expanded by $12 billion the Trade Adjustment Assistance Program, which provides both direct payments and training for workers whose jobs are lost because of enhanced trade. In short, even when opponents lose sequential battles against free trade, they can win significant concessions for their strongest supporters.

The Policy Explosion

Tied directly to the growth of interests is the great increase in the volume of national policy established since the 1930s, especially since the 1960s. In 1930, the reach of the federal government did not extend very far in terms of expenditures, taxation, or regulation. Congressional committee chairs may have been gaining independent power at this time, but they had very little to control.

Political analyst Michael Barone writes that "macroeconomic fiscal policy, redistribution of wealth, and government spending programs were not major issues [because] the federal government neither raised nor spent . . . much money in the late 1920s."[35] Most federal spending went to pay for the military, either in the form of current expenses, interest on the national debt incurred by borrowing to pay for past wars, or veterans' benefits. Of the $3.3 billion budget for 1930, less than $1 billion went to fund all other governmental activities.[36]

TABLE 3-1
Federal Spending, 1940-2004 (in billions, not adjusted for inflation)

Year	National Defense	Nondefense	Total (including interest on debt)
1940	$ 1.7	$7.8	$ 9.5
1950	13.7	28.8	42.6
1960	48.1	44.1	92.2
1970	81.7	114.0	195.6
1980	134.0	456.9	590.9
1990	299.0	848.9	1,151.8
1995	271.0	1,034.7	1,518.9
2000	294.5	1,594.3	1,788.8
2004 (est.)	390.4	1,839.0	2,229.0

Sources: Harold W. Stanley and Richard G. Niemi, eds., *Visual Statistics on American Politics,* 2nd ed. (Washington, DC: CQ Press, 1990), pp. 385–386, and Allen Schick, *The Federal Budget: Politics, Policy, Process* (Washington, DC: Brookings Institution, 1995), pp. 8, 33; *Congressional Quarterly Weekly Report,* February 11, 1995, p. 429; FY 2000 Budget and 2004 estimate, <www.access.gpo.gov/usbudget>.

Even after the increased spending commitments of the New Deal, domestic expenditures stood at just $7.8 billion in 1940 and $12.6 billion in 1946, the first post–World War II year. As late as 1954, domestic spending amounted to only $21.6 billion, a figure that almost doubled by 1960, the last year of the Eisenhower administration. Defense costs averaged $47 billion between 1952 and 1960; by 1960, the year of John F. Kennedy's election, total federal spending totaled $92 billion — a substantial increase since 1930, to be sure, but a figure that did not provide for much in the way of ambitious social programs.

The pent-up demand for more federal domestic intervention (such as Medicare) and more regulation (for example, the Environmental Protection Agency), along with continued requirements for high levels of Cold War defense spending (including Vietnam), produced great increases in both domestic and military spending during the 1960s (see Table 3–1). Still, the major story told in Table 3–1 is that of the great escalation in governmental expenditures during the 1970s and 1980s, when Republicans controlled the presidency for all but Jimmy Carter's 1977–1981 term.

No single explanation adequately accounts for burgeoning federal budgets, but the very existence of new programs in the 1960s and 1970s helped to create great pressures, both inside and outside the government, to increase spending levels. For example, the adoption of Medicare in 1965 produced a continuing rise in federal health-related costs over the next decade — from $9.9 billion in 1965 to $41.5 billion in 1975. More important than the mere cost, however, was the fundamental redefinition of health care as an issue in American politics. As one scholar notes, "By nationalizing a large portion of the bill, Medicare made health care inflation a public-sector problem and placed it on the policy agenda."[37] In 1996, the government's own estimates that Medicare would go broke by 2001 both made the issue central to congressional campaigns and placed it on the top of the agenda for the 105th Congress. Subsequently, Medicare funding has become an increasing problem for an American society with an aging population. But the number of powerful interests involved, from doctors to drug companies to hospitals to the elderly, have made it extremely difficult for Congress to agree on meaningful reforms.

Although the new policy commitments of the 1960s and 1970s often required more spending in such areas as health, education, and nutrition (in the form of food stamps), the reach of federal regulatory programs was at least as long. As shown in Table 3–2, from 1940 to 1980 the length of one year's body of regulations, printed in the *Federal Register,* grew almost twenty-fold, although the 1980 figure is artificially high; the Reagan administration cut back substantially on regulations but still managed to average 54,000 pages of *Federal Register* material per year. More importantly, most regulations stayed on the books, thus producing an overwhelmingly dense policy environment by the 1980s. Nor has the *Register*'s publication rate slowed down in the post-Reagan era (see Table 3–2).

TABLE 3-2
The Growth of Federal Regulation

Year	Number of Pages in *Federal Register*
1940	5,307
1950	9,562
1960	14,479
1970	20,032
1980	87,012
1990	53,618
2000	83,293

Sources: Harold W. Stanley and Richard G. Niemi, *Vital Statistics on American Politics,* 2nd ed. (Washington, DC: CQ Press, 1990), p. 248; Ornstein et al., *Visual Statistics on Congress,* 1995–1996, p. 165, *Federal Register,* 2000.

By the 1970s, Theodore Lowi described a national government that had fundamentally changed the nature of American political life. He saw the results as a "two-part model" of highly institutionalized politics, in which:

▶ "The national government by some formal action monopolizes a given area of private activity." This may be accomplished through spending, regulation, or other means.

▶ "Following that, a program is authorized and an administrative agency is put into operation to work without legal guidelines through an elaborate, sponsored bargaining process [between governmental agencies and specific interests]."[38]

In the end, tens of thousands of governmental units and interests have large stakes in countless discretionary decisions made within the bureaucracy, inside the presidency, by the judiciary, and on Capitol Hill. Lowi argues that there is virtually no accountability for most decisions; instead of clear policy and well-defined procedure, there is only process.[39]

This "process" has become the heart and soul of relations between organized interests, the bureaucracy, and the Congress. Robert Salisbury observes that much activity by groups and other interests emphasizes the monitoring of information sources: "Washington is, after all, the main source of what governmental officials are doing or planning to do. To get that information in a timely way, a continuous and alert presence . . . is vital."[40] Moreover, it is accurate information on political contingencies, not on policy alternatives, that is often most at a premium. Given its size and diversity, the Congress is ideally suited to provide such knowledge. Individual members and their staffs are well positioned to convey valuable political information to particular interests; in turn, these interests will have good reason to support their reelection bids. Through the 1980s, ideology played little role in the game. Rather, majority House Democrats became the vehicles for many business interests that wanted to "invest" in careerist legislators who would, it seemed, control the Congress, and especially the House, for the foreseeable future.[41] Of course, once Republicans won a majority of the House seats in 1994, such an arrangement lost much of its luster for many corporate and professional interests, whose support for the GOP increased dramatically, as we shall see in Chapter 4.

The Budget: Wrestling with an 800-Pound Gorilla

The growth of organized interests and the extended reach of national policies are developments that have reinforced each other. For the most part, both trends reflect an increased fragmentation of the decision-making context. Historically, the way the Congress appropriated funds also contributed to this decentralization. After the president proposed a unified budget, the House and Senate would break up the spending proposals into thirteen separate pieces, each initially considered by one House appropriations subcommittee. Only at the end of the legislative process, with the passage of thirteen distinct bills, would the Congress and the president know how much had actually been appropriated. This decentralized format worked reasonably well into the 1960s,[42] but by the early 1970s pressures began to mount for a more coherent congressional approach to the entire budget.

Legislators began to face major budgetary problems as a result of enacting numerous policies and having many groups capable of competing to influence them; policies cost money (obtained from taxes) in addition to conferring benefits. During the 1950s and 1960s, the appropriations committees could maintain a check on overall spending by the Congress, but by the early 1970s, this informal constraint had weakened substantially.[43] In the 1970s, the Congress provided itself with the staff and committee structure to increase its role in constructing annual budgets, which had been almost totally the province of the president and the well-staffed Office of Management and Budget.[44] After 1974, when Senate and House budget committees and the Congressional Budget Office were established in the Budget Reform Act, members of Congress could fight their "budget wars" with the executive branch on roughly equal footing.[45] This legislative capacity became especially important during the Reagan administration, when 1981 tax cuts meant that every succeeding budget would include a large deficit and result in great pressures on existing levels of spending.

Over the 1980s, a centralizing change that was implicit in the new budget arrangements modified the nature of congressional actions: the fiscalization of the policy process. In short, *fiscalization* simply means that the question of paying for services and programs has become the proverbial "800-pound gorilla," a beast that can sit wherever it wants. Within the contemporary Congress, this budgetary ape camps out in almost every committee room and leadership meeting. Controlling spending levels and the funding (or killing) of continuing programs have become the central issues of the postreform Congress. In sum, the budget has ceased to be an "empowering process," at least for federal initiatives. Rather, the contemporary budget "often appears to be a limiting process . . . [and it] crowds out genuine choice; it forces tomorrow's programs to give way to yesterday's decisions."[46]

With little ability to fund new programs, legislators sought to control the spending commitments that had already been enacted into law. The large annual deficits through the 1980s and into the 1990s demonstrated the difficulty of reducing expenditures; nonetheless, the post-1981 period has been dominated by budgetary politics. In several highly centralized budget summits from 1982 to 1993, congressional leaders negotiated with top executive-branch officials to arrive at acceptable spending and deficit levels. Thurber and Durst conclude that this will continue, in that "budget and party leaders will continue to build coalitions to formulate the budget and to negotiate with the president about spending priorities. [Current practices produce] a tighter zero-sum budget game with more control and with top-down, centralized budgeting by the congressional party leadership."[47]

This party-based, centralized process is what came crashing down on first-term Democratic Representative Marjorie Margolies-Mezvinsky as she came under intense pressures from the party leadership and the Clinton administration to vote in favor of the 1993 budget agreement, whose taxation provisions she had consistently opposed. The context for such pressures is a budget process that regularly produces high-visibility votes on the entire set of spending and taxing commitments for an entire year. Every increase in funding for one program must be taken out of the spending for some other governmental activity. Debate over policies thus turns more and more on fiscal considerations. Put bluntly, how much will each program cost? In such an environment, it is those who can survey the entire budget — members of the budget and appropriations committees and the party leadership — who have the most leverage in determining outcomes. The very nature of redistributive, or zero-sum, decision making is to empower those whose reach facilitates negotiations and whose power can enforce agreements, as long as they can convince even a bare majority of members to agree. Short of voting against the entire budget agreement, rank-and-file members of both parties can exercise little influence over the budgets that their leaders construct.

One notable exception lies in the Senate's post-1985 use of the Byrd Rule, named after Senator Robert Byrd (D-W.V.), who served as Appropriations Committee chair from 1987 through 1994. This rule subjects reconciliation bills (those that address total income and spending) to objections if language in the bill goes beyond the overall balancing of revenues and spending. Individual items can be challenged as extraneous, and a three-fifth's vote is required to sustain an item.

The politics of budgets shifted dramatically during the second term of the Clinton administration. The budget deficit first narrowed, then disappeared in the late 1990s, buoyed by a strong economy and the results of the 1990 and 1993 budget deals that restricted spending levels. Legislators such as House Budget Committee chair John Kasich (R-Ohio), who had spent their entire careers railing against budget deficits, needed to address new questions surrounding emerging surpluses.[48]

The prospect of a golden era of budget surpluses well into the twenty-first century proved illusory, however. The combination of a sharp economic slowdown, which began in 2000, the passage of major tax cuts in 2001, and the impact of post–9/11 spending requirements for security produced a rapid return to red ink for the federal government. For members of Congress, the reemergence of deficits meant that the long-term problems of funding Social Security and Medicare would become increasingly more difficult to address. Even as President Bush put forward a proposal to expand Medicare to cover some drug costs for the elderly, he found it essential to cut back on domestic appropriations for a large number of programs. Much as in the 1980s and early 1990s, budget choices continue to mean funding one activity at the expense of some other activity.

Can't Get No Respect: The Unpopular Congress

> *The very openness of the legislative process, which might otherwise be thought to endear Congress to the people, is much more likely to have the opposite effect. . . . Thus, while Congress is sometimes viewed by the public as an enemy, we wish to call attention to the fact that it is often viewed as an enemy because it is so public.*

John Hibbing and Elizabeth Thiess-Morse, *Congress as Public Enemy*

Let there be no mistake about congressional popularity: The legislative branch, despite its putative ties to "the people," has never won great adulation

FIGURE 3-1
Congressional Approval Ratings, 1990–2003

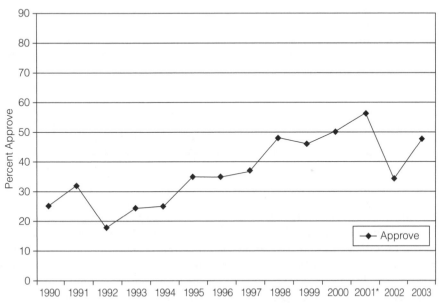

*Post–9/11.

Source: Annual Gallup polls, <www.gallup.com>, *Washington Post,* February 15, 1999; PollingReport.com and Karlyn Bowman, "POLLitics," *Roll Call,* August 8, 2002, p. 16.

from the public at large. Nor from editorial pages.[49] Historically, the Congress has been savaged by editorialists, much as it has been in more recent times. Most individual legislators do not help the situation, as they often engage in the practice of seeking reelection by running vigorously against the institution.[50]

The percentage of the population viewing the Congress in favorable terms has remained a minority since the mid-1960s; on average, during this period one in three adults has had a favorable image of the Congress at the time.[51] Adding insult to injury, evaluations of the president and the Supreme Court have been consistently more positive than those of the legislative branch, although approval rates improved somewhat in the late 1990s and continued to remain at reasonably high levels in the wake of the 2001 terrorist attacks (see Figure 3–1[52]). Still, Congress regularly receives lower levels of support than the president or the Supreme Court. Why is this so, we might well ask, especially since most incumbent members of Congress regularly win reelection? The evidence points to two complementary culprits: first, the Congress itself, and second, the media.

THE INHERENT PROBLEMS OF A POWERFUL, PUBLIC, AND PROFESSIONAL LEGISLATURE
Two sets of scholars have concluded that the modern Congress is its own worst enemy. One study observes that, "When Congress acts as it was constitutionally designed to act — passing major legislation and debating the issues of the day — it is rewarded by the public with lower levels of approval." In effect, congressional disapproval is built into our constitutional structure of decision making; to the extent that Congress does its prescribed job, it will remain unpopular. John Hibbing and Elizabeth Thiess-Morse flesh out this basic finding in *The Congress as Public Enemy*. Not only does the constitutional role of the Congress expose it to public criticism, the Congress has changed in various ways since the 1950s. They write:

> The elaborate institutional infrastructure, the committees, the subcommittees, the staffers, the partisanship, the nature of debate, the puffery, the boundaries, the sense of insularity, the lengthy careers, the perquisites, the salary, the maldistributed pork, and the special-interest representatives attracted to Congress like bees to honey all serve as tremendous turn-offs for large portions of the citizenry.[54]

Indeed, the very professionalism of the contemporary Congress, which we will examine in some detail over the remainder of the book, stands at the core of the public's contempt for the legislature. Both professional legislators and professional interest-group representatives win the scorn of the public, but more generally, "a surprising number of people . . . dislike being exposed to processes endemic to democratic government." Citizens desire a sanitized politics, without disagreement, without procedural wrangling — "in short . . . , a patently unrealistic form of democracy."

TABLE 3-3
High Approval for Members; Low Approval for Congress

Individual Members	Congress as an Institution
Serve constituents (usually done effectively).	Resolves national issues only with difficulty or not at all.
Run against Congress.	Has few defenders.
Emphasize personal style and outreach to constituents.	Operates as collegial body, difficult to understand.
Are reported on by local media in generally positive terms.	Is often reported on negatively by national media (scandals, etc.).
Respond quickly to most constituent needs/inquiries.	Moves slowly; cumbersome procedures limit rapid responses.
Are able to highlight personal goals and accomplishments.	Has many voices, but none can speak clearly for the Congress as a whole.

Source: Adapted from Davidson and Oleszek, *Congress and Its Members,* 4th ed., p. 444.

The denigration of Congress as an institution has contrasted sharply with the highly positive evaluations given individual legislators by their constituencies, as witnessed both by polling data (see Table 3–3) and the overwhelming proportion of incumbents who win reelection. Individual legislators can usually present themselves in positive terms, whereas the Congress as whole depends on the characterizations of others, especially those of the executive and the media. Although there are always interbranch tensions, the prevalence of divided government during the 1969–2002 period encouraged presidents to issue regular attacks on an allegedly obstructionist and partisan Congress.

THE MEDIA AS CRITICS AND CONDUITS OF CRITICISM   As much as interbranch bickering and congressional structure may contribute to disapproval, declining support for Congress may result from the nature of congressional press coverage in the post-Watergate era. "Over the years," concludes one study, "press coverage has moved from healthy skepticism to outright cynicism. . . . To believe the modern reporter or editor, legislators are egregiously overpaid, indulged, and indifferent to the problems of constituents who lack six-figure incomes and fantastic job perquisites."[56]

The press's relationship with Congress has become more complex over the years. In sheer numbers, the Washington press corps has grown steadily since about 1960, when it comprised fewer than 1,000 reporters who predominantly represented newspapers and periodicals. By 2000, more than 5,000 reporters were at work in the capital, with a slightly growing edge to those from television and radio.[57]

However significant the growth of the press corps and the rising importance of the electronic media, other developments have been equally telling. First, the nature of political reporting has changed since Watergate (c. 1973);

the historically cozy relationships between Washington politicians and reporters, although not disappearing, became more contentious, even adversarial — especially at the national level. Second, technical advances such as satellite linkages allow many members of Congress to communicate directly with their constituents, often through local television outlets that are far less critical than the national media.[58]

At the same time, the steady growth of cable television, which carries C-SPAN and its intense, unfiltered coverage of the Congress, and the popularity of talk radio, with its ability to generate thousands of letters and phone calls, have increased constituent pressures on members of Congress. Media sources are simply more varied and less subject to the control of any one voice, be it the president's or a legislative leader's. And many of the voices take a relentlessly negative approach to what they see as the needlessly complex and the insular context of Capitol Hill politics.

The capacity of talk shows to affect the Congress became clear in 1993. Then-Representative James Inhofe (R-Okla.), an obscure minority party congressman,[59] relentlessly traveled the talk show circuit, pushing his proposal to open up the process of prying a bill out of committee through the use of a discharge petition, which, to succeed, requires a majority of members' signatures. His campaign turned on the highly technical point that House members who signed the petition should have their names made public. The House leadership wanted to retain the cloak of anonymity on signees; such a practice allowed them privately to urge members not to sign, whereas public disclosure would increase pressures from outside interests to discharge a bill (and thus upset the leadership's control of legislative business). In a clever move, Inhofe constructed his own discharge petition to bring to the floor a bill that would open up the discharge process. Despite intense leadership opposition, this tactic succeeded, and the bill moved to floor debate and eventual approval. Representative Inhofe was subsequently elected to the Senate in 1994.

Only within the legislative branch would such public intervention into an arcane intra-institutional conflict be easily available as a tactic. Representative Inhofe and his supporters could defeat the Democratic leadership by campaigning vigorously through radio talk shows against the way the Congress conducted its own business. Despite the occasional airing of divisions within the executive and judicial branches, only the highly permeable Congress would change its internal rules because of public pressures orchestrated through the media from within the institution itself.

In a similar vein, Republicans captured control of the House in 1994 because they successfully campaigned not only against the Democratic majority but also against the entire organization of the House after forty years of Democratic control. And reporters were happy to present this narrative, which was both reasonably accurate and guaranteed to highlight an additional dimension of conflict, beyond the ordinary partisan battle.

CONGRESS IN CONTEXT

As a representative body, Congress necessarily responds to changes in its context, and we can best understand it within its contemporaneous environment. The strong state and local parties of the early 1900s helped produce well-disciplined legislative parties and the most powerful congressional leaders in the American experience (see Chapter 5). On regular occasions the electorate has modified its partisan preferences and thus changed the nature of Congress.[60] In such circumstances the usual condition of congressional elections as local contests is overwhelmed by national forces; the 1994 congressional elections reflect such an instance, even though the forty-year period of Republican minorities in the House does represent a historically unprecedented duration of such status. Subsequent elections may indicate the emergence of a new, competitive congressional alignment, with Republicans winning narrow majorities. Even so, both centrifugal and centripetal forces will shape the practices and policies of the contemporary Congress.

For the most part, tendencies toward centralization and decentralization *within* the Congress flow from *outside* forces that continually affect the legislature and its members. For example, local economies place tremendous constituency-based pressures on legislators who seek emergency aid for drought-plagued farmers, extended assistance for unemployed high tech workers, or subsidized loans for a global firm like Boeing, which must compete against the European Airbus consortium. As public policies and organized interests have grown in number and scope, lawmakers face increased lobbying pressures that can pit constituency against constituency. In the 1970s, the Congress created more and more subcommittees to address these interests, but this fragmentation has been curbed in the 1990s (see Chapter 8).

As we shall see, congressional reapportionment and redistricting in 1992 and 2002 have created a partisan alignment in which House members represent increasingly distinct constituencies — the Democrat's core liberal-to-moderate base and the conservative, both fiscally and socially, base of the Republicans. As the Clinton impeachment process demonstrated, House Republicans responded to their conservative constituents, even when it was almost certainly to the political disadvantage of the party. Enhanced partisanship has meant that both congressional parties have granted their leaders substantial powers, which has centralized the decision-making process.

The very responsiveness of individual members of Congress to specific constituencies may have rendered the Congress as an institution unresponsive to major long-term societal concerns such as Social Security and Medicare. Members of Congress know best how to serve constituents and groups with particular interests, even though they may desire to make large-scale changes to address broad societal problems. Given continuing budgetary restraints in either shaping new programs or eliminating old ones, legislators have contributed to a context that often breeds distrust and invites cynicism, a combination that makes coherent policy making all the more difficult. Into this breach has ridden an aggressive, ideological Republican Party in the House and, increasingly, in the Senate. The continuing question is whether this centralizing element in national politics and on Capitol Hill can constrain the centrifugal forces that remain ingrained in American life. So far, the answer has been Yes for the Republican majorities that have largely controlled the Congress under both Bill Clinton and George W. Bush.

As political scientist John Bader concludes after examining the agenda-setting powers of Congress: "A balance, however precarious and in need of adjustment, between heavy-handed leadership and fragmenting anarchy, should be maintained. . . . The ability to set priorities [by the Congress] fits into a larger set of factors that keep the system separated and in check."[61] Ironically, strong congressional leadership may contribute to an overall equilibrium among the many contending powers in American politics. Conversely, Sinclair observes that the 1990s have found the president and the Congress to be at best "hostile partners" as they confronted each other, even before the highly partisan politics of impeachment intervened.[62] In this context Republican President George W. Bush and the Republican-controlled 108th Congress face the task of providing a coherent agenda that can serve as the basis for legislative accomplishment.

CHAPTER BIBLIOGRAPHY

Baumgartner, Frank R., and Bryan D. Jones. *Agendas and Instability in American Politics*. Chicago: University of Chicago Press, 1993.

Berry, Jefferey M. *The Interest Group Society*, 3rd ed. Boston: Addison-Wesley, 1997.

Cigler, Allan J., and Burdett Loomis. *Interest Group Politics*, 6th ed. Washington, DC: CQ Press, 2002.

Hibbing, John, and Elizabeth Theiss-Morse. *Congress as Public Enemy: Public Attitudes toward American Political Institutions*. New York: Cambridge University Press, 1995.

Kingdon, John. *Agendas, Alternatives, and Public Policy*. Boston: Little, Brown, 1984.

NOTES

1. For examples of the earliest lobbying of the House and Senate, see Kenneth R. Bowling and Donald R. Kennon, eds., *The House & Senate in the 1790s: Pentioning, Lobbying, and Institutional Development* (Athens: Ohio University Press, 2002).

2. See John Mark Hansen, *Gaining Access* (Chicago: University of Chicago Press, 1991), pp. 57–58.

3. There is a very large body of literature here. For a contemporary summary, see James A. Thurber, "Dynamics of Policy Subsystems in American Politics," in Allan Cigler and Burdett Loomis, eds., *Interest Group Politics*, 3rd ed. (Washington, DC: CQ Press, 1991), pp. 319–344.

4. The "three pillars" of the sugar program include loans for the sugar

industry, import restrictions, and regulations, at times, of domestic sugar allotments for planting. See David Hosansley, "Florida Sugar Growers Edgy as Farm Bill Nears," *Congressional Quarterly Weekly Report,* May 13, 1995, pp. 1311–1315.

5. Kay Lehman Schlozman and John T. Tierney, *Organized Interests and American Democracy* (New York: Harper & Row, 1986).

6. David Vogel, *Fluctuating Fortunes* (New York: Basic Books, 1989).

7. Lawrence Brown, *New Policies, New Politics* (Washington, DC: Brookings Institution, 1983); see also Paul Light, *Thickening Government* (Washington, DC: Brookings Institution, 1995).

8. James Sundquist, *Politics and Policies* (Washington, DC: Brookings Institution, 1968).

9. Congressional scholars differ as to how effective legislators are in distributing their largesse to their geographic constituencies. In *Congress and the Bureaucracy* (New Haven, CT: Yale University Press, 1979), Douglas Arnold, summarizing several works, sees as too simplistic addressing only the variations in programs and policies as they affect members' districts (pp. 15–16). See also Robert M. Stein and Kenneth M. Bickers, *Perpetuating the Pork Barrel* (New York: Cambridge, 1995).

10. Randall B. Ripley and Grace A. Franklin, *Congress, the Bureaucracy, and Public Policy,* 5th ed. (Pacific Grove, CA: Brooks/Cole, 1991).

11. See, for example, Daniel J. Tichenor and Richard A. Harris, "Organized Interests and American Political Development," *Political Science Quarterly* 117 (Winter 2002–2003): pp. 587–612; and Burdett A. Loomis, "Interests, Lobbying, and the U.S. Congress: Past as Prologue," in Allan J. Cigler and Burdett A. Loomis,

eds., *Interest Group Politics,* 6th ed. (Washington: CQ Press, 2002), pp. 184–192.

12. See Raymond A. Bauer, Ithiel de sola Pool, and Lewis Anthony Dexter, *American Business and Public Policy* (Chicago: Aldine, 1963); and Lester Milbrath, *The Washington Lobbyists* (Chicago: Rand McNally, 1963).

13. Indeed, the number of active PACs has always been less than the total. As of 1992, there were 1,677 inactive PACs that made no contributions, of which 910 were defunct as organizations. See Paul Herrnson, *Congressional Elections* (Washington, DC: CQ Press, 1994), p. 109.

14. The preceding figures are cited in Mark Petracca, "The Rediscovery of Interest Group Politics," Mark Petracca, ed., *The Politics of Interests* (Boulder, CO: Westview Press, 1992), pp. 14–15.

15. Kevin Phillips, *Arrogant Capital* (Boston: Back Bay Books/Little, Brown, 1995), p. 43, cites James Thurber on the above figure. Thurber estimated a total of 80,000 in 1991, "off the top of [his] head," and Phillips provides data to demonstrate that this estimate was conservative.

16. Figure from *Government Affairs Yellow Book: Who's Who in Governmental Affairs* (Washington, DC: Washington Leadership Directories, Inc., 2002).

17. Schlozman and Tierney present data that demonstrate the rise of individual corporate representation, the decline of trade groups (as a percentage of all groups), and the decline of the percentage of citizens groups. At the same time, the overall number of groups with Washington representation had shot up, so that even labor unions, whose presence had decreased from 11 percent of all interests in 1960 to 2–3 percent in 1980, still increased in absolute numbers,

from about 55 groups in 1960 to more than 100 in 1980. Individual corporate representation, in contrast, rose from about 80 firms in 1960 to approximately 3,000 in 1980. Given differences among data, these comparisons may be a little loose, but the overall trends are clear. See Schlozman and Tierney, *Organized Interests and American Democracy*, p. 77.

18. Christopher J. Bosso, "Competition Among Interest Organizations: The State of the Literature and an Application to Environmental Advocacy," Paper presented at the Midwest Political Science Association meeting, Chicago, April 25–27, 2002.

19. See, in particular, Donald Haider's *When Governments Come to Washington: Governors, Mayors, and Intergovernmental Lobbying* (New York: Free Press, 1974) for the 1970s era and Beverly Cigler's "Not Just Another Special Interest: Intergovernmental Representation," in Allan Cigler and Burdett Loomis, eds., *Interest Group Politics*, 4th ed. (Washington, DC: CQ Press, 1995), pp. 131–153, for a perspective on the 1980s and 1990s.

20. Eric Uslaner, "All Politics Is Global," in Cigler and Loomis, *Interest Group Politics*, 4th ed.

21. Schlozman and Tierney, *Organized Interests and American Democracy*, p. 180.

22. Ibid., p. 155.

23. Almost all publications on Internet use for lobbying become obsolete quickly. Two good starting points are James A. Thurber and Colton Campbell, eds., *Congress and the Internet* (Upper Saddle River, NJ: Prentice Hall, 2003), and Christopher J. Bosso and Michael Thomas Collins, "Just Another Tool? How Interest Groups Use the Internet,"

in Allan J. Cigler and Burdett A. Loomis, eds., *Interest Group Politics*, 6th ed. (Washington: CQ Press, 2002), pp. 95–116.

24. Schlozman and Tierney, *Organized Interests and American Democracy*, p. 169. See also, Allan J. Cigler and Burdett A. Loomis, "From Big Bird to Bill Gates: Organized Interests and the Emergence of Hyperpolitics," in Cigler and Loomis, eds., *Interest Group Politics*, 5th ed. (Washington, DC: CQ Press, 1998), pp. 389–403.

25. Various scholars note these different forms of education. John Wright provides a good summary in his *Interest Groups and Congress* (Boston: Allyn & Bacon, 1996), pp. 88ff.

26. Jeffery Birnbaum, *The Lobbyists* (New York: Times Books, 1993), p. 6.

27. Richard L. Hall, "Lobbying as Legislative Subsidy," paper presented at American Political Science Association meetings, Washington, DC, August 31–September 3, 2000.

28. For a battlefield report, see Karen De Witt, "In Washington, Giving Is Now Art of Making Gifts Pass through the Eye of the Needle," *New York Times,* January 5, 1997, p. 10.

29. There is burgeoning literature here that is both useful and oversimplified. See, for example, Frank R. Baumgartner and Beth L. Leech, "The Multiple Ambiguities of Counteractive Lobbying," and David Austen-Smith and John R. Wright, "Theory and Evidence of Counteractive Lobbying," both in *American Journal of Political Science* 40 (May 1996): pp. 521–542 and pp. 543–565, respectively. Also, Marie Hojnacki and David C. Kimball, "Organized Interests and the Decision of Whom to Lobby in Congress," *American Political Science Review* 92 (December, 1998): pp. 775–790.

30. Christine DeGreggorio, *Networks of Champions* (Ann Arbor, MI: University of Michigan Press, 1999).

31. Keith Bradsher, "Foes Set for Battle on GATT," *New York Times,* October 3, 1994.

32. In *Home Style* (Boston: Little, Brown, 1978), Richard F. Fenno, Jr., concludes that the representativeness of the Congress makes it, at least most of the time, "the slow institution" (p. 245) — a description that should not be taken as criticism.

33. David Hosansky, "How Two Fervent Free-Traders Helped Set Back 'Fast Track,'" *Congressional Quarterly Weekly,* October 3, 1998, p. 2675.

34. For a comprehensive discussion of the coalitions on each side of the trade debate during the 1990s, see Wendy J. Schiller. "Has Free Trade Won the War in Congress, or Is the Battle Still Raging: A Study of the Influence of Industry Coalition Building on Congressional Trade Policy," in *NAFTA: Law and Business Review of the Americas* VI (2000): pp. 363–387.

35. Michael Barone, *Our Country* (New York: Free Press, 1990), p. 31.

36. Ibid., p. 31.

37. James A. Morone, *The Democratic Wish* (New York: Basic Books, 1990), p. 266.

38. Theodore Lowi, *The End of Liberalism,* 2nd ed. (New York: Norton, 1979), p. 278.

39. Ibid., p. 63.

40. Robert H. Salisbury, "The Paradox of Interest Groups in Washington — More Groups, Less Clout," in Anthony King, ed., *The New American Political System,* rev. ed. (Washington, DC: American Enterprise Institute, 1990), p. 203.

41. The key figure for congressional Democrats was Representative Tony Coelho, first in his role as chair of the Democratic Congressional Campaign Committee and then as Democratic Whip. Coelho brought Democratic House members and various business interests together to their mutual benefit. In 1989, Coelho resigned from the House after reports surfaced of his favored treatment in the purchase of bonds, although no charges were ever brought against him. In the 1990s, Coelho, as a managing partner of a New York investment firm, maintained contacts with the Democrats and emerged as a key adviser to President Clinton. See Brooks Jackson, *Honest Graft,* rev. ed. (Washington, DC: Farragut, 1990), and Ruth Shalit, "The Undertaker," *New Republic,* January 2, 1995, pp. 17–25.

42. In his 1966 book, *The Power of the Purse* (Boston: Little, Brown), Richard F. Fenno, Jr., could characterize the appropriations process in the Congress as a system. Within a few years, that system had broken down in terms of controlling expenditures and priorities, and Congress was unable to limit presidential intervention, as Richard Nixon aggressively used his informal powers to withhold or "impound" funds as a means of altering congressional spending priorities. See James Pfiffner, *The President, the Budget, and Congress* (Boulder, CO: Westview Press, 1979).

43. See various works by Allen Schick and later editions of Aaron Wildavsky's *The Politics of the Budgetary Process* (Boston: Little, Brown).

44. There is a vast literature here. A good starting place is Allen Schick's *Congress and Money* (Washington, DC: Urban Institute, 1980).

45. Allen Schick introduces the term *budget war* in reference to the 1966–1974

period, but there has scarcely been a peace after the adoption of the Budget Reform Act. See Schick, *Congress and Money.*

46. Allen Schick, *The Federal Budget* (Washington, DC: Brookings Institution, 1995), p. 2.

47. James A. Thurber and Samantha L. Durst, "The 1990 Budget Enforcement Act: The Decline of Congressional Accountability," in Lawrence C. Dodd and Bruce I. Oppenheimer, eds., *Congress Reconsidered,* 5th ed. (Washington, DC: CQ Press, 1993), p. 391.

48. The budget surplus reflects the merging of both regular income and Social Security income. Some analysts and members of Congress argued that Social Security surpluses unduly inflated income figures, but most legislators, the president, and both the Congresssional Budget Office (CBO) and the executive-branch Office of Management and Budget (OMB) operated under income definitions that produced substantial surpluses. Indeed, both CBO and OMB predicted that, absent tax cuts or disproportionate spending increases, the entire non–Social Security debt of the federal government could be erased by 2014.

49. In Loomis's classes on Congress, he has a standing wager that no one will be able to bring in a post-1970 cartoon that depicts the institution in an unambiguously positive light. In more than ten years, no student has yet collected.

50. Of the many key findings in Fenno's *Home Style,* none was more important or more surprising than his conclusion that campaigning against the Congress was a ubiquitous strategy (p. 168). This contradicted the notion that members of Congress felt a strong sense of "institutional loyalty" to their body.

Although this norm of loyalty may have had some continuing impact in Washington, it had virtually no impact on members' behavior back in their home districts.

51. Among others, see Glenn Parker, *Characteristics of Congress* (Englewood Cliffs, NJ: Prentice Hall, 1989), chap. 3; and Roger H. Davidson and Walter J. Oleszek, *Congress and Its Members,* 4th ed. (Washington, DC: CQ Press, 1994). Most recently, see John Hibbing and Elizabeth Thiess-Morse, *Congress as Public Enemy* (New York: Cambridge, 1995), chaps. 2 and 3.

52. In 1993, the following percentage of respondents expressed a "great deal of confidence" in the three branches of government: the Supreme Court, 31 percent; the executive branch, 12 percent; and the Congress, 7 percent. In 1973, the Congress had received a 24 percent confidence rating in a similar survey. (*Source:* National Opinion Research Center surveys, cited in Karlyn Bowman and Everett Ladd, "Public Opinion toward Congress," in Thomas E. Mann and Norman J. Ornstein, eds., *Congress, the Press, and the Public* [Washington, DC: AEI/Brookings, 1994], p. 54.)

53. Robert H. Durr, John B. Gilmour, and Christina Wolbrecht, "Explaining Congressional Approval," *American Journal of Political Science* 41 (January 1997): p. 199.

54. Hibbing and Thiess-Morse, *Congress as Public Enemy,* p. 161.

55. Ibid., p. 147.

56. Mark J. Rozell, "Press Coverage of Congress," in Mann and Ornstein, *Congress, the Press, and the Public,* pp. 109–110.

57. Harold W. Stanley and Richard G. Niemi, *Vital Statistics on American*

Politics, 2nd ed. (Washington, DC: CQ Press, 1990), p. 52, and Phillips, *Arrogant Capitol,* p. 45.

58. See Timothy Cook, *Making Laws and Making News* (Washington, DC: Brookings Institution, 1989), and his "PR on the Hill: The Evolution of Congressional Press Operations," in Christopher Deering, ed., *Congressional Politics* (Chicago: Dorsey, 1988), pp. 62–89.

59. In something of an upset, Representative Inhofe won a Senate seat in 1994, but the Republican sweep was probably more responsible than any

credit that he could claim from his discharge petition triumph.

60. David Brady, *Critical Elections and Congressional Policy Making* (Stanford, CA: Stanford University Press, 1988).

61. John Bader, *Taking the Initiative* (Washington, DC: Georgetown University Press, 1997), p. 223.

62. Barbara Sinclair, "Hostile Partners: The President, Congress, and Lawmaking in the Partisan 1990s" (paper presented at "Congress and the President in a Partisan Era," Texas A&M University, College Station, Februrary 5–6, 1999), p. 13.

Four

CONGRESSIONAL ELECTIONS: ROOTS OF THE CENTRIFUGAL CONGRESS

I n 1992, tremendous change rocked the U.S. House of Representatives. Extensive redistricting in the wake of the 1990 census and widespread abuse of check-cashing privileges at the House Bank induced many members to retire, led to nineteen primary election defeats and twenty-four general election losses by incumbents, and resulted in the largest total turnover since 1948 — 110 newcomers (63 Democrats and 47 Republicans), or more than a quarter of the chamber's 435 representatives. Republicans did gain some House seats, but, much to their dismay, Democrats continued to hold substantial majorities in both the House and Senate.

Two years later, however, Republicans picked up fifty-two additional seats in the House and eight seats in the Senate to gain control of both bodies for the first time in forty years.[1] If the number of 110 new House members represented the most important aspect of the 1992 elections, in 1994 the central result was that all Republican incumbents in both houses waged successful bids for reelection (among Democrats, however, thirty-four Representatives and two senators were defeated[2]).

In sum, the 1992 and 1994 elections shook up much of the conventional wisdom about congressional elections in the postreform era, a conventional wisdom that emphasized stability, incumbency, and the insularity of sitting legislators from effective challenges. Moreover, few scholars or political professionals had viewed the Democratic House as vulnerable to a Republican takeover. Nonetheless, on January 3, 1995, Republican Newt Gingrich was sworn in as the presiding officer of the House — a House in which more than half the members had served for four years or less.

The 1996 and 1998 elections represented something of a return to the incumbency-dominated electoral politics that have become the norm for the U.S. Congress. Even though the Republicans maintained narrow majorities in the House and a 55-45 margin in the Senate, the electoral verdicts of 1996 and 1998 indicated no clear national trends. Rather, the local politics of congressional districts and individual states came to the fore, despite vast spending by independent groups and national political parties to influence results across the country.

The 2000 election illustrated the emerging parity that exists between the Republican and Democratic Parties at the congressional and presidential levels.

The Republicans retained the majority in the House with a precarious six-seat margin and the Senate elections produced a 50-50 tie in party control. The Republicans controlled the Senate as the majority in 2001 because Vice President Dick Cheney, a Republican, counted as the fifty-first vote when the Senate was organized into a majority and minority party structure. With such a slim margin, Senate Republicans had to negotiate with the Democrats to agree on committee ratios that favored the majority by only a single vote (see Chapter 5). In June 2001, Senator James Jeffords left the Republican Party and effectively gave the Democrats a 51-49 governing majority. With his switch, the Democrats assumed majority control of the committees as well.

The 2002 elections reflect the results of congressional redistricting in which district boundaries were redrawn in ways that often protected incumbents and left relatively few (thirty or so) House seats in actual competitive play. However, given the parity between the two parties, even modest changes in either chamber can make the difference in majority control. Ultimately, the Republicans in the House picked up 6 seats, and now govern with the same 229-205-1 margin that they did in 1995; in the Senate, the Republicans regained the majority with a margin of 51-48-1 (effectively 51-49).

This chapter explores a fundamental building block of the centrifugal Congress — the politics of congressional elections. In the postreform era, this has meant the politics of reelection, given that the vast majority of successful candidates are sitting representatives and senators. After the partisan upheaval of 1994, when the Republicans firmly captured control of both houses, elections have trended less and less toward clear party majorities. In turn, party leaders have placed even more pressure on members of Congress to consider the partisan control implications of _every vote they cast_. But partisan tendencies run headlong into political realities, at least for many legislators. Because members harbor the goal of reelection, they rarely put the collective policy good ahead of their own electoral future. Indeed, the very success of this strategy represents part of a perplexing problem. Writing before the 1992 and 1994 elections, scholar Gary Jacobson observed that "political incapacity and stalemate are encouraged by a peculiar shortcoming of contemporary congressional election processes. They give us representatives and senators who are individually responsive but collectively irresponsible."[3]

Ironically, the voters as a whole — the _electorate_ — can succeed where _individual voters_ may fail. As Robert Erickson and Gerald Wright conclude:

> The average voter knows little about his or her representative and only a bit more about his or her senators. House challengers are almost invisible, and only a portion of the electorate has even a modest amount of information about senatorial challengers. Nevertheless, the electorates that candidates and parties face are smart and discerning, and they reward faithful representation. [In listening to and anticipating the electorate's wishes,] candidates . . . work to give them what they want. Elections bring about much higher levels of policy representation than most observers would expect based on the low levels of citizen awareness.[4]

In one way then, congressional elections present a continuing set of puzzles because every two years a new Congress is forged as a result of local forces that may or may not converge with national policy trends. Local forces often seem to dominate congressional decision making, as lawmakers protect their constituents' particular interests, ranging from grazing rights for cattle to shipbuilding to the aerospace industry. Occasionally national issues displace these centrifugal forces such that the legislative and executive branches respond to the electorate by moving significant policy initiatives through the complex and slow process of lawmaking. This occurred dramatically as a result of the election of 1994, during the initial months of the 104th Congress. Not only did Republicans win majorities, they proved themselves capable — at least in the House — of passing an impressive array of legislation, much of it drawn from a single campaign document, the Contract with America. Despite subsequent failures to push much of this program into law, House Republicans did succeed in shaping the terms of many national policy debates (e.g., welfare reform in 1996).

This chapter first examines the forces of fragmentation — localism, incumbency, and campaign finance — that have grown increasingly important in congressional elections since the 1970s. Then, more general forces are explored to see how much a Congress might reflect a "national verdict"[5] on hotly contested issues. If a national message is clear, congressional leaders and the president may well be able to overcome, or at least balance, the tendencies of members to look homeward in developing their policy positions.

LOCAL ELECTIONS FOR A NATIONAL OFFICE

All politics is local.

Former Speaker Thomas P. (Tip) O'Neill

Much of the fragmentation on Capitol Hill lies in the profoundly local nature of congressional elections, especially for representatives whose districts remain relatively homogeneous (even as they have become less dominated by a few interests over time). To be sure, a few constituencies cover immense areas, such as the whole of Alaska, Montana, and Wyoming, each with a single representative. Other districts reflect highly diverse populations, such as those metropolitan seats that include substantial numbers of the urban poor, various racial and ethnic groups, small-business owners, and wealthy suburbanites. Nonetheless, when compared with a presidential campaign or a Senate race in a large state, most congressional races are fought within a narrow, well-defined local context.

Members of Congress often speak of their constituents as if they know exactly who these individuals are. In fact, all legislators relate to several different, overlapping constituencies. Richard Fenno finds that "each member of Congress perceives four concentric constituencies: geographic, reelection, primary, and personal."[6] Roughly speaking, the geographic constituency reflects the physical boundaries of the district; the reelection constituency comprises the number of voters, and their preferences, that have provided (and will provide) electoral success; the primary constituency is that group which "each congressman believes would provide his last line of electoral defense in a primary";[7] and the personal constituency consists of those long-time intimates whom the legislator can trust to offer unvarnished advice and useful political information.

Geographic Constituencies

In the wake of a series of key Supreme Court decisions and voting rights legislation in the 1960s, all congressional districts have had roughly equal populations;[8] post-2000 districts average about 650,000 as a result of the regular decennial apportionment, which allocated seats to states in accord with their populations. Thus, California's House delegation grew from forty-five in the 1980s to fifty-three in 2002, and each district has a total population of a little more than 639,000.[9] In that congressional seats are awarded to states through a mathematical formula and districts cannot cross state lines, population variations from state to state can be much more substantial. For example, in 1991 the state of Montana filed an unsuccessful suit over the loss of one of its two congressional districts in the 1992 reapportionment process, which left the state with a single constituency of almost 800,000. In 2002, Montana has 902,195 constituents but still only has one at-large congressional district. In contrast, Iowa's congressional districts consist of 585,000 residents, about 10 percent less than the national average.[10] Absent some mass migration to Iowa, the state will likely lose one congressional seat after the 2010 census.

Members of the House all represent roughly the same number of constituents with roughly the same resources (see Chapter 9 on congressional enterprises). This ensures a substantial fragmentation within the House, given the great differences in culture, race, ethnicity, age, wealth, and so forth, across the nation. Over the past two decades, the issue of racial representation has become a major element of redistricting, both through the 1965 Voting Rights Act (extended in 1982) and a series of court cases. The 1982 legislation required that redistricting — the actual redrawing of congressional districts, usually by state legislatures after reapportionment — not dilute minority voting strength. Minorities were explicitly defined as African Americans and Latinos. Congressional redistricting in 1991–1992 thus produced a slew of "minority-majority" districts that elected fifty-eight minority representatives in 1992, up from thirty-eight in 1990.[11] Minority populations were concentrated in districts by legal gerrymandering; that is, many odd-shaped districts were created specifically so that minority legislators would be elected. These expectations were fulfilled, in that "sixteen new black elected officials joined the 1992 Congress, each from a majority black district."[12]

In many ways, the emphasis on the racial composition of districts has turned the notion of gerrymandering on its head. Although gerrymandering — drawing political boundaries to benefit one candidate, party, or population grouping — has a long history in the United States, it has always been considered unethical.[13] The Voting Rights Act of 1965 and a series of important Supreme Court decisions in the mid-1960s established a "one-person, one-vote" rule that opened up the electoral system to minorities, but the impact of minority voters often appeared diluted. For example, in North Carolina, African Americans made up 22 percent of the population in 1990, but the state had elected no minority member to Congress in this century. The state's 1992 redistricting produced two districts designed to send an African American to Washington. Gerrymandering to concentrate minority voting strength had become an officially sanctioned policy.[14]

In fact, the most remarkable example of racial gerrymandering came in North Carolina's "I-85 district," so labeled "because it consists of a series of urban black areas, many of them poor, partially connected by a line sometimes no wider than I-85, splitting adjacent districts in two"[15] (see Figure 4–1). The government-sanctioned gerrymander worked; African American candidates, both Democrats, won the seats that had been carved out for them.

The Supreme Court has begun to closely examine oddly drawn geographic districts that are designed to give minority populations majority power within a congressional district. Although the legal gerrymandering of North

FIGURE 4-1
North Carolina's Twelfth Congressional District — 1992 and 1998

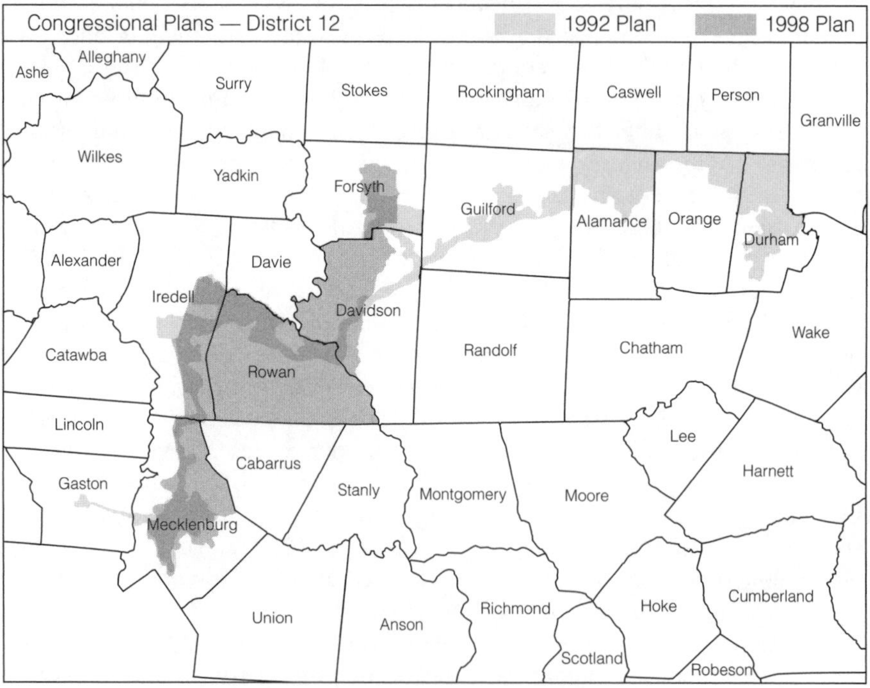

Source: State of North Carolina, <www.nega.state.nc.us>, January 20, 1999.

Carolina's First District survived judicial scrutiny, the Supreme Court struck down the Twelfth District's lines as well as mandated the alteration of the racially based "majority-minority" seats in other Southern states (Georgia, Louisiana, Texas), where boundaries had reduced the emphasis on their racial composition.[16] In 1995, the Supreme Court reaffirmed its 1993 ruling (*Reno v. Shaw*) that cast doubt on any district lines drawn to take race into account as "the predominant factor."[17]

Protecting and preserving minority representation continues to be a crucial element of American politics, but the old routes to accomplishing full minority representation have attracted increased scrutiny. In recent years, some scholars have challenged the effectiveness of majority-minority districts both in terms of producing policies that are favorable to minorities and sending more minority representatives to the House.[18] If the purpose of majority-minority districts is to elect more minority members of Congress, the current system can be counter-productive by marginalizing the electoral prospects of minority candidates. Thus, after a series of recent court decisions, the 2002 election season witnessed two instances of African American candidates competing against each other for their party's nomination in majority-minority districts. In Alabama's Seventh District, Representative Earl Hilliard, elected in 1992 as the first African American elected from the state in over a century, lost to another African American, Earl Davis, who went on to win election in the predominantly black district. Georgia Representative Cynthia McKinney was defeated by Denise Majette in a hotly contested party primary. Rather than making each of these four African American candidates viable across four different districts, they were forced to compete with each other for two seats. And in each instance the candidate perceived as the more moderate emerged victorious.

At the same time, two Georgia seats that appeared favorable to African American nominees (both Democrats) ended up in Republican hands. To an extent, these results were upsets, but they also demonstrated the need for strong candidates in districts that fell short of majority-minority status.

Because minority candidates have overwhelmingly aligned themselves with the Democrats, these representatives are disadvantaged in an era of Republican dominance in the House. Recognizing this disadvantage, and the fact that minority voters are not as geographically concentrated as they were in the past, some black leaders have joined in court cases to advocate that minority voters be more dispersed across congressional districts.[19]

The Other Constituencies: Behavior and Perception

If the geographic constituency is unambiguous (if irregular) in its boundaries, the other constituencies identified by Fenno are subjectively defined. Even in the same district, no two incumbents would put together the same reelection constituency. Nor would we expect their primary supporters or their personal backers to be the same. In particular, personal constituencies are unique; Fenno recalls sitting in the living room of one member's top district staffer and best friend:

> watching an NFL game with the congressman, the district aide, the state assemblyman from the congressman's home county, and the district attorney of the same county. The last three were among the five people with whom the congressman had held his first strategy meeting four years earlier. . . . Between plays and at halftime, over beer and pretzels, the four discussed every aspect of the congressman's campaign. . . . Ostensibly they were watching the football game. Actually, the congressman was exchanging political advice, information, and perspectives with three of his oldest and closest political associates.[20]

Examining the evolution of constituencies within a single congressional district demonstrates both how the geographic boundaries can change through redistricting and how a series of incumbents construct their own unique bases of support. From 1971 through 2002, for example, Kansas's Second Congressional District has changed its representative stripes as much as any seat during the country; six different individuals have held the seat during that period. Not only was the district redrawn in 1972, in 1982, and in 1992, but also each of the incumbents developed his or her own set of personal, primary, and reelection constituencies (see Table 4–1).

Over this twenty-eight-year period, the population of the Second District grew dramatically — from a low of 454,000 in the 1970s to 672,098 in 2002 (Kansas lost one of its five House seats after the 1990 census) — and its geographic configuration changed as much. Historically, the district had encompassed a relatively compact area of northeast Kansas; since 1992, however, its reach has extended from the Nebraska border on the north to the Oklahoma line on the south.

Even more significant have been the changes in the reelection, primary, and personal constituencies represented by the six incumbents. A district with roughly the same geographic boundaries elected two fairly liberal Democrats, a moderate-to-conservative Democrat, a conservative Republican, and two extremely conservative Republicans — each with his or her own set of personal supporters and winning reelection coalition.

Incumbents also develop their own funding constituencies, often bringing in hundreds of thousands of dollars from *outside* the confines of their physical districts. With a seat on the powerful Energy and Commerce Committee, Representative Jim Slattery proved especially adept at obtaining substantial PAC funding from groups with little direct interest in Kansas's Second District. In his last two campaigns (1990 and 1992) he spent a total of $1,169,000, with $767,000 (or 66 percent) coming from PACs. Republican Representative Jim Ryun, in contrast, has not had to raise or spend as much money to keep his office. In 2000, for example, he raised $443,593 ($222,404 from PACs), spent only $284,404, and won reelection with a healthy 67 percent of the vote.[21] The difference may

TABLE 4-1
Changing Constituencies in a Single Congressional District:
The Kansas Second, 1971–2003

Member/Term	Constituency Type			
	Geographic	*Reelection*	*Primary*	*Personal*
Bill Roy (D), 1971–1975	479K, NE 1/4 of KS, rural/urban	Democrats/ Independents/ Moderate Republicans	Kansas City, KS, Democrats; federal/state employees	State legislators' support, medical doctors
Martha Keys (D), 1975–1979	454K, NE 1/4 of KS, rural/urban	Democrats/ Independents/ Moderate Republicans	McGovern Democrats	Antiwar Democrats, 1972 campaign
Jim Jefferies (R) 1979–1983	454K, NE 1/4 of KS, rural/urban	Republicans/ Conservatives	Conservative Republicans	Reagan backers in 1976
Jim Slattery (D), 1983–1995	472K, NE 1/4 of KS, rural/urban	Democrats/ Independents/ Moderate Republicans	Topeka and Moderate Democrats	Loyalists from state legislature days
Sam Brownback* (R) 1995–1996	619K, east 1/3 of KS, except suburban Kansas City	Republicans/ Perot supporters/ Reagan Democrats	Traditional Republicans	Agricultural community, Kansas State University, family media base
Jim Ryun (R) 1997–	672K, east 1/3 of KS, except sub-urban Kansas City	Most Republicans/ Christian Right	Christian Right	Personal friends with religious and athletic ties

*Won the Senate seat vacated by Senator Robert Dole in 1996.

Source: Almanac of American Politics, various editions.

very well be that Representative Ryun is an overall better ideological fit with his district and thus did not attract as strong a challenger as did Representative Slattery. Indeed, Ryun fought vigorously to keep the liberal university town of Lawrence out of his district during the 2002 redistricting process.

Careful cultivation of Fenno's four concentric constituencies (geographic, reelection, primary, personal), as well as maintaining a strong funding base, allows incumbents considerable latitude in deciding how to represent their districts, especially if they are skilled at explaining their positions. Nevertheless, there are real limits to this flexibility. As Democratic House members discovered in 1992 and 1994, incumbents can face problems as a result of unpopular votes, well-funded opponents, strong national trends, scandals of their own making, or some combination of the above. Even the most successful members are risk averse, and most incumbents run as if the next election could be their last. In this way, the nature of representation has become intertwined with the dynamics of election campaigns. The days are long gone when campaigning and governing occurred in separate periods.

ELECTIONS IN A CAREERIST CONGRESS

If a group of planners sat down and tried to design a pair of
American electoral assemblies with the goal of serving
members' electoral needs year in and year out,
they would be hard pressed to improve on what exists.

David Mayhew, *Congress: The Electoral Connection*

Over the course of the past one hundred years, the Congress has developed into an institution that fosters long careers. This may be changing, as formal and informal pressures for term limits affect legislators' choices, but over the course of the twentieth century, extended careers became the norm. Between 1911 and 1971, the number of "careerists" (legislators serving ten or more terms) rose steadily, from 2.8 percent to 20 percent. After substantial turnover in the 1970s, the percentage of careerists stabilized at about 15 percent of the House for almost twenty years, then the post-1990 elections witnessed enough turnover (often through Democratic retirements and defeats) to reduce the careerist numbers to fifty-five, or 13 percent in the 105th Congress, but the number rebounded to sixty-eight (15.6 percent) in the 106th Congress (1999–2000). In 2003, the average tenure of House members stands at five terms, and the typical senator's length of service is roughly similar — eleven years.[23]

Careerist legislators want to remain in office; thus, every two (or six) years they must win reelection. Unsurprisingly, with the careerist, professional Congress has come both increased incentives to run for reelection and enhanced capacities for incumbents to emerge victorious. Since 1950, 90 percent of House incumbents ordinarily run for reelection and well over 90 percent of them win.[24] Incumbency success rates rose to what were then historic highs in the 1984–1990 period, when House members won a staggering 97 percent of their bids for reelection. Even in 1992, with anti-incumbency sentiment running at a fever pitch and the House Bank scandal in full bloom, almost nine in ten (88 percent) of those seeking reelection were returned to office. House members won reelection at a 94 percent rate in 1996, a figure exactly in line with the overall 1968–1994 average. Six years later, in 2002, the rate of reelection for incumbents had exceeded levels from the mid-1980s; 98 percent of incumbents who ran for reelection in the House won their seats.[25]

Sitting senators are more vulnerable than House incumbents, with the 1952–1992 period producing an overall reelection rate of 80 percent. From 1982 on, Senate incumbents have won more than 86 percent of their races, indicating a trend toward a greater safety that roughly mirrors that in the House. Indeed, in 1996, 95 percent of sitting senators won their reelection bids, slightly outpacing their House counterparts (94 percent success rate that year). In 1998, twenty-six of twenty-nine Senate incumbents who ran won reelection; in 2000, twenty-four of twenty-eight Senate incumbents who ran won reelection; in 2002, twenty-three of twenty-seven Senate incumbents won reelection, and three candidates, John Kerry (D-Mass.), Jack Reed (D-R.I.), and Pat Roberts (R-Kans.), ran without facing any major party opponent. On average, throughout the past decade, more than 90 percent of Senate incumbents won reelection.[26]

Why are incumbents so difficult to unseat? And what difference does it make that they remain relatively safe? The answers to both these questions are central to understanding the fragmentation, or atomization, of the U.S. Congress. Most of our attention will be directed at House elections, given the greater safety of House members and the extensive research that has focused on these contests.

House Incumbents and the Structure of Competition

Although House members have consistently won reelection at high rates, there have been major changes in how this has occurred in the past forty years, especially since the early 1970s. First, incumbents' margins rose substantially over this period; second, freshman members, who were historically more vulnerable than their more experienced colleagues, improved their success rates to match those of the chamber as a whole.

Increasing Margins and the "Slurge"

In the 1960s and 1970s, scholars and political observers began to take note of the fact that fewer congressional races were won by narrow margins. By historical standards the "marginals," or closely contested seats in which the winning candidate receives no more than 55 or 60 percent of the vote, were vanishing.[27] This stark observation, illustrated in Figure 4–2, set off a scramble to find a "smoking gun" explanation for this phenomenon.

Political scientist Morris Fiorina concluded in 1977 that "the bureaucracy did it," as legislators created a series of programs to which they could subsequently control access (thus winning credit for their assistance in providing benefits).[28] Over the next decade, numerous scholars weighed in with their own assessments of the growing margins, as they looked at congressional redistricting, the growth of the congressional enterprise and its resources (such as staff, franking, and trips home), levels of casework, and patterns of campaign funding[29] (see Chapter 9). Basically they sought to identify shared advantages that all incumbents had over their challengers. This cottage industry of research found no *single* cause for the sharply reduced number of marginal seats, but a rough consensus has formed about several main explanations for the reduced levels of congressional competition in the 1970–2002 era.[30] Findings include the following:

▶ *Redistricting has had little, if any, systematic effect in initially reducing competition.* The conventional wisdom through 1990 was that although some incumbents may have been protected, redrawing district lines after decennial censuses did not cause increasing margins.[31] But the 1992 redistricting did produce both heavily Democratic majority-minority districts and many new seats in which Republicans could and did compete

FIGURE 4-2

House Vote in Districts with Incumbents Running, 1948 and 1972

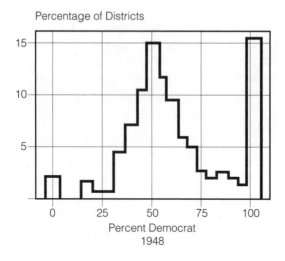

Percentage of Districts

Percent Democrat
1948

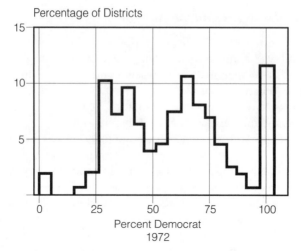

Percentage of Districts

Percent Democrat
1972

Source: Morris P. Fiorina, "The Decline of Collective Responsibility in American Politics," reprinted by permission of *Daedalus,* Journal of the American Academy of Arts and Sciences, from the issue entitled "The End of Consensus?" Summer 1980, Volume 109, Number 3.

effectively. Subsequently, in 2002, a somewhat different kind of gerrymandering occurred, which served to protect incumbents of both parties in state after state. Thus, there were no truly competitive districts in the entire fifty-three-member California delegation.

▶ *The "personal vote" has grown.* That is, while broad partisan and national trend bases for voting in congressional elections have declined or remained minimal, the "personal" component has steadily increased.[32] Incumbency represents a large component of the personal vote, even without considering campaign spending or constituency service; incumbents are almost always better known than challengers. In campaigns during the 1980s, for example, almost half of the electorate (47 percent) recalled the name of their sitting member of Congress, but only one in five (19 percent) recalled the challenger's name.[33]

▶ *Constituency service is important, but there are 435 ways to do it.* In reviewing research on constituency service, various studies have found no relationship between electoral results and casework, federal spending in the district, travel back to the district, or size of staff. "The latest academic research," Fiorina incredulously wrote in 1989, "appears to show that members of Congress can close up their district offices, dismiss their staffs, spend weekends in Washington with their families, quit doing casework, abandon their quest for federal funds, discontinue their newsletters . . . and *nothing will happen to them.*"[34] This is patently absurd, but the variety among districts, individual members' home styles, and the required levels of effort in safe and potentially marginal districts combine to deny incumbents any surefire formula to improve their percentage of the vote.

▶ *Campaign spending is important, but mainly for challengers.*[35] If a challenger can spend enough money to gain substantial recognition, the chances of a close race rise sharply. But the amount of money required merely to stage a legitimate challenge is daunting. In the 1980s, a challenger needed about $400,000 simply to have a one-in-five chance of defeating an incumbent.[36] By 1998, the few challengers who were successful spent an average of $1,175,823.[37]

▶ *The incumbent's most effective electoral strategy is to discourage serious opposition.*[38] So-called high-quality challengers — state senators, mayors, previous losers who did reasonably well — start out with substantial name recognition and may well be able to raise funds more easily than neophytes. Incumbents thus seek to maximize their victory margins, raise substantial sums of campaign funds, and provide excellent service at home in hopes of discouraging strong potential candidates from making what could prove to be a serious challenge.

Margins of victory began to increase sharply in the late 1960s and even more so through the 1970s, but the entrenched nature of incumbency really became evident during the 1980s. By this time, only the occasional scandal provided a likely avenue for challenger success.[39] Incumbents continued to worry about their survival, however, as almost every election provided a vivid example of some seemingly safe member going down to an unexpected defeat.[40] Survey data demonstrated that increasing numbers of voters held their own representative, and not just the Congress as a whole, responsible for the ills of society, such as large budget deficits and high crime rates. Still, it is easier to win an open seat than to defeat an incumbent, and winning open seats has been the major avenue for partisan electoral gains over the past decade.

FUNDING CAMPAIGNS AND SUPPORTING INCUMBENTS

Along with the increasing official resources available to sitting members and the rising number of federal programs to which members could provide access and ombudsman services, the structure of campaign financing helped increase the margins and safety of House incumbents in the wake of 1974 campaign reform legislation. The 1974 amendments to the Federal Election Campaign Act, which had limited individual donations to $1,000 per campaign, and a 1976 Supreme Court decision (*Buckley v. Valeo*) that struck down limits on campaign spending, combined to encourage the proliferation of PACs, which could give congressional candidates up to $5,000 for each separate election (for example, a primary in August followed by the general election in November). Although labor unions and a few other groups had long given money to candidates through PACs, the 1974 legislation opened the door to businesses (such as oil companies[41]); trade associations (for example, realtors); and ideological groups,[42] such as the National Rifle Association, to raise funds and make contributions to congressional campaigns.

Since the 1974 reform legislation was enacted, campaigns have grown much more expensive. Candidates have come to rely more heavily on PACs and individual contributions, and much greater roles have opened up for national interest groups and parties in local campaigns through the use of "soft money" and "issue ads." Economic and ideological groups took advantage of the opportunity to contribute more money to candidates for the House and Senate, and with the rising significance of television advertising in campaigning, that money grew in importance. In turn, as the role of money became much more pronounced in winning a congressional seat, incumbents learned to use the powers of their office to raise campaign funds, and contributors learned that campaign contributions could frequently buy access to specific legislators. Although scholars have yet to demonstrate a direct connection between campaign contributions and vote outcomes, a consensus exists around the notion that campaign contributions facilitate access to House and Senate members.[43] This political dance benefits incumbents, because challengers do not have anything to offer contributors except their future "potential" support if they win the election. Even in 1994, with the sweeping victory of a large number of Republican challengers, much of the funding for those campaigns came through electorally secure Republicans in the House who established their own PACs designed to help fellow Republican challengers.

Rising Costs

Although inflation has affected campaign expenses in the post-1974 period, the overall growth in campaign expenditures remains striking. In 1976, the average House candidate spent $73,000 on his or her campaign; by 1982 that figure had tripled, to $228,000, and it almost doubled again in the next ten years, to $410,000 in 1992.[44] In 2002, the average House candidate spent

TABLE 4–2
Average Campaign Expenditures in the House and Senate (in dollars*)

	House			
	1976	*1982*	*1992*	*2002*
All	73,000	228,000	409,000	624,000
Incumbent	79,000	265,000	595,000	831,000
Challenger	51,000	152,000	168,000	256,000
Open Seat	124,000	284,000	436,000	1,044,000
	Senate			
	1976	*1982*	*1992*	*2002*
All	596,000	1,782,000	2,877,000	4,061,000
Incumbent	623,000	1,858,000	3,852,000	4,072,000
Challenger	452,000	1,217,000	1,825,000	2,401,000
Open Seat	757,000	4,143,000	2,939,000	7,445,000†

* Numbers are rounded to nearest 1,000.

† In 2002, Republican candidates running for open seats spent almost twice as much as their Democratic opponents, $9,201,000 as opposed to $5,690,000.

Sources: Norman Ornstein, Thomas Mann, and Michael Malbin, eds., *Vital Statistics on Congress 1984–1985* (Washington DC: American Enterprise Institute Press, 1985); Norman Ornstein, Thomas Mann, and Michael Malbin, eds., *Vital Statistics on Congress 1995–1996* (Washington DC: CQ Press, 1995); Norman Ornstein, Thomas Mann, and Michael Malbin, eds., *Vital Statistics on Congress 1999–2000* (Washington DC: American Enterprise Institute Press, 2000); Federal Election Commission, <www.fec.gov>, "Financial Activity of General Election Congressional Candidates, 1990–2002," January 2003.

$624,000 (see Table 4–2). Looking at average expenditures is misleading, however, in that spending by incumbents has increased much more sharply than has that by challengers.

Between 1976 and 1982, challengers' total spending amounted to about 65 percent of what incumbents spent; twenty years later, this proportion has decreased to 31 percent. In 2002 incumbents spent an average of $831,000, while challengers spent $256,000. In the Senate, there is less of a difference between challenger and incumbent campaign spending. There are several reasons for the closer fund-raising and spending totals in Senate races. First, the longer six-year period of time to raise money allows challengers to plan in advance. Second, challengers to Senate races tend to have more visibility like Hillary Clinton (D-N.Y.), have previously won local or statewide office like Lamar Alexander (R-Tenn.), or have independent financial resources like Jon Corzine (D-N.J.).[45]

Incumbents and challengers alike need immense amounts of money, and such a requirement makes almost all serious candidates highly attentive to, if not beholden to, their contributors. In effect, these individuals and groups compose another constituency for a candidate, beyond those within his or her district. Much funding reinforces the local forces that shape representation (such as a tobacco PAC's funding of a North Carolina legislator), but many contributions come from interests far beyond the district's confines. On balance, this trend increases congressional fragmentation by creating a new set of influential constituents whose interests must be taken into account. In a study of campaign funding and its revolutionary practitioner Representative Tony Coelho (D-Calif.), who served as chairman of the Democratic Congressional

Campaign Committee (DCCC) during the 1980s, journalist Brooks Jackson concluded that:

> increasingly . . . House Members were acting as ombudsmen not only for their constituents but also for their donors. Those who gave money came to be [another] constituency, one not envisioned by the drafters of the Constitution. Coelho interceded for a donor from another state as naturally as he would have for a businessman from Modesto, in his district. One was entitled to help by virtue of residence, the other by virtue of his currency.[46]

At best such constituencies of contributors compete for a legislators' attention with their districts' voters. At worst, notes campaign reform advocate Senator Russ Feingold (D-Wis.), "the very notion of representative democracy [is lost]. Money cuts the link between the representative and the represented."[47]

Campaign Contributions and the Rise of PACs

In 1972, PACs contributed a bit more than $8.5 million to congressional candidates, about 17 percent of all House campaign spending in that year. Twenty years later, PACs gave more than $127 million to House candidates, a fifteen-fold increase; PAC funds amounted to 38 percent of all campaign spending.[48] As dramatic as these changes appear, they mask even more significant patterns in PAC funding of congressional campaigns.

In the post-1974 era of campaign financing, PACs gave disproportionately to incumbents and to Democrats, and in the 1980s these patterns became more pronounced. As many businesses and trade associations organized PACs in the 1970s, Republicans increased their reliance on PAC funds from 10 percent in 1974 to 30 percent in 1984, but the tendency of these groups to back incumbents held overall Republican support from PACs to approximately the 30 percent level. Democrats, on the other hand, moved from 22 percent PAC support in 1974 (mostly from long-standing labor groups) to an average of 45 percent in 1990–1992. Overall, House Democrats have proven the prime beneficiaries of PAC financing in the contemporary era of congressional electoral politics. Such patterns changed, however, in a post-1994 era of Republican majorities. In 1994, for example, PACs gave two-thirds of their contributions to House Democratic congressional candidates; after two years of Republican control, House Republicans received slightly more than 50 percent of all PAC funding,[49] and in 1998, this advantage rose to 52 percent.

Changing PAC Support Patterns: 1980–2002

In 1980, although incumbents received the lion's share (69 percent) of all PAC contributions, Republican challengers could realistically hope for some significant support from this source. Aside from labor groups, which funded only Democratic challengers, PACs provided substantial funds to the most viable Republican challengers and open-seat candidates (those with no incumbent to challenge). A decade later things had changed dramatically, as Table 4–3 illustrates. Total PAC contributions had tripled, with 80 percent going to

TABLE 4-3
Political Action Committee Contributions to House Candidates, 1990-2002

PAC Type	Amount Contributed (in millions)	Percentage of Contributions*					
		Incumbent		Challenger		Open Seat	
		D	R	D	R	D	R
1990							
Corporate	35.4	49	38	1	3	3	6
Labor	27.6	66	6	11	0	16	0
Association	332.5	52	33	2	2	3	8
Nonconnected†	8.5	44	21	7	6	6	6
Other	4.4	61	27	1	2	4	5
Total	108.5	54	26	4	2	8	5
1994							
Corporate	44.3	50	33	<1	6	33	6
Labor	31.4	75	3	9	<1	13	<1
Association	37.1	50	30	2	5	5	8
Nonconnected	11.1	49	18	4	10	10	9
Other	4.7	60	26	2	4	4	4
Total	126.6	56	24	4	4	7	5
1996							
Corporate	53.2	30	59	1	3	3	6
Labor	40.2	49	7	29	0	15	<1
Association	45.4	27	51	4	4	5	8
Nonconnected	15.6	23	38	14	8	6	10
Other	5.4	24	46	4	4	4	6
Total*	159.9	32	41	10	3	7	6
1998							
Corporate	50.3	30	58	<1	3	2	6
Labor	37.3	62	8	14	<1	15	4
Association	48.3	32	50	2	4	4	7
Nonconnected	20.0	25	33	6	15	7	14
Other	2.9	39	43	2	6	4	7
Total*	158.8	38	40	5	4	6	6
2000							
Corporate	62.1	34	54	<1	3	<1	8
Labor	43.5	62	7	18	<1	12	1
Association	55.0	35	48	3	4	2	8
Nonconnected	27.0	24	31	10	11	8	15
Other	5.6	40	44	3	4	2	7
Total*	193.4	39	38	7	4	6	7
2002							
Corporate	68.2	32	55	<1	2	2	8
Labor	44.4	62	8	11	<1	17	<1
Association	57.2	34	48	2	2	4	10
Nonconnected	32.2	25	32	7	7	10	17
Other	4.9	39	49	<1	2	2	7
Total*	206.9	38	40	4	2	7	8

* Percentages may not add to 100 due to rounding.

† Independent committees.

Sources: Modified from data in Norman J. Ornstein, Thomas E. Mann, and Michael J. Malbin, eds., *Vital Statistics on Congress, 1995-1996* (Washington, DC: CQ Press, 1995), and Federal Election Commission, "PAC Contributions to Federal Candidates, January 1, 1995–December 31, 1996," January 1, 1997–December 31, 1998, January 1, 1999–December 31, 2000, January 1, 2001–December 31, 2002, at <www.fec.gov>.

incumbents, and it remained at about 80 percent through the 2002 election cycle. Republican challengers had garnered $5.25 million in PAC contributions in 1980, compared with $2.17 million ten years later. Open-seat patterns witnessed a similar reversal, although it was not so dramatic. What happened in the 1980s?

Much of the change in the pattern of PAC contributions can be explained by the strategic decision of some Democratic Party leaders in the House. Specifically, Representative Tony Coelho (D-Calif.) became chair of the Democratic Congressional Campaign Committee in 1981, after the Democrats had suffered serious losses in the congressional elections of 1978 and 1980. Coelho not only possessed a gift for prying funds from contributors, he rapidly increased donations from PACs representing businesses and trade associations — the Republicans' natural allies. Coelho's job was to convince the business and trade PACs of two things: that Democrats would control the House for the foreseeable future and that business and trade interests could work effectively with Democratic Party and committee leaders. Organized interests often see great advantages in supporting potential leaders, who have little trouble soliciting contributions for their own PACs. Coelho and his lieutenants worked hard to reassure key PAC managers that the Party would help them, while holding in reserve the real threat that House Democrats might well look unkindly toward interests that did not contribute.

The resulting monies provided a great edge to Representative Coelho personally, who contributed $570,000 to House candidates prior to his election by the caucus as the Democratic whip, and to Representative William Gray (D-Pa.), who spread around more than $60,000 in his successful 1988 bid to chair the Democratic caucus.[50]

Until the election of 1994, the strategy of Coelho and his successors at the DCCC proved successful in retaining Democratic House majorities, weathering the Reagan–Bush period of Republican presidents, and maintaining expectations that the Democrats would control the House for years to come. Despite some indications that incumbents had grown increasingly vulnerable in 1990 and 1992, Democrats emerged from the 1992 elections with a seemingly healthy 258-176 margin in the House of Representatives. Even so, Democrats looked ahead to the 1994 congressional elections with some trepidation for the following reasons:

- ▶ Given control of the presidency, their party could be held responsible for the actions of the national government.

- ▶ President Bill Clinton received only 43 percent of the 1992 vote, while independent Ross Perot's antigovernment rhetoric helped him garner 19 percent.

- ▶ The president's party generally loses seats at midterm elections, and Democrats had already lost ten seats in 1992, despite the Clinton victory.

- ▶ As November 1994 approached, less than 40 percent of the electorate expressed the opinion that President Clinton was doing either an "excellent" or "good" job.

THE ELECTORAL EARTHQUAKE OF 1994 AND ITS AFTERSHOCKS IN 1996 AND 1998

Assessing the 1994 congressional elections, in which Republicans captured control of the Congress by gaining fifty-two House and eight Senate seats, various analysts reached for metaphors to communicate the breadth and depth of the change on Capitol Hill. All observers had predicted some gains for House Republicans, but almost none, save for GOP partisans, foresaw the Democrats losing their majority.[52] The House Republicans needed to win forty seats to gain control; their fifty-two-seat swing represented the largest shift since 1946, when Democrats suffered a fifty-five-seat loss. The Republicans' 1994 triumph was all the more significant because it came in an era of enhanced incumbent safety (despite some decline in 1990 and 1992) and it swept Democrats out of office all across the country. In 1994 at least, all politics was not local.

The nationalization of the 1994 election was no random event. Rather, congressional Republicans infused traditionally local congressional elections with national themes and national issues. Representative Newt Gingrich, the minority whip at the time, worked with the National Republican Congressional Committee (NRCC) and Republican-affiliated PACs on behalf of Republican candidates on a district-by-district basis. Indeed, Gingrich helped recruit many members of the Republican majority, instructed them on key issues, campaigned for most of them, and raised money for their campaigns. Through GOPAC, a Gingrich-directed group, funds and campaign assistance flowed to Republican candidates, and the NRCC could guarantee the maximum allowable contribution of $25,000 to any seriously competitive candidate. Overall, Republicans spent more than half their funds (51 percent) on challengers in competitive races, a tactic that allowed them to counter the PAC receipts of Democratic incumbents.[53] In this way, Gingrich followed his Democratic counterpart, Tony Coelho, in using leadership PAC money to consolidate political power in his own party.

The efforts at nationalizing the 1994 elections culminated in the Contract with America, a campaign pledge document that all but three Republicans signed. In conjunction with political consultant and pollster Frank Luntz, Gingrich announced early in the year that on September 27, 1994, Republican House candidates would gather on the steps of the Capitol to offer their support for a ten-item "Contract with America," which would explicitly lay out the changes they would propose in the first one hundred days of the new Congress. Although most voters neither knew nor cared about what was in the Contract, it provided a succinct and clear message that the Republicans would govern the House as a unified majority party. The Republicans capture of the House came one district at a time, with each individual new member owing a great deal to Gingrich for the assistance he provided. For Gingrich, the Contract nationalized the voting decision and offered him, as incoming Speaker, a useful vehicle to push a series of reforms. In the end, the national themes and the leader's expertise, funding, and energy all contributed to a great unity among first-term members in particular and the entire Republican majority in general.[54]

Republican Senate candidates, whether incumbents or challengers, did not join in the Contract with America nor did they actively campaign with their House colleagues. Although the Republicans' 1994 Senate triumph, which produced a 53-47 margin (gaining eight seats in the election and adding the partisan defection of Alabama Democrat Richard Shelby), was noteworthy, it was not a great surprise in that Senate elections have proven much more competitive than House contests and the Republicans had controlled the upper chamber as recently as January 1987. Nonetheless, Republicans who ran for Senate in 1994 benefited from the general campaign theme that the Republicans would govern as a more unified and more effective majority party than the Democrats did in the 103rd Congress. Moreover, GOP Senate candidates were also helped by the House Republicans' persuasive argument that the long-term Democratic control of the Congress had rendered the entire institution highly suspect, if not corrupt.

From 1996 to the 2000 elections, the Republicans held their House majority, albeit with some seat losses in 1998 that reduced their margin. Republicans retained their majority in part because they learned quickly that a great deal of politics is still local. Republicans who were elected in 1994 on a national platform in ideologically friendly districts understood that ideology alone would not get them reelected; constituents in all districts still expected services and projects brought back to their communities. As Jacobson notes, vulnerable GOP House members operated much as incumbent Democrats had for four decades: "run as independent champions of local district issues."[55] In particular, Republicans moved away from their initial emphases on revolutionary change by endorsing various policy and budgetary compromises (on education and welfare, for example) in the second session of the 104th Congress. At the same time, House Republicans aggressively used their status as majority party incumbents to raise large sums of money, both to ward off powerful challengers and to conduct expensive campaigns. (See Table 4–3.) Not only did they tap PACs, they also became increasingly reliant on large soft money contributions to the parties. And Democrats followed suit, to the point that they relied more on soft money than did their counterparts.

The 2000 congressional elections were more remarkable for their outcome in the Senate than the House, which remained in Republican control. In the Senate, the parties each held fifty Senate seats, and Vice President Cheney could thus preside over the Senate and give Republicans a fifty-first vote when they needed it. The subsequent shift of one GOP senator to the Democratic camp ended the reliance on Cheney, but the 2002 races brought majority control back to the Republicans in the Senate. And the House GOP picked up six seats to increase their margin in that chamber. Again, most of these results flowed from localized conditions, but President Bush did campaign aggressively in targeted districts and states with strong Republican candidates.

Indeed, the commentary on the 2002 elections focused primarily on how the results reflected President Bush's popular support and the loyalty to him among the core base of Republican voters.

One continuing important trend in both parties since 1994 reflects the use of individual legislator PACs to curry favor with other members. By 2001–2002, 149 sitting legislators had formed leadership PACs, and these organizations funneled $23.5 million into other candidates' campaigns. These contributions came on top of the large volume of funds transferred from one campaign to another. Given that leaders (actual and would be) use PACs to help them win or hold their positions, these organizations can assist in centralizing their power, as with Majority Leader Tom DeLay's substantial contributions to moderate Republicans.

In the Senate, leadership PACs have also proliferated, often because so many senators have presidential aspirations. For example, in the 2001–2002 electoral cycle, Senator Joseph Lieberman's PAC raised $2.9 million and spent $2.5 million, much of it going to other campaigns and various party units, to support his quest for the 2004 Democratic presidential nomination. Despite this continuing trend, most leadership PACS serve to assist representatives and senators within their own chambers.

Still, given that many legislator PACs are not controlled by party leaders themselves, the tendency toward fragmentation remains important.[56] As congressional scholar Ross Baker concluded in an early study of these organizations, the PACs will "magnify the influence of individual members, . . . [who], armed with their own checkbooks, [will make] harder the job of party leaders as they try to manage the delicate balance and often frustrating task of building party majorities."[57] In the House and, especially, the Senate, where every legislator can hope to exercise some policy leadership, the additional resource of personal PACs can work against the centralization that strong parties have imposed on the postreform Congress. Still, Representative DeLay and his lieutenants have increasingly used leadership PACs to enforce party discipline.

Campaign Finance Reform

Perhaps the most remarkable electoral development in 2002 was the passage of campaign finance reform legislation, which President Bush signed in March 2002 and which went into effect immediately after the November election. The Congress had considered campaign finance reform several times since the 1980s, but the two parties could never agree on contribution limits from specific sources. Democrats had traditionally received more money from PACs, while Republicans had more success among independent contributors. But after 1994, the two parties reached more parity in the distribution of funds from these sources (see Table 4–2).

The origins of the 2002 legislation date back to 1995, when Senators John McCain (R-Ariz.) and Russell Feingold (D-Wis.) introduced a bill that banned PAC contributions and provided free advertising time to candidates who agreed to spending limits. A companion measure, with similar provisions, was introduced in the House by Representative Christopher Shays (R-Ct.) and Martin Meehan (D-Mass.).

The role of money in campaigns had intensified in the mid-1990s for several reasons. First, a 1996 Supreme Court ruling largely freed political parties at the state and national levels from restrictions of spending so-called soft money directly on behalf of federal candidates' campaigns. For example, in the weeks immediately prior to and following the 1996 general elections, Republicans and Democrats combined to raise more than $38 million, much of which went directly into advertising for congressional candidates.[58] In addition, many congressional leaders funneled money from their own campaigns or from their personal PACs into tight races. Second, organized interests spent enormous amounts of "independent expenditures" on behalf of individual candidates. The AFL-CIO embarked on the most visible campaign — at least $35 million spread across fewer than fifty districts. Other soft money expenses were equally substantial, if not so focused; at least thirty-four businesses, unions, and trade associations each contributed more than $1 million in 1996, led by Philip Morris's $2.7 million plus.[59] In 1998, independent expenditures fell somewhat, as groups reduced their advertising spending, but many — especially unions — invested heavily in get-out-the-vote efforts. At the same time, party-based soft money funding rose sharply. With a maximum of about thirty House seats in play, parties could concentrate their resources on a small number of races. In 1994 (the previous off-year election), Democrats and Republicans raised $49 million and $53 million, respectively, in soft money; four years later the totals roughly doubled, to $89 million and $111 million.[60]

If 1996 was the "year of the loophole," in which independent expenditures from interest groups affected a host of individual House races, 1998 was the "year of soft money," in which the parties took advantage of court rulings to pour funds into a handful of competitive races around the country. Democrats directed $22.5 million to their congressional candidates in 1998, and Republicans offered more than $18 million. Despite the overwhelming strength of incumbents in both 1996 and 1998, national funds from groups and parties have been directed into a small number of key races. Even when competition levels are low and incumbents dominate, national funds from groups and parties can still play a great role in determining the balance of power in a Congress that continues to be closely divided. The number of close contests for congressional seats may have diminished, but the battles for those seats are as intense as ever, and the parties have not hesitated to concentrate their funds on winning them, often at the expense of the message of the individual candidate.

It was not until after the 2000 elections and the Enron scandals that real pressure was brought to bear on the House and Senate to remedy the skyrocketing costs of campaigns and the role of money in federal politics. In 2001, the Senate passed a version of campaign finance reform that banned soft money contributions to national political parties but allowed smaller amounts to be given to state and local parties, limited issue advertising by interest groups to the period up to sixty days before Election Day, required full disclosure of sponsorship of issue ads, and raised individual contribution limits. The House passed the bill in February 2002, and the Bipartisan Campaign Reform Act became law the next month to take affect in November 2002.

The biggest impact from the bill is bound to be felt by the national political party organizations. Prior to the bill, parties could raise unlimited amounts of money from individual contributors and distribute them to any number of candidates in the party. In this way, soft money became an alternative gateway of access to legislators via the party organizations and strengthened the influence of the party over individual legislators as a result. With the closing of that gateway, (as of November 6, 2002), national parties will have to use alternative resources to forge strong ties with House and Senate members.

Given that this law profoundly affects the very livelihoods of members of Congress, the legislation mandated expedited review by the Supreme Court, which will be able to review any lower court decision on the bill well before the November 2004 general election. Until then, however, the new rules may well benefit congressional Republicans, who have capitalized on their advantage in raising "hard money" in increments up to $2,000 per individual contribution, or twice what the previous law had allowed.[61]

LOCAL CAMPAIGNS FOR NATIONAL OFFICE: THE MIX OF FORCES

Buoyed both by the late former Speaker Tip O'Neill's homey advice that "all politics is local" and by dozens of academic studies that explain or assume the power of incumbency, a strong conventional wisdom about the reduced competition in congressional elections emerged during the early 1970s and held sway for more than twenty years.[62] Bolstered by PAC funds and the contributions of interests and individuals who wanted to invest with the majority party, Democrats succeeded in sheltering their House members and, to a lesser extent, their senators from the winds of national politics that filled the sails of Republican presidential candidates in five of six elections between 1968 and 1988.[63]

As marginal seats vanished, less opportunity existed for powerful national forces to sweep large numbers of new members into office.[64] In part, however, this resistance to change had its foundation in the assumption of a continuing Democratic majority in the House of Representatives. Such an assumption no longer holds, and the underlying structure of competition has changed substantially. For example, the contest to control a majority of House seats usually rests on the outcomes in fewer than fifty districts and sometimes in just twenty or so. But more important than party control, the very capacity of a challenger to successfully defeat an incumbent has diminished over time. The forces that buffer all incumbents have grown to the point that the electoral playing field is grossly uneven. Incumbents from both parties have become more and more entrenched. Combined with the unvarnished partisan views of many new arrivals on Capitol Hill, the role of parties in congressional politics continues to grow stronger from its electoral roots.

As of the 108th Congress, and for the first time in almost fifty years, the Republican Party won control of the House, the Senate, and the presidency. Unified party control can be a blessing when the party stays unified and enacts a set of policies that wins approval among voters. Conversely, it can become a curse when those policies are not successful and voters can clearly assign blame to a single majority party. Republicans will either continue to gain seats, and keep the White House, or they will end up repeating the outcomes of the 1994 elections, when the unified majority Democratic Party lost control of both the House and Senate.

CHAPTER BIBLIOGRAPHY

Ahuja, Sunil, and Robert Dewhirst. *The Roads to Congress*. Toronto: Wadsworth Group, 2002.

Fenno, Richard F., Jr. *Going Home*. Chicago: University of Chicago Press, 2003.

Gierzynski, Anthony. *Money Rules: Financing Elections in America*. Boulder, CO: Westview Press, 2000.

Tate, Katherine. *Black Faces in the Mirror: African Americans and Their Representatives in the U.S. Congress*. Princeton, NJ: Princeton University Press, 2003.

NOTES

1. A ninth Senate seat came to the Republicans through the November 1994 party switch of Alabama Democrat Richard Shelby. They added a tenth seat with Colorado Senator Ben Nighthorse Campbell's switch in March 1995.

2. Beyond the thirty-four Democratic incumbents who lost in the general election, two more lost in Democratic primary contests.

3. Gary Jacobson, *The Politics of Congressional Elections,* 3rd ed. (New York: HarperCollins, 1992), p. 2.

4. Robert S. Erickson and Gerald C. Wright, "Voters, Candidates, and Issues in Congressional Elections," in Lawrence C. Dodd and Bruce I. Oppenheimer, eds., *Congress Reconsidered,* 6th ed. (Washington, DC: CQ Press, 1997), p. 156.

5. Ibid., p. 91.

6. Richard F. Fenno, Jr., *Home Style* (Boston: Little, Brown, 1978), p. 27.

7. Ibid., p. 18.

8. The Constitution mandates the reapportionment of House seats among the states every ten years, after the decennial census. Each state must then redraw its district lines to comply with equal representation requirements. For a good contemporary overview of the redistricting and reapportionment, see David Butler and Bruce Cain, *Congressional Redistricting* (New York: Macmillan, 1992).

9. National Committee for an Effective Congress, Redistricting Resource Center, <www.ncec.org>, November 2002.

10. Ibid.

11. See Jon Meacham, "Voting Wrongs," *Washington Monthly,* March 1993, p. 28. Of the fifty-eight minority House members, fifty-two came from minority-majority districts.

12. Lani Guinier, "Don't Scapegoat the Gerrymander," *New York Times Magazine,* January 8, 1995, pp. 36–37.

13. See Butler and Cain, *Congressional Redistricting,* pp. 1ff.

14. Several legal cases challenged this policy; in its 1997 session, the Supreme Court had approved maps in Louisiana and Georgia that reduced the role of race in redistricting.

15. Michael Barone and Grant Ujifusa, *The Almanac of American Politics 1994* (Washington, DC: National Journal, 1993), p. 969.

16. Linda Greenhouse, "High Court Voids Race-Based Plans for Redistricting," *New York Times,* June 14, 1996, A1.

17. Holly Idelson, "Court Takes a Harder Line on Minority Voting Blocs," *Congressional Quarterly Weekly Report,* July 1, 1995, p. 1944.

18. For two excellent studies of the current state of majority-minority districting, see David I. Lublin, *The Paradox of Representation: Racial Gerrymandering and Minority Interests in Congress* (Princeton, NJ: Princeton University Press, 1997), and David T. Canon, *Race, Redistricting, and Representation: The Unintended Consequences of Black-Majority Districts* (Chicago: University of Chicago Press, 1999).

19. Robert Hanley, "Judges Uphold New Districts in New Jersey," *New York Times,* May 2, 2001, B5.

20. Fenno, *Home Style,* p. 25.

21. *National Journal* Web site, <www.nationaljournal.com>, accessed February 12, 2003. In 2002, Representative Ryun was reelected with 60 percent of the vote.

22. This is not new. For an earlier analysis of electoral uncertainty among House members, see Thomas Mann, *Unsafe at Any Margin* (Washington, DC: American Enterprise Institute, 1978).

23. Charles S. Bullock III, "House Careerists: Changing Patterns of Longevity and Attrition," *American Political Science Review* 66 (1972): pp. 1295–1305. See also Donald Matthews, "Legislative Recruitment and Legislative Careers," in Gerhard Loewenberg, Samuel C. Patterson, and Malcolm E. Jewell, eds., *Handbook of Legislative Research* (Cambridge, MA: Harvard University Press, 1985), pp. 17–56, and seniority lists in *Congressional Quarterly Weekly Report,* various years.

24. Gary Jacobson, *The Politics of Congressional Elections,* 4th ed. (New York: Longman, 1997), pp. 19ff.

25. *Roll Call* and Election Data Services, December 2002.

26. Senator Paul Wellstone, the incumbent Democrat from Minnesota, died while campaigning.

27. David R. Mayhew, "Congressional Elections: The Case of the Vanishing Marginals," *Polity* 6 (1974): pp. 295–317.

28. Morris P. Fiorina, "The Case of the Vanishing Marginals: The Bureaucracy Did It," *American Political Science Review* 71 (1977): pp. 177–181.

29. Among an avalanche of studies, see the summary presented in Bruce Cain, John Ferejohn, and Morris Fiorina, *The Personal Vote* (Cambridge, MA: Harvard University Press, 1987), pp. 121ff.

30. The best brief summary here can be found in Morris Fiorina, *Congress: Keystone of the Washington Establishment,* 2nd ed. (New Haven, CT: Yale University Press, 1989).

31. Among others, see John Ferejohn, "On the Decline of Competition in Congressional Elections," *American Political Science Review* 71 (March 1977): pp. 166–176. More generally, see the discussion in Jacobson, *Politics of Congressional Elections,* 4th ed., pp. 19ff.

32. See Cain, Ferejohn, and Fiorina, *The Personal Vote.*

33. Jacobson, *Politics of Congressional Elections,* 3rd ed. p. 118. The same tendency holds for name recognition: 92 percent for House incumbents, 54 percent for challengers.

34. Fiorina, *Congress,* pp. 94–95.

35. Jacobson, p. 50. For a differing view, see Donald P. Green and Jonathan S. Krasno, "Salvation for the Spendthrift Incumbents," *American Journal of Political Science* 32 (1988): pp. 844–907.

36. Jacobson, *Politics of Congressional Elections,* 3rd ed., p. 50.

37. Federal Election Commission, <www.fec.gov>, February 11, 1999.

38. Jacobson, *Politics of Congressional Elections,* 3rd ed., p. 55.

39. Ibid., p. 29.

40. See Mann, *Unsafe at Any Margin.*

41. In particular, the Supreme Court ruled in 1976 that Sun Oil Company could absorb the administrative costs of its political action committee, thus freeing virtually all the funds it raised to be distributed to candidates. This decision encouraged many corporations and trade associations to establish PACs. For a good overview of the first ten years of PAC activity, see Larry Sabato, *PAC Power* (New York: Norton, 1984).

42. *Nonconnected* means literally not connected to any parent group, such as a corporation or a trade association such as the American Medical Association or the American Trucking Association.

43. Darrell M. West and Burdette A. Loomis, *The Sound of Money* (New York: W. W. Norton, 1999).

44. Norman Ornstein, Thomas Mann, and Michael Malbin, eds., *Vital Statistics on Congress, 1995–1996* (Washington, DC: CQ Press, 1995), p. 75. All other figures and tables in this chapter come from the same source, pp. 75ff., save as noted.

45. Gary Jacobson, *Politics of Congressional Elections,* 5th ed. (New York: Longman, 2001).

46. Brooks Jackson, *Honest Graft* (Washington, DC: Farragut, 1990), p. 107.

47. Quoted in Shulte and Enda, "Fund Raising Is Always on Political Agenda." Feingold tested this notion in 1998, as he limited his spending to $3.8 million and actively discouraged outside funding from the national Democratic Party. His opponent, Representative Mark Neumann, spent $4,316,928. Feingold won reelection, with just over 50 percent of the vote.

48. These figures include general election candidates' spending in both the primary and the general elections. Defeated primary candidates are not included. These figures and others in this section are from Ornstein, Mann, and Malbin, *Vital Statistics on Congress,* chap. 3. (1995–1996).

49. Federal Election Commission, "PAC Activity Increases in 1995–96 Election Cycle," news release, April 22, 1997, p. 2; 1998 data from <www.fec.gov>. See also Gary W. Cox and Eric Magar, "How Much Is Majority Status in the U.S. Congress Worth?" *American Political Science Review* 93 (June 1999): pp. 299–310.

50. Ross K. Baker, *The New Fat Cats* (New York: Priority Press, 1989), pp. 35–40.

51. This margin was later trimmed, through special elections to fill vacant seats, to 256-178, with one independent.

52. Two weeks before the 1994 election, then-Minority Leader Gingrich put the odds at two to one that Republicans would win the House. Katharine Q. Seelye, "With Fiery Words, Gingrich Builds His Kingdom," *New York Times,* October 27, 1994, p. A1.

53. Paul Herrnson, "Money and Motives: Spending in House Elections," in Lawrence C. Dodd and Bruce I. Oppenheimer, eds., *Congress Reconsidered,* 6th ed. (Washington, DC: CQ Press, 1997), p. 101.

54. For detailed discussions of Republican Party governance in the 104th Congress, see James G. Gimpel, *Legislating the Revolution : The Contract with America in Its First 100 Days,* (Boston: Allyn & Bacon, 1996), and Richard F. Fenno Jr., *Learning to Govern: An Institutional View of the 104th Congress,* (Washington, DC: Brookings Institution Press, 1997). A good analysis of the fates of the freshman Republican class of 1995 can be found in Linda Killian's book, *The Freshmen: What Happened to the Republican Revolution?* (Boulder, CO: Westview Press, 1998).

55. Gary C. Jacobson, "The Congressional Elections of 1996," *Extension of Remarks/ Legislative Studies Newsletter,* January 1997.

56. Albert D. Cover and David R. Mayhew, "Congressional Dynamics and the Decline of Competitive Congressional Elections," in Lawrence Dodd and Bruce Oppenheimer, eds., *Congress Reconsidered* (New York: Praeger, 1977), pp. 54–74.

57. Gary Jacobson, *Politics of Congressional Elections,* 4th ed., p. 24.

58. Jonathon D. Salant, "Million-Dollar Campaigns Proliferate in 105th," *Congressional Quarterly Weekly Report,* December 21, 1996, p. 3449.

59. David E. Rosenbaum, "In Political Money Game, the Year of Big Loopholes," *New York Times,* December 26, 1996, p. A11. Soft money represents funds meant ostensibly for so-called party-building activities.

60. Federal Election Committee, press release, January 26, 1999, <www.fec.gov>.

61. *Washington Post National Weekly,* March 3–10, 2003.

62. See the list in the previous section on the "slurge."

63. Some voters may well have chosen to balance a Republican president with a Democratic Congress, and many have grown comfortable with it, but to see divided government as an explicit choice of rational voters may push the interpretation a bit too far. For a coherent discussion, see Gary Jacobson, *The Electoral Origins of Divided Government* (Boulder, CO: Westview Press, 1990), especially pp. 119–120.

64. For a useful summary of the relative import of national and local forces, see James Campbell, *The Presidential Pulse of Congressional Elections* (Lexington: University Press of Kentucky, 1993).

Five

PARTIES AND LEADERSHIP: CAPTURING THE CONGRESS

The Contract [with America] can be understood as an effort to introduce responsible party government into a legislature that has heretofore been described as an inchoate collection of atomized interests.

James Gimpel, *Fulfilling the Contract*

April 7, 1995. Speaker of the House Newt Gingrich and many, though not all, of his fellow Republican representatives marched out to the Capitol steps to proclaim the success of their hundred- (actually ninety-three) days forced-march passage through the House of all but one (term limits) of their Contract with America agenda. Speaker Gingrich, supported strongly by old and (especially) new House Republicans, had captured the congressional agenda, even if only two Contract items had become law by the April rally.

November 6, 1998. Speaker of the House Newt Gingrich resigned his post as Speaker and his seat in the House of Representatives. The Republicans surrendered five seats in the 1998 midterm elections, in spite of the historical trend that predicted a loss for the president's party (the Democrats). Coupled with the constant battles against President Bill Clinton, which culminated in impeachment proceedings, this loss ultimately proved too detrimental to the public image of the House Republican majority, whose members responded by effectively ousting Speaker Gingrich. Waiting in the wings was Representative Bob Livingston (R-La.), a man who owed his chairmanship of the all-powerful Appropriations Committee to Speaker Gingrich (see Chapter 8). With a mere twelve-vote majority in the 106th Congress, Republican House members sought an astute legislative leader, rather than a fading partisan revolutionary like Gingrich.

But Livingston himself was undercut by the very same behavior that had led to the impeachment of President Clinton. Larry Flynt, publisher of the salacious *Hustler* magazine, was ready to publish details of several of Livingston's extramarital affairs. Livingston resigned and thus left the Republican House majority without a Speaker for the next Congress.

Representative Dennis Hastert (R-Ill.) emerged as a consensus candidate for the Speakership in the wake of Livingston's resignation, in part because of his own qualifications and experience (as chief deputy whip), and in part because of the almost desperate need for House Republicans to coalesce around a single figure. With his 223-211 majority and a weakened Republican Party, both in the legislature and in national polls, Speaker Hastert had his work cut out for him in the 106th Congress.

The rise and fall of Newt Gingrich as minority party whip and then Speaker of the House illustrates the role of party leaders in the House. Party leaders must gain their colleagues' confidence and craft a party message that secures their party's majority status. Party leaders may amass great power in this effort, and as long as the party retains the majority, the rank and file will stay loyal. But as Gingrich discovered, those members will withdraw their support for a strong Speaker if they judge that their party's majority or its programs are at risk.

Over the same period of time in the Senate, the only transition in leadership was voluntary: Senator Robert Dole (R-Kans.) left the post of majority leader to run for president in June 1996, and Senator Trent Lott (R-Miss.) assumed the post of Senate majority leader. Senator Tom Daschle (D-S.D.) had become Democratic leader in 1995 and he and Senator Lott ran the Senate throughout the 1990s in these positions until Senator Jeffords, a Republican from Vermont, switched his party affiliation to Independent and gave the Democrats a one-vote majority in 2001. With the November election results of 2002, Senator Lott regained his position as majority leader, and Senator Daschle resumed his post as Democratic leader. In December 2002, however, Senator Lott was forced to resign as majority leader over his comments about segregation in the South, and Senator Bill Frist (R-Tenn.) was elected majority leader.

This chapter focuses on the history of party leadership in the House and Senate and how that leadership has evolved over time. In the House, majority party leaders are granted substantial agenda-setting and committee appointment powers by the rank-and-file membership of the party. In contrast, Senate party leaders hold less power over the Senate floor agenda and limited power over committee appointments. The House, under Democrats and Republicans alike, encourages strong party leadership, while the Senate, despite some increased partisanship, continues to preserve individual powers, often at the expense of the party leaders.

THE CONGRESSIONAL PARTY: CENTRALIZATION IN CONTEXT

Legislatures, like all institutions, must function with some overall coherence. Political parties provide much of the glue that holds together the disparate ambitions of 535 legislators, buttressed by their enterprises, as well as the fragmented collection of committees, subcommittees, and special interest caucuses. Yet in the United States, political parties have proven much weaker and less capable of producing strong centripetal effects within the legislature than have parties in most other Western-style democracies, and especially those with parliamentary systems.[1]

Assessing the role of parties in the early 1960s, a strong committee era, Richard F. Fenno, Jr., concluded that parties "organize decision making across committees and across stages [of the legislative process], thereby functioning as a centralizing force in the making of House decisions." Although most members shared emotional attachments to their party and regarded it as one means to exercise power, Fenno noted, "the . . . party label masks a pluralism of geographic, social, ideological, and organizational sources of identification, support, and loyalty. The roots of this pluralism lie outside the chamber, in the disparity of conditions under which the members are elected and in the decentralized organization of the parties nationally."[3] Congressional parties thus grow stronger when partisan divisions within the electorate increase. In 1994, for example, congressional election results reflected strong partisan forces that helped form the basis for strong party leadership under new Republican Speaker Gingrich. By the time the 2000 elections occurred, the electorate was evenly divided and, along with a close presidential election, produced a 50-50 Senate with a Republican vice president to serve as the tie-breaking vote. The 2002 congressional elections gave the Republicans some modest gains, but effective parity remained in the 108th Congress. In the end, the best opportunities to exercise effective party leadership on Capitol Hill have depended on forces largely beyond the control of the leaders, forces that emanate from the society and the electorate.

Not only does the diversity of constituencies constrain the impact of congressional parties, so too does the very resolution of issues that occasionally, but temporarily, divide the country into two broad, party-based factions. Periods of strong, centralized leadership and high levels of partisan voting on Capitol Hill reflect polarization between the parties in the electorate.[4] Circa 1900, Republican Speakers Thomas Reed and Joseph Cannon benefited from electoral results built on clear philosophical differences between two legislative parties that shouldered responsibility for ruling and accountability for their actions. In that era, individual representatives, having won their seats "on the basis of a party's platform," were expected to "support party positions, even against personal convictions or desires."[5] Internal allegiances to a party leader fit neatly into a world in which party machines controlled the candidate selection process.[6] Opposing the party might well mean that a legislator would be denied renomination, and thus reelection, especially in an era before the widespread adoption of primary elections as the means of choosing nominees.

If party machines and a polarized electorate provided the external context for strong direction, the Speaker could act forcefully on party issues within the House.[7] Reed (1889–1891, 1895–1899) and Cannon (1903–1911) each combined their extensive formal prerogatives under the rules with their status as Speaker to carry out their legislative agendas. Speaker Cannon, for example, chaired the Rules Committee and his majority leader headed Ways and Means — at the time, the two most powerful committees in the chamber. He appointed *all* committee members and *all* chairs and could delay making these appointments until well after the Congress had convened. He controlled the legislative schedule with an iron hand and used his power of recognition to reduce opponents' capacity to participate meaningfully in floor debate. Moreover, the Speaker was also a party leader who could define those issues appropriate for partisan position taking. Straying from the party might well mean that a dissident would be disciplined by the Speaker through removal from a powerful committee or the rejection of his preferences in fashioning a key piece of legislation. At worst, the Speaker could encourage the dissident's local party organization to reject him as a candidate in the next election.

Why should we care much about century-old congressional party politics and voting alignments? (See Table 5–1.) Whatever the importance of the policies made at the time, this period's practices allow us to assess the actual possibilities for centralization with Congress. Given an external context that

TABLE 5-1
The First and Last Congresses of the Twentieth Century

	57th Congress	106th Congress
Party Identification		
House	199 R	222 R
	151 D	211 D
	8 Other	1 Other
Senate	55 R	55 R
	31 D	45 D
	4 Other	0 Other
Average Age		
House	49	53
Senate	58	58
Average Number of Previous Terms		
House	2	4
Senate	1	1
African Americans	0	38
Women	0	65
Most Common First Name	William (45)	John (40)
Most Common Last Name	Smith (7)	Smith (6)
Members Named Elijah	1	1
Members Named Nehemiah	1	0
Members with Military Experience	28%	33%
Most common Former Profession	Lawyer (90%)	Lawyer (40%)
Former Blacksmiths	1	0
Former Plastic Surgeons	0	1
Members from Alaska, Ariz., Hawaii, N.M., or Okla.	0	28

Sources: Roll Call, January 18, 1999.

produces opposing voting blocs, legislators may opt to strengthen the hand of party leaders by providing them with the tools to lead forcefully, as the Democrats did in the 1980s, with Republicans following suit after winning control of Congress in 1995. Indeed, the Gingrich Speakership left congressional scholars grasping for parallels in the modern Congress. For example, political scientist Charles Jones observed that the House Republicans' domination of the agenda, at least in the first year of 104th Congress, had no precedent in this century, including during the Cannon Speakership.[8]

If the context of congressional politics can produce strong leadership and intense partisanship, it can also set conditions for relatively weak parties. In fact, from the 1920s through the early 1960s, parties within the Congress often reflected a social stalemate over the scope of governmental actions and, particularly, the role of federal involvement in matters of race and other domestic matters such as education and health care. To the extent that Americans were split by both ideology and region on these issues, so too were their representatives in Congress, where three party blocs developed in the wake of the policy initiatives of Franklin Roosevelt's first term (1933–1937) as president: Republicans, Northern Democrats, and Southern Democrats.

As the majority party, Democrats organized both the House and Senate for all but two Congresses between 1933 and the 1960s.[9] This means they named the Speaker, the majority leader, various other majority party offices, and all the committee chairs, as well as holding a majority of seats on all legislative committees. But this "procedural majority," which ensured Democratic control in formal terms, often vanished when important, substantive issues came to a vote.[10] Not only was the Congress fragmented among constituencies in ordinary pluralistic ways, but it also frequently split sharply along the related lines of region and ideology, as Southern Democrats joined with Republicans to form a "Conservative Coalition" that opposed the liberal initiatives of Democratic presidents and their Northern Democratic allies in the Congress, especially on civil rights and social welfare policies.[11]

As Brady and Bullock point out, "Understanding how the Conservative Coalition works furthers our understanding of the [Congress] as a whole. The voting alliance begun in 1937 between Southern Democrats and Republicans . . . greatly reduced the ability of the majority Democratic Party to function as a governing party."[12] Although Republicans and Southern Democrats did consult with each other, the alliance remained informal. Key Republicans such as House Minority Leader Joseph Martin (R-Mass.) and influential Southern Democrats such as Senator Richard Russell (D-Ga.) would communicate casually, if purposefully, with their allies and encourage the formation of a voting coalition.[13] The party and committee leadership, with moderate-to-conservative Texan Sam Rayburn as Speaker, was heavily weighted with Southerners who ordinarily deferred to the coalition.

Rayburn's greatest strengths as Speaker did not derive from his formal powers, which were modest at best. He could not control the Rules Committee;

it had been captured by the Conservative Coalition during the 1950s under the strong-willed chairmanship of conservative Democrat Howard Smith (D-Va.), who owed his position to his seniority on the committee. More generally, the seniority principle had become so firmly entrenched within the Congress that advancement on committees was virtually automatic, regardless of one's loyalty to the party. Nor did Rayburn control the initial assignments of Democrats to committees.[14] In short, Rayburn possessed few of the leadership tools that Cannon had wielded so effectively to control the agenda and legislative results of the House.[15] Yet legislators almost universally viewed him as a powerful Speaker. How could this be so?

Rayburn did retain significant, if limited, formal powers and the discretion to recognize whom he wanted on the House floor. He also controlled the leadership organization, which kept him well informed on most issues. Rayburn could dominate the final scheduling of legislation, and he often used his position to trade favors with other members — both Republicans and Democrats.[16] Favors such as campaigning for a fellow Democrat, postponing a vote to mollify a freshman Republican, and supporting a new dam for a marginal-seat member allowed the Speaker to build up positive "balances" in his exchanges with legions of representatives (including those in the minority). As a result of past favors, Rayburn could request assistance on a specific issue from various legislators who would be hard-pressed to rebuff him.[17] In addition, Rayburn's work ethic, his absolute integrity, and his total dedication to the House provided strong foundations for his politicking on given legislation items.

The years between 1956 and 1961 proved to be a watershed for the Democratic Party in Congress. As Senate majority leader, Lyndon Johnson forcefully asserted himself in forming a cohesive coalition among liberals and southern conservatives, but it was a fragile coalition at best.[18] The influx of northern liberal Democrats to both the House and Senate presented a challenge to conservative dominance. With the election of a Democratic president, and the departure of Lyndon Johnson from the Senate, the Democrats became a more powerful party in government but now faced a growing chasm between southern conservatives and northern liberals. With the exception of large Democratic majorities in the 89th Congress (1965–1966), which ushered in President Johnson's sweeping Great Society programs, internal conflicts among Democrats in both houses prevented the party from governing effectively.[19]

Over the course of the 1960s and early 1970s, the Democratic Party in the House continued to fracture on issues ranging from voting rights to the Vietnam War, which resulted in a weakened party leadership and a decentralized policy making. It was simply too difficult to craft a set of party policies that would command the loyalty of a majority of the Democratic Party over and over again. Neither of the two Speakers who followed Rayburn — Representatives John McCormack (D-Mass., 1961–1969) and Carl Albert (D-Okla., 1969–1977) — proved forceful or effective in countering these decentralizing forces. Senator Mike Mansfield, who was the Senate majority leader from 1961 to 1977, practiced a restrained leadership style that failed to unify his Democratic colleagues, though he retained great personal popularity and respect from them.

Beginning in the 1960s, the more liberal members of the House Democratic caucus began a concerted effort to empower party leaders who shared their policy ideas in order to reduce the power of the bloc of conservative members who held many of the important committee chairs. Using their base in the Democratic Study Group (one of the first informal groups on Capitol Hill), liberals continuously prodded the Democratic caucus to reduce the autonomy of full committee chairs and increase the authority of the leadership and the full caucus, which the northern Democrats increasingly dominated.[20] In particular, the Democratic caucus gave the Speaker the power to appoint members of the Rules Committee, thus making the committee a loyal "arm of the Leadership."[21] Next, the caucus moved the committee assignment responsibility to the party leadership–dominated Steering and Policy Committee and thus greatly enhanced the leaders' roles in this process. Finally, to coordinate policy making within the fragmented committee system, the Speaker was granted broad powers to refer bills to multiple committees, often in a well-defined sequence that imposed deadlines on committee action.[22]

Even as subcommittees proliferated, individual enterprises grew, and new norms encouraged the participation of all members in the late 1970s, party leaders slowly gained more leverage and influence. During his decade-long tenure as Speaker (1977–1986), Representative Thomas P. (Tip) O'Neill (D-Mass.) and his lieutenants created a new leadership style within a House that encouraged more individual participation from virtually all members, but especially those of the majority party.[23] In this democratized context leaders became service providers, more than ever, to their colleagues; by offering meaningful support to incumbents, by keeping all the Democratic legislators well informed, and by granting any number of particular favors, the leadership demonstrated its responsiveness. At the same time, the Democratic leaders greatly increased their ability to structure the decision-making process through their formal powers to schedule bills and dominate the Rules Committee. Collectively, congressional Democrats were willing to allow their leadership considerable leeway here, as long as its actions did not conflict with clear membership preferences. Finally, the leaders consciously adopted an inclusive strategy, bringing large numbers of members into the leadership during the late 1970s, both in permanent positions (for example, as whips) and in ad hoc capacities (such as task force heads and members).

By the end of 1986, Democrats were willing to accept a strengthened leadership that would allow Jim Wright to become, in 1987–1989, one of the House's most powerful Speakers. The party had become more dominated by northern and midwestern Democrats, as the South began its transformation to a Republican-dominated region. At the same time, the Republicans grew increasingly united and vocal in their protests against both the Democrats' policy positions and their use of procedures to limit meaningful minority participation within the House.[24] By acting as aggressive, effective partisans, the House Democrats simultaneously offered Republicans a model of strong leadership and a clear target for the opposition's efforts to gain control of the House.

In the Senate, party control changed hands twice. From 1977–1980, the Democrats ran the Senate under the leadership of Robert Byrd (D-W.V.), who invoked his limited formal powers to try to bring together the disparate members of his party. In 1981, the Republicans took control of the Senate, first under the leadership of Howard Baker (R-Tenn.) and then in 1985, Robert Dole (R-Kans). Both Baker and Dole sought to shepherd President Ronald Reagan's policies through the Senate and to lead negotiations with the Democratic House. In 1987, the Democrats recaptured control of the Senate, and again, Senator Byrd served as majority leader. Although the House Democratic caucus had moved over time to consolidate and strengthen the powers of their party leaders, Senate leaders' powers remained modest at best. Senators from both parties were more interested in preserving their individual power than giving their leaders the power to pass a set of unified party-based initiatives.

Caucus-Based Centralization in the House: The Democratic Model, 1981-1994

Notions of party leadership, partisanship, and party voting overlap within the Congress. Party leaders often structure votes and other decisions to take advantage of party majorities, but they must also take into account the preferences of their followers. Partisanship in voting does not necessarily flow from a stronger, more centralized party leadership; intense partisanship depends as much on electoral patterns as any set of practices within the Democratic caucus or the House as a whole. Over the period of 1981–1994, the composition of the Democratic Party changed in the House. The traditional conservative southern Democrats declined in numbers and impact, to be replaced increasingly replaced by southern Democrats from urban areas and districts with high percentages of African American voters. As the Democratic Party overall moved to the left, conservative southern ("Yellow Dog") Democratic voters gradually switched to the Republican Party and elected Republicans in rising numbers.[25] The result was more uniformity within both the Democratic and Republican Parties, and a more stark division between them.

Overall, the postreform Congress has become a highly partisan place, particularly in the House. In assessing the strength of political parties within the Congress, political scientists frequently analyze changes in two different but related measures of partisanship on roll-call votes.[26] From 1983 on, there is no question that both the proportion of party-based votes and the level of party loyalty on these votes have increased considerably (see Tables 5–2 and 5–3).

TABLE 5-2
Party Unity Average Scores

Average Scores for Each Party in Both Chambers of Congress					
Year	*Democrats*	*Republicans*	*Year*	*Democrats*	*Republicans*
1961	71%	72%	1982	72	71%
1962	69	68	1983	76	74
1963	71	72	1984	74	72
1964	67	69	1985	79	75
1965	69	70	1986	78	71
1966	61	67	1987	81	74
1967	66	71	1988	79	73
1968	57	63	1989	81	73
1969	62	62	1990	81	74
1970	57	59	1991	81	78
1971	62	66	1992	79	79
1972	57	64	1993	85	84
1973	68	68	1994	83	83
1974	63	62	1995	91	80
1975	69	70	1996	87	80
1976	65	66	1997	82	88
1977	67	70	1998	83	86
1978	64	67	1999	84	86
1979	69	72	2000	83	87
1980	68	70	2001	85	90
1981	69	76	2002	86	89

Sources: Congressional Quarterly Weekly Report, December 31, 1994, p. 3658; December 21, 1996, p. 346; January 9, 1999, p. 92; January 6, 2001, p. 67; and December 14, 2002, p. 3240. *Congressional Roll Call 2001*, p. B-17.

As the composition of Southern Democrats has changed, their party-voting scores rose steadily, from an average 53 percent party unity score in the 94th Congress (1975–1976) to an average of 78 percent in the 100th through 103rd Congresses (1987–1994).[27] Congressional scholar David Rohde observes, "in 1971–2, the *average* southern Democrat supported his or her party less than half the time on those votes that divided party majorities. From that point on, southern unity began a gradual increase to almost 80 percent in recent years."[28]

Bearing in mind Fenno's conclusion that we get the kind of Congress that the members give us,[29] we got a postreform Congress in which, from the early 1980s to 1994, the Democratic caucus empowered its leaders to act aggressively as its agents. This was accomplished in two related ways: (1) through an initial set of decisions at the beginning of each Congress and (2) through continuing conversations between party leaders and Democratic members, both in groups and one on one. These two developments came together within the Democratic caucus, where an increasingly homogenous membership could communicate its wishes to the leadership.[30] The caucus granted party leaders more tools for leadership and the leaders in turn accrued more experience in employing these instruments (restrictive rules, suspensions of the rules, sequential referrals of legislation to committees).

TABLE 5-3
Proportion of Partisan Roll Calls

How Often a Majority of Democrats Voted against a Majority of Republicans											
Year	*House*	*Senate*	*Year*	*House*	*Senate*	*Year*	*House*	*Senate*	*Year*	*House*	*Senate*
1954	38%	47%	1966	41%	50%	1978	33%	45%	1990	49%	54%
1955	41	30	1967	36	35	1979	47	47	1991	55	49
1956	44	53	1968	35	32	1980	38	46	1992	64	53
1957	59	36	1969	31	36	1981	37	48	1993	65	67
1958	40	44	1970	27	35	1982	36	43	1994	62	52
1959	55	48	1971	38	42	1983	56	44	1995	73	69
1960	53	37	1972	27	36	1984	47	40	1996	56	62
1961	50	62	1973	42	40	1985	61	50	1997	50	50
1962	46	41	1974	29	44	1986	57	52	1998	56	56
1963	49	47	1975	48	48	1987	64	41	1999	47	63
1964	55	36	1976	36	37	1988	47	42	2000	43	49
1965	52	42	1977	42	42	1989	55	35	2001	40	55
									2002	43	45

Source: Congressional Quarterly Weekly Report, December 31, 1994, p. 3659, December 21, 1996, p. 3462; January 9, 1999, p. 93, and December 14, 2002, p. 3240. *Congressional Roll Call 2001*, p. 3240 B–18.

At the outset of a new Congress, in January of each odd-numbered year, members of the legislative parties select their respective leaders. In the postreform era, House Democrats elected the Speaker, the majority leader, and chief majority whip[31] and voted to approve all full-committee chairs, as well as each of the thirteen appropriations subcommittee chairs. In short, the membership possesses a biennial opportunity to defeat any top party or committee leader who has lost the caucus's confidence. Between 1975 and 1993, Democrats unseated six committee chairs, eased another one out of his position, and, equally important, delivered numerous warnings to many other committee heads through negative votes.[32] For the party and committee leaders, this process can be unnerving, but it is highly valuable because these individuals receive the explicit endorsement of their peers. In an era when party leaders enjoyed great formal powers, such as the Speaker's Rules Committee appointments, his chairmanship of the Policy and Steering Committee, and his domination over legislative scheduling, this endorsement by the party's legislators gave Democratic leaders wide latitude in setting agendas and providing specific assistance to individual members. Yet the grant of authority remained contingent on the continuing support of a firm caucus majority, as Speaker Jim Wright learned in 1988. Speaker Wright was forced to resign his post as Speaker ostensibly over charges of ethics violations, but it was widely accepted that the caucus felt Wright had overstepped the bounds of the powers afforded to him by his party and he was replaced by Tom Foley (D-Wash.), a popular but less forceful leader.

The active Democratic caucus both empowered and restrained the party's leaders. By the early 1990s, a fairly large core group of leaders emerged as the day-to-day directors of House business. The traditional leaders — the Speaker, the majority leader, and the whip — were joined by three chief deputy whips, along with the caucus chair and vice chair. In addition, political scientist Barbara Sinclair notes, "as the leadership has become more central to the legislative process, members' desires for *representation* in the leadership have intensified."[33] Indeed, when Speaker Foley split the chief deputy whip's office into three positions, he appointed a woman (Barbara Kennelly, Conn.), a Southerner (Butler Derrick, S.C.), and an African American (John Lewis, Ga.), and in 1993 he added a fourth slot for Bill Richardson (N.M.), a Latino. Beyond these attempts to include more factions within the party leadership, this trend toward representation is important in that committees have historically served as the principal agents of representation. Given the emphasis on an expanded, inclusive leadership, however, the centrifugal forces of representation have grown stronger within the House's bastion of centralization.

The core leadership, aided by a formidable staff, serves as information source, sounding board, strategic and tactical decisionmaker, and, under divided government, interbranch negotiator. Nevertheless, given its highly inclusive style of operation, even an expanded core leadership could not maintain adequate communication lines with more than 250 House Democrats, so the Democrats established a much more extended leadership apparatus, which included almost half of the party's 256 legislators in the 103rd Congress. Of special note has been the systematic expansion of the whip system, which acts as a conduit for information between members and leaders and as an organization for mobilizing votes on the House floor.

In the 103rd Congress (1993–1994), the whip system included the majority whip, four deputy whips, a floor whip, an "ex-officio whip" (Representative Joe Moakley, then Rules Committee chair), eleven deputy whips, two "whip task force" chairs, fifty-six leadership-appointed at-large whips, and eighteen assistant whips elected by members of regional zones. The whip system alone included ninety-two Democratic members, well over a third of the party's ranks in the House. But the expansion in the ranks of Democratic leaders did not stop with the whip system. Rules Committee members clearly occupied leadership slots, as did the chair of the Budget Committee and a host of ad hoc task force heads appointed by the majority leader to organize party efforts on specific legislative initiatives.[34] In addition, the chairmanship of the Democratic Congressional Campaign Committee (DCCC) represented an important leadership position.

At first with great hesitancy, and later with vigor and conviction, the Democratic majority came to structure the context of decision making in the House, which meant that the minority Republicans became less and less able to influence outcomes.[35] The movement toward strong party leadership in a weak-party era illustrates the trends toward more ideological cohesiveness within parties in the House, as well as in members' cost–benefit calculations, which increasingly led them to encourage leaders' latitude in structuring decisions.[36] Strong party leadership remained contingent on these calculations by the members and on the ideological divisions between the two parties, however, and Democratic leaders became more and more dependent on manipulating the agenda and structuring floor votes through the aggressive use of the Rules Committee.[37] Many, if not most, Republicans found themselves holding no stake in the institution of the House; with little remorse they would seek to tear down the House that the Democratic majority had constructed.

Postreform Politics in the Republican Mold

Given the stunning results of the 1994 elections, Republicans gained control of the House after forty years as the minority. We shall explore in some detail the strong, centralized leadership adopted by the GOP. First, however, let us examine how the party operated as a minority within the contemporary House.

THE DILEMMA OF BEING THE MINORITY OPPOSITION   For the forty years that they were in the minority, the Republicans were relatively unified, voting as a party block about 70 percent of the time (see Table 5–2). As members of a long-standing minority in the House, Republicans found themselves holding little authority, which freed them to pursue a variety of strategies in seeking to affect policy outcomes.[38] Simple hard-boiled opposition always served as one alternative, of course, but historically many Republicans opted to cooperate with the Democratic majority, hoping to affect policies in committee or by providing key votes on the floor. The Rayburn-era House presented frequent opportunities for committees' ranking minority members to become important forces in shaping congressional policies. For example, in the 1950s and 1960s, Appropriations Committee Chair Clarence Cannon (D-Mo.) consulted not just regularly, but almost continuously, with ranking minority member John Taber (R-N.Y.) in reaching agreements on spending bills.[39]

During the 1970s and 1980s, House Republicans found themselves in increasingly difficult straits. First, they were often expected to support the policies of a Republican president, even though their minority status denied them any effective means to implement the executive agendas articulated by Nixon, Reagan, and Bush. Second, Democratic majorities, especially after 1982, acted in highly partisan ways within committees and on the House floor. Republicans could do little in the face of Rules Committee decisions to structure floor debates and votes, and the Speaker's control of scheduling allowed them little voice in decision making on either policies or procedures. A strong Democratic leadership and an increasingly unified set of Democratic members meant that House Republicans enjoyed few opportunities to influence outcomes.

In step with its generally conservative membership and often in reaction to the strengthened, sometimes arrogant, Democratic leadership, the House minority frequently chose confrontational strategies through the 1980s and into the 1990s. Indeed, the well-publicized actions of Representatives Newt Gingrich (R-Ga.), Robert Walker (R-Penn.), and Richard Armey (R-Tex.), among many others, heightened tensions in the increasingly partisan House. Gingrich enlisted other young, activist representatives to join him in the Conservative Opportunity Society, an informal group that functioned simultaneously as in-House think tank and guerrilla base in challenging the established powers of both parties.[40]

Two decisions — one imposed by the Democrats, the other taken by the Republican conference — demonstrated the growing strength of the con-frontational elements within the GOP. On May 1, 1985, following an extended and highly partisan process, the House opted in a partisan vote to give a con-tested seat to an Indiana Democratic incumbent, even though the state had certified the Republican challenger as the winner of the November election. Every Republican House member marched out of the chamber in protest; even the most moderate, least confrontational Republicans found this decision too much to swallow. Representative Vin Weber (R-Minn.), a Gingrich ally, observed, "it was essential to Newt and his success to drive home the point that after [thirty] years . . . something corrupting had happened to Democratic rule and it was just not in our interest to be in bed with the Democrats."[41]

The second decision came from within the Republican conference four years later. President Bush tapped House Minority Whip Dick Cheney (R-Wyo.) to become secretary of defense. The ensuing leadership contest pit-ted Gingrich against veteran Representative Edward Madigan (R-Ill.). Buoyed by early support from some frustrated moderates such as Nancy Johnson (R-Conn.), Gingrich won the whip post in an 89-87 count. By this narrowest of margins, the Republican conference had decided to move in a more con-frontational direction.

In the early 1990s, Republicans sought to link the unpopularity of the Con-gress with its Democratic leadership, especially in the House, thus laying the basis for partisan message politics to become the dominant method of internal governance. In a comprehensive broadside, Representatives Richard Armey (R-Tex.), Jennifer Dunn (R-Wash.), and Christopher Shays (R-Conn.) published an extensive attack on an unresponsive and allegedly corrupt Democratic House. They concluded, for example, that:

> forty years of single party control of the House of Representatives has cre-ated a *corrupt institution isolated from public sentiment* . . . (emphasis added) the ruling party has collectively used [its] powers to partisan ends. It has unleashed its investigatory power on enemies in the other party, while turning a blind eye and a deaf ear to equal or worse violations by some of its own. It has used its power over support institutions [such as the House Post Office] to give jobs to its supporters and to cover up scan-dals within them.[42]

In sum, members of the Republican House minority chose to use increas-ing aggressiveness and hostility, as they sought to link an unpopular postre-form Congress with its Democratic leadership. Given that Republicans became the majority and that no Republican incumbent lost his or her seat in the 1994 midterm elections, the conclusion can be drawn that they succeeded, at least in the short term. Over the longer haul, the increasing levels of partisan hostility and attacks on the House itself may have reduced the possibility of civil discourse and serious deliberation on Capitol Hill.

THE REPUBLICANS WIN THE HOUSE AND REORGANIZE, 1994–   In the wake of the 1994 sweep, which gave Republicans a gain of fifty-two seats and a 230-204-1 margin in the House,[43] the Republican conference approved rules for the party and the chamber that centralized leadership authority more firmly than at any time since the overthrow of Speaker Cannon. Building on the examples and structures provided by congressional Democrats in the postreform era, the Republican membership empowered Speaker Newt Gingrich to dominate the reconfiguration of many House practices and procedures, as well as giving him great power in selecting committee chairs and making committee appointments.

Moreover, the House Republicans demonstrated overwhelming unity throughout the highly publicized first one hundred days, in which they passed nine of ten items in their so-called Contract with America. The House cast 302 recorded votes in its first three months, and Republican levels of party unity reached near unanimity on all but a few issues such as term limits. On Contract items, 141 of 230 House Republicans voted with the party 100 percent of the time, and of seventy-three GOP freshmen, fifty-three compiled perfect records and seventy-one voted with the party at least 94 percent of the time.[44] This unity came in part from the momentum of capturing the House and having an agenda that had been developed through polling and focus groups, as well as in long discussions among Republicans for more than a decade; Gingrich was also credited for his skillful handling of both the seventy-three first-term members and the moderate wing of the party within the House. Indeed, "Gingrich has sought to encourage, rather than suppress the activist tendencies of the freshmen" by providing key committee appointments to the Appropriations, Budget, and Ways and Means Committees, as well as meeting with a different group of Republican freshmen every week.[45] Moderate Representative Sherwood Boehlert (R-N.Y.) observed that Gingrich proved a good listener, as "he challenges the moderates to unite, talk things over and come up with a plan."[46]

Beyond the Contract and a policy vision of a smaller national government, Gingrich's 1995 backing in the conference derived in large part from two perceptions: (1) Many junior members concluded that they owed their elections to him because of financial support, a nationalized election, and, for a lot of them, personal campaign visits; and (2) almost all House Republicans understood that they would not have won control in 1994 save for Gingrich's persistence and majority-building activities over the previous decade.

The first few months of the 104th Congress gave the impression that the Congress, at least in the House of Representatives, had become a parliamentary body; that is, the majority party could move its agenda through the legislature on its own schedule, essentially ignoring the minority Democrats. Indeed, Speaker Gingrich's role model as a party leader was Benjamin Disraeli, the

Tory leader who not only controlled the British House of Commons, but who created his own majority through the rough and tumble of electoral politics.[47] Given the enthusiasm, homogeneity, and tactical advantages of the GOP majority, if the House alone could have decided which bills, in what form, would become law, the unified Republicans[48] would have passed substantive legislation that truly would have been revolutionary — going beyond the Contract to eliminate several Cabinet department positions and to enact far-reaching restrictions on federal regulations.

But the U.S. House is not a parliamentary body, nor was Speaker Gingrich a prime minister. The Republican majority had to contend with the constitutional constraints embodied in a Democratic president and a Senate that often requires a supermajority (sixty votes to break a filibuster) to work its will (see below and Chapter 6).[49] As 1995 wore on, the euphoria of the first hundred days gradually changed to exhaustion brought on by endless negotiations over the unresolved budget issues and a series of continuing resolutions to fund the government for short periods of time (from a few days to a few weeks, during the fall of 1995).[50] As with the strengthened Democratic leadership of the 1980s, the Republican version of enhanced party leadership remained constrained by the preferences of the party's membership. As one GOP House member put it, "We tried to do too much, and there was no exit strategy when the government shut down. And we had a whiner [Gingrich] for a spokesman."[51]

The narrow Republican majorities of the Gingrich Speakership (230-204 in the 104th Congress, 228-206 in the 105th, both with one independent) allowed the Republican leader little leeway. Even when party voting reached historically high levels, Republicans found themselves at a great disadvantage in dealing with a generally united Democratic Party in the House, a politically astute Democrat in the White House, and a Senate Republican majority that could not overcome Democratic filibusters. As for House Republicans, former Gingrich aide Tony Blankley noted, "There is no point in declaring war when you've got a squad and you need a battalion."[52] Although moderate Republicans could and did hold the majority hostage to their demands, on occasion, it was the die-hard conservatives, who had provided the margin of the GOP's (and Gingrich's) initial 1994 victory, that caused the lion's share of trouble for the leadership. Indeed, as congressional scholar Dan Palazzalo concluded, Gingrich's military allusions did not fit the partisan situation, in that "political parties aren't armies. They're fractious organizations."[53]

By the time Dennis Hastert assumed the post of Speaker in December 1998, the party was barely holding on to its slim majority. The 106th Congress began in 1999 and was essentially a standoff between the Republicans and an embattled President Clinton. In 2000, presidential candidate George W. Bush distanced himself from House Republicans, which was an additional signal that the congressional Republican Party was in a bit of disarray. Nevertheless, it is important to keep in mind that the Republicans continue to maintain consistently high party unity; even now they vote together close to 90 percent of the time, in contrast to 70 percent unity when they were in the minority (see Table 5–2).

The leadership of Speaker Hastert and Representative Tom DeLay (first as whip, then majority leader) has succeeded in maintaining a Republican House majority that can dictate most major policy decisions within the House. But legislative politics remain bicameral, and even stronger partisanship in the Senate cannot ordinarily overcome the tendencies toward delay and individualism in that chamber.

The Senate: Every Senator for Himself or Herself

The same partisan forces that strengthened both Democratic and Republican House leaders in the 1980s and 1990s did not infiltrate the Senate to nearly the same degree. As an institution, the Senate is designed to preserve the powers of individual senators at the expense of party leaders. Unlike the House, where the majority party can use the Rules Committee to dictate which bills get to the floor and which amendments can be offered to them, the Senate has no such gatekeeper. The majority leader is selected by fellow partisans, and heads the majority party. The powers of the majority leader are limited at best. The majority leader has the right of first recognition by the presiding officer and typically brings bills up for consideration on the floor. But any individual senator, whether of the majority or minority party, can block a bill by simply objecting to its consideration. This power stems from the right of senators to speak on the Senate floor.[54] It is from this right of speech that the power to filibuster (delay indefinitely) originates, and senators use it as a threat and in full force when it serves their political purposes. Moreover, senators use this same right of speech to offer amendments to any bill, and they can do so (with a few exceptions) at any time, in any order. This is strikingly different from the way that the House organizes itself, where the majority party leadership strictly controls access to the floor.

Senate leaders operate under rules that do not allow them to dictate the pace of floor debate or the content of amendments offered by individual senators.[55] Unlike the House, the Senate is not a majoritarian body. A determined minority of forty-one senators can stop the body in its tracks through the filibuster, and a single member can often hold the Senate hostage by rejecting a request for a unanimous consent agreement that governs the conduct of floor debate on a given issue. Unlike their House counterparts, Senate leaders cannot easily structure votes or schedules, nor can they routinely set time limits for debate. Rather, leaders must cajole their colleagues, privately and publicly; compromise with them; and provide consideration for a hundred different schedules, preferences, and egos.

Historically, the Senate as an institution has discouraged strong collective partisanship in favor of preserving individual senators' political flexibility. Even the strongest majority leaders, in the tradition of Lyndon Johnson, relied more heavily on persuasion than outright control to win votes on the Senate floor.[56]

Each Senate party elects a floor leader and a whip, as well as chairs of committees on policy, committee assignments, and campaigns.[57] Although Republicans have traditionally distributed these jobs more widely than have Democrats, the fact is that, aside from the majority and minority leader positions, no one slot is especially important. Undeniably, Senate party leaders possess many fewer weapons than do their House counterparts. Rather than controlling the chamber's schedule, the majority leader endlessly negotiates and renegotiates the order of business. The minority leader serves as the chief sparring partner in these sessions,[58] and the leaders must represent the interests of their own party's members. Nor do Senate party caucuses provide broad grants of authority to their respective leaders; rather, the fundamental expectation of party leaders is to serve "the *personal* political needs of party colleagues."[59] Fred Harris, writing in 1993, argued that party conferences (or caucuses) grew in strength within the Senate of the 1980s and 1990s, but that these groupings have largely allowed individual senators, all with their own agendas, to influence leaders who continually seek consensus.[60]

Senators are generally less partisan because they represent larger districts than House members, for longer periods of time. These fundamental differences in electoral environments translate into different incentives within the Senate. Senators have more individual power than House members, and are therefore judged on a more comprehensive basis than simple party-line voting. Because they represent states with populations ranging from 600,000 to 37 million, senators have to appeal to wide ranges of constituent opinions and ideologies. Their longer terms also insulate them from pleas and threats from party leaders; party control can shift every two years, but a senator's term is triple that. In addition, senators have to deal with another colleague from the same state, who may or may not share his/her party affiliation. These senators often have to work together, even if they come from opposite parties. It is therefore in a senator's interest to maintain working relationships with many colleagues in both parties.

The Senate stayed resistant to strong partisan division until Majority Leader George Mitchell began to run the Senate in a more partisan fashion in the early 1990s. He did so by trying to structure committee bills and floor debates to emphasize policy differences between the Senate Democrats and President Bush. In 1994, when the Republicans took back control of the chamber under the leadership of Senator Robert Dole (R-Kans.), the environment in the Senate changed in two important ways. First, the Republicans assumed control of both chambers at the same time, which had not happened in forty years. The second significant change was that the Republicans reached parity with the Democrats in most southern states, which changed the composition of the Senate. The division within the Democratic Party between north and south subsided, because conservative Republicans replaced southern conservative Democrats. In the north, moderate Democrats often won seats previously held by liberal Republicans. Consequently, the differences between the two parties in the Senate became greater than the differences within each party. Greater interparty ideological differences gave rise to opportunities for stronger partisan leadership than had existed in the Senate in the past.[61]

As Senator Dole began his second tenure as majority leader of the Senate in 1995, his Republican majority was different than it had been ten years earlier when he had first served as leader. The southern conservative Republicans, many of whom had come from the House, agitated for more aggressive party leadership and majority rule in the Senate. They signaled this by electing Senator Trent Lott as assistant majority leader rather than Senator Alan Simpson (R-Wyo.).

Ultimately, Senator Dole, preoccupied by his campaign for president, resigned his post as majority leader (and his Senate seat) in June 1996, clearing the way for Senator Lott to take over the position of majority leader. Although Lott quickly proved himself a skillful deal-maker, he also reflected a style of leadership that was honed in the House, first as a staffer to Representative William Colmer (D-Miss.), then as a backbencher (1973–1980), and subsequently as minority whip, a position he captured after only four terms in office. Giving up his House leadership position, Lott won his Senate seat in 1988. Lott structured the Senate leadership in a more collegial, participatory way than did Dole, who often tended to keep his own counsel as floor leader.[62] Led by Majority Leader Lott, Republican senators, while defending their individual rights within the institution, moved to mute some of the intense individualism that had characterized the Senate of the previous twenty years. At the same time, in 1996 twelve moderate Republican and Democratic senators announced their retirements from the Senate, and their replacements in both parties were more partisan. Subsequently, the character of the Senate became more ideological, and much more partisan.

This trend is illustrated in the patterns of partisan voting, which culminated in historically high levels during the 104th Congress and has remained very high since then. Most notably, during the second session (1996) of the 104th Congress, Senate Republicans compiled a higher party unity score (89 percent loyalty on all party votes) than did their House colleagues (87 percent), and the 89 percent figure represented the highest level of partisan voting by either party in the Senate for more than forty years.[63] Thus, even in a year that produced substantial legislative compromises between the Congress and President Clinton, Senate voting patterns reflected a historic level of partisanship. Since then, both parties have maintained these historic highs in unity on roll-call voting (see Table 5–4).

Throughout the 1990s, party leaders have responded to the increasingly partisan composition of the Senate by crafting party messages and coordinating party communication and fund-raising strategies. In some ways, the Senate party leaders adopted the tactics of House party leaders a decade earlier. Senators responded to party-based message politics, came to identify more closely with their party's policy positions and have voted accordingly on the Senate floor.[64] Both Senator Lott and Senator Daschle, the Democratic minority leader, used their powers over committee appointments and floor schedules to struc-

TABLE 5-4
Senate and House Party Unity Scores:
1969-1972, 1989-1992, 1995-1998, and 1999-2002

Chamber and Party	1969-1972 Unity*	1989-1992 Unity*	1995-1998 Unity*	1999-2002 Unity*
House Democrats (all)	71%	86%	81%	83%
House Southern Democrats	48	78	74	78
House Republicans	74	80	88	89
Senate Democrats (all)	73	81	76	87
Senate Southern Democrats	51	72	90	78
Senate Republicans	73	81	87	87

* Four-year averages. Scores reflect the percentage of occasions that members vote with a majority of their fellow partisans on votes in which most (>50 percent) Democrats vote against most (>50 percent) Republicans.

Sources: Norman J. Ornstein, Thomas E. Mann, and Michael J. Malbin, eds., *Vital Statistics on Congress, 1997–1998* (Washington, DC: CQ Press/AET, 1998), pp. 211–212; Norman J. Ornstein, Thomas E. Mann, and Michael J. Malbin, eds., *Vital Statistics on Congress, 2001–2002* (Washington, DC: CQ Press/AEI, 2002), pp. 173; *Congressional Quarterly Weekly Report,* January 9, 1999, pp. 79–81, 93–94; *Congressional Quarterly Weekly Report,* January 6, 2001, p. 67, December 14, 2002 p. 3281; *Congressional Roll Call Vote,* 2001 p. B–17.

ture debate in the Senate along clearer party lines. Perhaps the most important change in the Senate party leadership is the emphasis they place on representing the party and the Senate to the media, and in negotiations with the president.[65] Both parties now have coordinated messages of the day, and senators in both parties are assigned the task of making speeches and framing the party's position to the media. Senators have become more willing to let their party leader negotiate on behalf of the party with the president on major policy initiatives. Individual senators are more strongly discouraged from publicly disagreeing with the party leaders because it dilutes the clarity of policy differences between the parties.

Still, the Senate as an institution requires a lot of consultation and collegiality in order to function — any senator can block or hold a bill up for any number of reasons. Even at the height of partisan rancor during the 1999 Clinton impeachment trial, Senator Lott and Senator Daschle kept the Senate in order and on track by virtue of their constant communication. The bottom line for Senate party leaders is that their job is primarily to sell their party's position to their caucuses and to the public at large, but their power is derived from winning the public relations battle rather than any internal structure that allows them to control outcomes on the Senate floor.

At the same time, the Senate governs itself under a rule that limits the power of majorities to work their will. On most major issues, forty-one senators (often from one party) can hold up Senate business indefinitely. Only if sixty senators vote in favor of cloture will debate be limited and votes forced to resolve difficult issues. Filibusters have changed and grown over the years, but their central import for the modern Senate is that sixty votes are often required to move along many key pieces of legislation.

The mid-session shift in majority control in 2001 nicely illustrates the benefits and limitations of majority party power in the Senate. The net effects of the switch in majority control were felt most of all in committees, where all committee chairs changed hands thus enabling Democrats to block many of President Bush's proposals and judicial nominations. But on the Senate floor, things did not look all that different, as the majority leader still negotiated with the other ninety-nine senators to move Senate business along the legislative track. Moreover, during the 1980–2003 period, party control in the Senate shifted six times — 1981, 1987, 1995, 2001 (twice), and 2003. Thus, the senatorial shoe is often on the other foot. In 2001–2002, it was the Republicans who exercised their individual rights as senators to offer amendments and filibuster the Democratic majority's preferred policies. The elections of 2002 returned Senate control to the Republicans, who made changes in seat allocations and chairs across most Senate committees.

Despite the shifts in party control of the Senate throughout the last forty years, the power of the individual senator relative to the party has remained consistently strong. That is why Senate leaders can rarely take full credit for making their institution run even passably well. Rather, a functioning Senate, no matter how slow and inefficient, requires that its leaders act more as facilitators than as aggressive commanders. In the final analysis, the notion of strong party leadership in the Senate remains largely a contradiction in terms within an institution that continues to serve its individual members.

PARTY AND THE LIMITS OF CENTRALIZATION IN THE POSTREFORM CONGRESS

Given the high levels of partisan voting in the contemporary Congress, it is tempting to see the congressional party, especially the House majority, as dominating the legislative process — at least on many of the most salient issues. When legislative parties consist of homogeneous groups of partisans (e.g., mostly conservative Republicans and liberal Democrats), and the gap between them is wide, it makes sense that individual legislators, at least in the House, are willing to give up some individual power in order to give the larger group — the legislative party — more power. Both Democratic and Republican rank-and-file members have voted to restrain, and even replace, their leaders. At the same time, leaders have strong incentives to hold party majorities together, to the extent that those majorities reflect their members' policy preferences.[66]

The very individualism of the Senate provides one clear set of limitations on the potential for strong, centralized leadership within the Congress. In the House, however, party leadership has grown extremely strong, as evidenced by partisan voting levels, the extended whip system, and the formidable powers that leaders possess to control appointments, schedules, and legislative procedures. Nonetheless, both the House and Senate are national institutions consisting of individuals elected locally. There have been a number of issues over recent years that have generated division within parties in Congress, including campaign finance reform and homeland security. However, partisan divisions on a single issue such as free trade or campaign finance reform rarely lead to irreconcilable splits. Party leaders in both the House and Senate spend a great deal of energy building cohesion on a wide range of issues, and in an era of close parity between the parties, neither majority nor minority leaders can afford to shut out any members because of their opposition on a single issue.

Members of the House and Senate must constantly balance their partisan affiliation and ideology with the national party's objectives, as well as the best interests of their local constituents. There will always be examples of national party leaders asking their rank and file to support a policy that is not beneficial to members' constituents. However, they try to set agendas to avoid such choices because on those occasions where a member is asked to choose constituency or party policy, constituency often prevails. Constituency pressures, contributors' concerns, and the entreaties of organized interests demonstrate the continuing power of local forces on House members both as individuals and as a bloc within their caucus.

Party leadership in the contemporary U.S. Congress is surely stronger than it was between the 1920s and the 1970s, but many real constraints remain firmly in place, especially in the highly individualistic Senate. In the House, strong centralized leadership is possible, even likely, and partisanship has risen sharply in the postreform era. Nevertheless, such leadership remains based on power willingly but not unreservedly granted by individual representatives.[67]

CHAPTER BIBLIOGRAPHY

Cox, Gary W., and Matthew McCubbins. *Legislative Leviathan.* Berkeley: University of California Press, 1993.

Rae, Nicol C., and Colton C. Campbell, eds. *New Majority or Old Minority?: The Impact of Republicans on Congress.* Lanham, MD: Rowman & Littlefield, 1999.

Rhode, David. *Parties and Leaders in the House of Representatives.* Chicago: University of Chicago Press, 1991.

NOTES

1. Parties in most parliamentary systems possess the power to select candidates rather than relying on primary elections to bestow the party label on a candidate.

2. Richard F. Fenno, Jr., "The Internal Distribution of Influence: The House," in David B. Truman, ed., *Congress and America's Future* (Englewood Cliffs, NJ: Prentice Hall, 1965), p. 61.

3. Ibid., pp. 61–62.

4. Joseph Cooper and David W. Brady, "Institutional Context and Leadership Style: The House from Cannon to

Rayburn," *American Political Science Review* 75 (June 1981): pp. 411–425.

5. Ibid., p. 413.

6. Peter Swenson, "The Influence of Recruitment on the Structure of Power in the U.S. House, 1870–1940," *Legislative Studies Quarterly* 7 (February 1982), pp. 7–36.

7. The following discussion relies in part on Cooper and Brady, "Institutional Context and Leadership Style," pp. 412ff. See also, relevant chapters in Roger H. Davidson, Susan Webb Hammond, and Raymond W. Smock, eds., *Masters of the House* (Boulder, CO: Westview Press, 1998.)

8. Comment made at American University forum on Congress and the president, April 17, 1995, televised on C-SPAN.

9. The exceptions were narrow Republican majorities in both houses for the eightieth and eighty-third Congresses (1947–1949 and 1953–1955, respectively).

10. David S. Cloud, "Speaker Wants His Platform to Rival the Presidency," *Congressional Quarterly Weekly Report,* February 4, 1995, p. 331.

11. See John Manley, "The Conservative Coalition in Congress," *American Behavioral Scientist* 17 (1973): pp. 223–247; Mack C. Shelley, *The Permanent Majority: The Conservative Coalition in the United States Congress* (Tuscaloosa: University of Alabama Press, 1983).

12. David W. Brady and Charles S. Bullock III, "Coalition Politics in the House of Representatives," in Lawrence Dodd and Bruce I. Oppenheimer, eds., *Congress Reconsidered,* 2nd ed. (Washington, DC: CQ Press, 1981), p. 201. According to Brady and Bullock the coalition began to operate in 1937, but the forces that produced this cooperation had existed for some time.

13. Joseph Martin, *My First Fifty Years in Politics* (New York: McGraw-Hill, 1960), p. 84.

14. Traditionally, Democratic members of the House Ways and Means Committee had served as the party's "committee on committees." In 1975, this power was transferred to the Steering and Policy Committee, where party leaders possessed much more influence on appointments.

15. For a brief summary of the tools of powerful leadership, see Robert L. Peabody, *Leadership in Congress* (Boston: Little, Brown, 1976), pp. 41–47. See also Ronald M. Peters, Jr., *The American Speakership* (Baltimore: Johns Hopkins University Press, 1990).

16. Peters, *The American Speakership,* pp. 42–46; see also Lewis L. Gould and Nancy Beck Young, "The Speaker and the Presidents: Sam Rayburn, the White House, and the Legislative Process, 1941–1961," in *Masters of the House,* pp. 181–221.

17. These tactics were similar to those used by former Ways and Means chair Representative Wilbur Mills (D-Ark.), as detailed by John Manley, "Wilbur Mills: A Study in Congressional Influence," *American Political Science Review* 63 (June 1969): pp. 442–464. Mills served as Ways and Means chair from 1958 through 1974.

18. Robert A. Caro, *Master of the Senate: The Years of Lyndon Johnson* (New York: Knopf, 2002). Also see Ralph Huitt, "Democratic Party Leadership in the Senate," *American Political Science Review* 55 (1961): pp. 333–344.

19. David Mayhew, *Party Loyalty among Congressmen* (Cambridge, Mass.: Harvard University Press, 1966).

20. Arthur G. Stevens, Arthur H. Miller, and Thomas E. Mann, "Mobilization of Liberal Strength in the House: 1955–1970: The Democratic Study Group," *American Political Science Review* 68 (1974): pp. 667–681.

21. Oppenheimer, "The Rules Committee: New Arm of Leadership in a Decentralized House," in Lawrence C. Dodd and Bruce I. Oppenheimer, eds., *Congress Reconsidered,* 5th ed. (Washington, DC: CQ Press, 1995), p. 1977.

22. See Gary Young and Joseph Cooper, "Multiple Referral and the Transformation of House Decision Making," in Dodd and Oppenheimer, *Congress Reconsidered,* pp. 211–236.

23. The following discussion draws on Barbara Sinclair, *Majority Leadership in the U.S. House,* (Baltimore: Johns Hopkins University Press, 1983), pp. 28–29, as well as Sinclair, "Tip O'Neill and Contemporary House Leadership," in *Masters of the House,* pp. 289–318.

24. The Republican position was thoroughly articulated in a paper issued by Representatives Richard T. Armey (R-Tex.), Jennifer Dunn (R-Wash.), and Christopher Shays (R-Conn.), "It's Long Enough: The Decline of Popular Government under Forty Years of Single Party Control of the U.S. House of Representatives" (Washington, DC: House Republican Conference, 1994).

25. "Yellow Dog" Democrats were so named because they would sooner vote for a cur than a Republican.

26. Most, though not all, important votes are recorded. If twenty-five House members or one-fifth of the senators present request a roll-call vote, the chamber goes on the record. This was not always the case; through the 1960s, many key issues were decided on "unrecorded teller" votes, in which Representatives would signify their vote by lining up and walking past vote counters on the Aye or Nay side of a given proposal. In the early 1970s, the House ceased this practice and installed an electronic voting system. The number of roll-call votes rose from an average of 175 annually in the 1960s to more than 600 per year in the 1970s. Subsequently, the average declined to about 450 in the 1980s. Virtually all major decisions are still on the record, however. In the Senate, the patterns have been similar, although the rise has been more gradual and the number of roll-call votes has averaged 100 to 200 fewer per year since the late 1970s.

27. Figures from Norman Ornstein, Thomas Mann, and Michael Malbin, *Vital Statistics on Congress, 1993–1994* (Washington, DC: CQ Press, 1993), pp. 201–202, and *Congressional Quarterly Weekly Report,* December 31, 1994, p. 3659. See also David W. Rohde, *Parties and Leaders in the Post-Reform House* (Chicago: University of Chicago Press, 1991), p. 57.

28. Rohde, *Parties and Leaders in the Post-Reform House,* p. 55; Rohde's emphasis.

29. Richard F. Fenno, Jr., "If, as Ralph Nader Says, Congress Is the 'Broken Branch,' How Come We Love Our Congressmen So Much?" in Norman Ornstein, ed., *Congress in Change* (New York: Praeger, 1975), p. 287.

30. For an extended discussion of strong legislative leadership in parties that are relatively weak outside the legislature, see Barbara Sinclair, *Legislators, Leaders, and Lawmaking: The U.S. House of Representatives in the Postreform Era* (Baltimore: Johns Hopkins University Press, 1995), especially pp. 300–306.

31. The whip was appointed until a 1985 rules change mandated election by the caucus.

32. Leroy N. Rieselbach, *Congressional Politics,* 2nd ed. (Boulder, CO: Westview Press, 1995), p. 93.

33. Barbara Sinclair, "House Majority Leadership in an Era of Divided Control," in Dodd and Oppenheimer, *Congress Reconsidered,* p. 243, emphasis added.

34. On task forces, see Sinclair, *Majority Leadership in the U.S. House.*

35. On the theory of partisan control, see Gary W. Cox and Matthew McCubbins, *Legislative Leviathan* (Berkeley: University of California Press, 1993); for a Republican analysis of Democratic control of the House, see Representatives Armey, Dunn, and Shays, "It's Long Enough."

36. Barbara Sinclair, "The Emergence of Strong Leadership in the 1980s House of Representatives," *Journal of Politics* 54 (August 1992): pp. 657–684.

37. Rohde, *Parties and Leaders in the Post-Reform House,* p. 174.

38. See Charles O. Jones, "Somebody Must Be Trusted: An Essay on Leadership of the U.S. Congress," in Herman J. Ornstein, ed., *Congress in Change,* p. 266.

39. Richard F. Fenno, Jr., *The Power of the Purse* (Boston: Little, Brown, 1966).

40. For a pre-Republican majority view of the party as minority, see William F. Connelly, Jr., and John F. Pitney, Jr., *Congress' Permanent Minority?* (Lanham, MD: Littlefield, Adams), 1994.

41. Quoted in Dan Balz and Charles R. Babcock, "How Newt Climbed the Hill," *Washington Post National Weekly Edition,* January 9–15, 1995, p. 11.

42. Richard T. Armey, Jennifer Dunn, and Christopher Shays, "It's Long Enough: The Decline of Popular Government under Forty Years of Single Party Control of the U.S. House of Representatives," (Washington, D.C.: House Republican Conference, 1994) p. 131.

43. Democrats actually won 204 seats, but Bernard Sanders (Ind.-Vt.) caucused with them. By late 1995, the defections of Democratic representatives raised the Republicans' ranks to 234.

44. Donna Cassatta, "Republicans Bask in Success in Rousing Performance," *Congressional Quarterly Weekly Report,* April 8, 1995, p. 990.

45. Carroll J. Doherty, "Time and Tax Cuts Will Test GOP Freshman Solidarity," *Congressional Quarterly Weekly Report,* April 1, 1995, p. 916. See also James G. Gimpel, *Fulfilling the Contract* (Boston: Allyn & Bacon, 1996).

46. Cassatta, "Republicans Bask in Success of Rousing Performance," p. 990.

47. Ronald M. Peters, "The Republican Speakership" (paper presented at the 1996 American Political Science Association meetings, Chicago), p. 9.

48. On party votes (Table 5–2), House Republicans supported the party position more than nine times out of ten in 1995, the highest figure in the post–World War II House.

49. On the limitations imposed by constitutional constraints and Senate rules, see Keith Krehbiel, *Pivotal Politics* (Chicago: University of Chicago Press, 1998).

50. This is a complex and difficult story, best told, perhaps, in Elizabeth Drew's dense, insider account, *Showdown: The Struggle between the Gingrich Congress and the Clinton White House* (New York: Touchstone, 1996).

51. Quoted in Richard E. Cohen, "On the Brink," *National Journal,* February 22, 1997, p. 368.

52. Katherine Q. Seelye, "Gingrich Draws Fire from the Right," *New York Times,* October 25, 1998, A22.

53. Dan Palazzalo, quoted in Seelye, "Gingrich Draws Fire from the Right," p. A22.

54. Floyd M. Riddick and Alan S. Frumin, *Riddick's Senate Procedure* (Washington DC: Government Printing Office, 1992), pp. 1092–1097.

55. See Steven Smith, *The American Congress* (Boston: Houghton Mifflin, 1995), pp. 232ff, for an excellent extended example of the problems inherent in making the Senate move with even moderate speed on a major issue.

56. Ralph K. Huitt, "Democratic Party Leadership in the Senate," *American Political Science Review,* 55 (June 1961): pp. 333–344.

57. Roger Davidson and Walter Oleszek, *Congress and Its Members,* 4th ed. (Washington, DC: CQ Press, 1994), p. 192.

58. A brief period of viewing C-SPAN II's coverage of the Senate will flesh out this description. Majority Leader Bill Frist (R-Tenn.) and Minority Leader Tom Daschle (D-S.D.), along with a handful of other interested senators, often converse at length about how the schedule will proceed. Nothing is resolved until all actors are satisfied with the arrangements.

59. Steven S. Smith, "Forces of Change in Senate Party Leadership and Organization," in Dodd and Oppenheimer, *Congress Reconsidered,* p. 262; emphasis added.

60. Fred R. Harris, *Deadlock or Decision: The U.S. Senate and the Rise of National Politics* (New York: Oxford University Press, 1993), pp. 184ff.

61. Barbara Sinclair, "The Senate Leadership Dilemma: Passing Bills and Pursuing Partisan Advantage in a Nonmajoritarian Chamber," in Colton C. Campbell and Nicol C. Rae, eds., *The Contentious Senate* (Boston: Rowan and Littlefield, 2001).

62. Donna Cassatta, "Lott's Task: Balance the Demands of His Chamber and His Party," *Congressional Quarterly Weekly Report,* March 8, 1997, pp. 567–571.

63. Figures drawn from *Vital Statistics on Congress, 1995–1996,* Norman J. Ornstein, Thomas E. Mann, and Michael J. Malbin, eds. (Washington, DC: CQ Press/AEI, 1995), 213–214; *Congressional Quarterly Weekly Report,* December 21, 1996, p. 3461.

64. C. Lawrence Evans and Walter Oleszek, "Message Politics and Senate Procedure," in Campbell and Rae, *The Contentious Senate.*

65. This list comes from Roger H. Davidson, "Senate Leaders: Janitors for an Untidy Chamber?" in Lawrence C. Dodd and Bruce I. Oppenheimer, *Congress Reconsidered*, Third Edition (Washington, D.C.: CQ Press, 1985), p. 236. Steven Smith, writing in 1993, eight years after Davidson's article, depicts leaders' responsibilities in terms of more partisan expectations of the members; although many of these relate to individual re-election campaigns and other personal needs, there exists at least the possibility of substance-oriented leadership. See Smith, "Forces of Change in Senate Party Leadership and Organization."

66. There is extensive theoretical literature about the importance of parties, their capacity to organize the legislative chamber, and their ultimate impact on policy outcomes. See, among others, John H. Aldrich and David W. Rohde, "The Transition to Republican Rule in the House: Implications for Theories of Congressional Politics," *Political Science Quarterly* 112: Winter, 1997–1998 pp. 541–567, and Aldrich and Rohde, "The Consequences of Party Organization in the House" (paper presented at "Congress and the President in a Partisan Era," Texas A&M University, February 5–6, 1999).

67. Rohde, *Parties and Leaders in the Post-Reform House,* chap. 6.

Six

PRESIDENTIAL-CONGRESSIONAL RELATIONS: FOCUS, AUTHORITY, AND NEGOTIATION

A s the first president of the twenty-first century, George W. Bush faced a difficult task entering office in 2001 with a disputed election and a less than overwhelming professional reputation. Nevertheless, he took full advantage of his presidential powers, buttressed by his own party's control of the House and Senate, to shape the national policy agenda with a simple but ambitious plan — cut taxes and reform education. President Bush succeeded in getting congressional support for a sweeping tax cut package in 2001 and managed to win approval for a modified version of his "No Child Left Behind" initiative, all before his party lost control of the Senate in June 2001.

As the 108th Congress convened in January 2003, President Bush found himself in a solid political position but forced to govern in a world made more unstable by terrorist threats, large deficits, and a flagging economy. Aside from the fact that the U.S. was preparing to go to war against Iraq, a move that the Congress had previously ratified, President Bush proposed another round of extensive tax cuts, a restructuring of Medicare and prescription drug coverage, and a budget with huge deficits, just three years after large surpluses had flowed into the Treasury. Although the Republicans had regained control of the Senate (51–49) and thus the Congress as a whole in the 2002 elections, their majorities were not large enough that the president could rely solely on his own party to pass his agenda. Still, early in his term, after the 2001 terrorist attacks, and in the wake of the 2002 election, he put forward aggressive sets of policies for congressional action.

In his systematic study of presidential leadership of Congress, political scientist George Edwards concludes "the president is not the ruler of the American state but a vital centralizing force, providing direction and energy for the nation's policy making."[1] Setting the agenda is only one aspect of the president's ability to direct the actions of an often-fragmented Congress. With the growth of programs, regulations, and spending since the New Deal, the institution of the presidency has held the responsibility for making sure that prospective legislation, specific appropriations, and budget decisions compose a roughly coherent whole.

Ronald Reagan's performance as president demonstrates the potential for central coordination of the policy-making process. Immediately after winning the presidency in 1980, President Reagan placed a large tax cut on the legislative agenda, and he lobbied consistently for its passage.[2] The Congress had little choice but to act on this initiative, although there was much politicking and posturing on the exact nature of the reductions. In the end, President Reagan won much of what he desired, even though most legislators did not agree with his "supply-side" economic assumptions. His large-scale tax cut proposals dominated the agenda, and lawmakers came under withering pressure to pass the legislation.

The executive's agenda-setting power can also work to keep items from receiving serious legislative consideration. Along these lines, President Reagan simply refused to consider reauthorization of clean air legislation, which the Congress was scheduled to address in 1982. Given his opposition to this legislation, the Congress kept the 1977 provisions intact through his tenure and waited until 1989–1990 to negotiate with a more receptive Bush administration on a revised clean air bill.[3]

The president's ability to dominate the agenda results in part due from his control over the Office of Management and Budget (OMB).[4] With its power to review all executive-branch regulations and thus ensure their compliance with presidential priorities, the OMB can thwart the legislative intent of laws, directing executive agencies to carry out specific policies that in fact differ in substantial ways from the legislative intent of the laws enacted by Congress. In going about its business, Congress must regularly peer over its collective shoulder, beyond Capitol Hill to the White House. No matter who occupies 1600 Pennsylvania Avenue or which party organizes the congressional proceedings, legislative outcomes are shaped by the chief executive's preferences and the authority for program and budget review held by OMB.[5] In the post–Franklin Roosevelt era of large-scale government, presidents cannot always get their way, but their wishes, as expressed in policy agendas or control of the regulatory process, must still be taken into account.[6]

Even as the presidency has consistently grown in size and power, Congress has remained — both constitutionally and politically — central to national policy making. Political scientist Mark Peterson points out, "both presidents and the public must learn to recognize Congress as the executive's legislative partner."[7] As in any partnership, the actors play distinctive roles; Peterson argues that presidents:

> should exploit the vantage point of their lofty position to bring coherence to policy making by functioning as agenda *focusers.* . . . Ideas for the nation's agenda will have originated in Congress and elsewhere in the nation. . . . Rather than attempting to be the government and the repository of all solutions for all problems, presidents would identify the problems, challenge others to respond, and work with other participants in the process to craft possible policy solutions.[8]

Reagan's determined support of a tax cut and his consistent opposition to renewed clean air legislation illustrate two ways in which the president can focus congressional attention. On the tax cut, his strong emphasis essentially required the Congress to respond to his initial proposal. Both in terms of modifying his proposal and addressing the issue with great speed, the Congress reacted directly to Reagan's focusing efforts. On the other hand, his unwillingness to consider further clean air legislation gave the Congress the freedom to explore potential courses of action during the 1980s. Thus, when President George Bush signaled his willingness to negotiate seriously on clean air in 1989, the Congress could move with reasonable speed toward a productive legislative partnership in that it had hashed out many disagreements during extensive deliberations over the 1981–1989 period.[9]

In the end, presidents can hope to exercise no more than partial and temporary influence over legislative actions and outcomes. Presidents such as Franklin Roosevelt, Lyndon Johnson, and Ronald Reagan won great victories, but all suffered serious setbacks. Others, such as Dwight Eisenhower, sought to exercise influence largely in private ways. Nonetheless, even the weakest post–World War II president, Republican Gerald Ford, who rose from serving as an unelected vice president to face a hostile, activist Democratic Congress in the wake of Richard Nixon's resignation, exercised considerable power. In his 1974–1976 tenure, he set much of the legislative agenda through his budget-writing authority, and he regularly exercised his constitutional weapon of the veto, thereby affecting legislative consideration of controversial matters.

And, as we have seen, despite apparent weaknesses, both Bill Clinton and George W. Bush have proven formidable at shaping the congressional agenda as well as placing their own stamp on the implementation of laws passed by previous congresses. President Bush has turned back much of Clinton's environmental policy by reversing various Clinton directives and reinterpreting legislation. Moreover, as one 2003 analysis concluded, "Bush's appointees to federal regulatory bodies like the Federal Communications Commission and the Securities and Exchange Commission have, of course, been as ardently antiregulation as Reagan's, and Bush has been, if anything, more willing to brandish executive powers to accomplish deregulatory missions that might face a hard time in Congress."[10]

This chapter emphasizes the core elements of presidential-congressional relations, ranging from constitutional roles to the centralization of policy making that derives from deficit-based budget policies. In addition, the impact of divided government (when the presidency and the Congress are controlled by opposing parties) is explored. Related to — but different from — divided government is the notion of *gridlock,* or the extent to which presidential-congressional relations encourage deadlock, regardless of whether one party controls both branches of government or not.[11] Finally, we consider the temporary nature of any president's capacity to provide focus and direction to the necessarily messy business of writing laws. The president may win numerous legislative victories and suffer his share of defeats, but many bills pass with little presidential expression of interest. And although the OMB can monitor regulation writing, it has neither the staff nor the authority to control the entire process. In short, the modern presidency, no matter its size and reach, cannot dominate either the policy debates or the outcomes of all policy initiatives.

THE PRESIDENT AS CHIEF LEGISLATOR

The Congress, with its potential for fragmentation and individualism, can ordinarily benefit from focus and direction. Although in 1995 the Speakership of Newt Gingrich offered a historic alternative to strong presidential leadership, in contemporary American politics it has been the president whose position has provided the best chance of generating a coherent vision of where the nation should be headed. Convincing the Congress to act on this vision is quite another matter, however.

As a rule, no member of Congress is as important a legislator as is the chief executive, although the strong partisanship of the postreform era has certainly increased the power of party leaders, especially those in the majority. Whether in setting the congressional agenda, twisting a lawmaker's arm to support a favored measure, or threatening to veto an unsatisfactory bill, the president can affect the legislative process more forcefully, and in more ways, than the most influential senator or representative. But does this mean that presidents get what they want? Hardly. A generation of research in presidential-congressional relations has demonstrated that neither partner can overwhelm the other. Rather, as Richard Neustadt observed in 1960 and Charles Jones confirmed more than thirty years later, the separate institutions of the Congress and the presidency must both share and compete for power.[12]

The Constitution offers only modest guidance in defining presidential-congressional relations. For example, Article I gives the Congress the power to declare war, but in the post–World War II era, presidents have committed American troops to warlike conflicts (in Korea, Vietnam, and the Persian Gulf) without any formal declaration of war. Congress did agree to the actions in both legislation and appropriations, but its attempt through the 1973 War Powers Act to wrest effective control from the executive branch of most decisions to commit troops has proved notably unsuccessful.[13] Likewise, the presidential power to veto legislation is a potent formal weapon, but one that is often most effective when used sparingly. Gerald Ford, for example, regularly employed the veto during his two-plus years as president, but largely as a defensive tool against the overwhelmingly Democratic Ninety-fourth Congress.[14] More creative use of veto power is available to most presidents.[15] By making credible threats to veto unacceptable bills, presidents can enhance their capability to shape legislation, thus turning a negative power into a positive tool to influence policy making on Capitol Hill.

Agenda Setting and the Prospects for Presidential Influence

The core of presidents' legislative strength lies in their ability to influence national policy agenda issues in both ordinary and extraordinary ways. The most consistent and predictable impact of the presidency comes through the centralization of the annual budget and the executive's capacity to monitor and pull together disparate proposals that bubble up within dozens of separate bureaucratic units. Indeed, the governmental agenda is ordinarily full; that is, there are always many issues, initiatives, and problems for presidents and legislators to consider. As Charles Jones observes:

> Since it is not possible to treat all issues at once, members of Congress and others anxiously await the designation of priorities. These presidential choices are typically from a list that is familiar to other policy actors. Nonetheless, a designator is important, even if he is a Republican having to work with a Democratic Congress. As in any organization, there is a need for someone in authority to say: "Let's start here."[16]

Aside from designating certain issues as priorities in the course of normal policy making, almost all presidents offer up some major initiatives that depart markedly from past policies. Such proposals — Nixon's welfare reforms, Carter's energy plans, Reagan's tax cuts, Clinton's health care proposals, Bush's education package — require large-scale changes in existing policies and have the potential to disrupt established policy subsystems made up of congressional committees, interest groups, and bureaucratic units.[17] The president can move only a limited number of major items on to the legislative agenda; all presidents must therefore be careful in what they choose to push as their own legislative agenda.

The annual State of the Union message and upcoming year's budget are the earliest and most visible statements of a president's policy agenda. It is through these public pronouncements that presidents have the opportunity to direct the policy agenda within the Congress as well as the public at large.[18] Ordinarily, the president can focus the attention of the press and the public on a few key issues; on occasion, as with Franklin Roosevelt and Lyndon Johnson, the context permits a broad agenda of large-scale changes. But even for these energetic, forceful leaders who enjoyed the favorable circumstances of large Democratic congressional majorities, the windows of opportunity for focusing legislative attention were relatively brief.[19]

Regardless of political circumstances, presidents are well advised to set the agenda on major issues early in their terms — either "move it or lose it."[20] Delay is the enemy of change, and as an institution the Congress encourages delay at every turn in a legislative process that requires a succession of majorities — in committees, in both chambers, and often on conference committee reports. Moreover, presidents begin their terms of office with election victories that provide them with substantial amounts of political capital. Rarely do they increase this store of assets; rather, the longer they wait to introduce key pieces of legislation, the lower the chance of passage.[21]

Even Bill Clinton, a president elected with 43 percent of the popular vote in an era of $200 billion annual budget deficits, could move comprehensive health care reform on to the congressional agenda, though he failed to achieve his policy goal. Leading the 535 legislative horses to the trough does not mean that Clinton or any other president can make them drink. In the final years of his presidency, Clinton did not have the political clout to move major items through the legislative process, even though his skills at legislating had surely grown over his two terms as president. At the same time, despite much congressional opposition, he still retained the role of commander-in-chief and could prosecute a military action against Serbia in 1999. Likewise, in 2002–2003, George W. Bush's escalating, well-focused attention on Iraq as a highly dangerous nation demonstrated how effective a president could be on foreign policy matters. Bush made it difficult for members of Congress to mount any effective opposition to his position on war against Iraq.

In the end, both presidential and congressional dreams of major change produced only limited movement during the late 1990s. In the wake of the budget battles in the 104th Congress, "Clinton and the Democrats had to adjust to the New Republican agenda, [while] Republicans had to compromise and learn that the president has substantial power through the veto and public opinion."[22] In various ways, President George W. Bush has attempted to test the idea that great changes should not (or could not) be built on slender majorities. Although his domestic security proposals have generally fared well in the wake of the September 2001 terrorist attacks, extensive domestic policy victories, such as privatization of Social Security or the thorough reform of Medicare, are much less likely to win approval.[23]

Legislating and the Contexts of Presidential Influence

No matter how successful presidents are in focusing public, media, and congressional attention on a major initiative, they and their aides must continue to participate in the process of lawmaking. The independent power of Congress — whether in its fragmented, contentious mode of the 1970s; its committee-based, conservative mode of the 1950s and early 1960s; or its more partisan mode since the mid-1980s — has imposed great limitations on the ability of presidents to achieve their objectives. Indeed, even a renowned "focuser" like Ronald Reagan, who was widely admired for his single-minded emphasis on tax cuts in 1981, subsequently produced a series of budgets that the Congress felt free to ignore, labeling them "dead on arrival" on Capitol Hill.[24]

In the wake of extended scholarly debates over the nature of presidential influence on Congress, a rough consensus has emerged, which paints presidential power within the legislative process as an important force but subject to many limitations. At a minimum, some restrictions include those of the "pure context" of a separation-of-powers system. Political scientist Keith Krehbiel has identified key supermajority "pivot points," where gridlock caused either by Senate filibusters or the threat of presidential vetoes can be overcome.[25] Such constitutional restraints are magnified by relatively weak political party organizations and electorally independent, well-staffed legislators who need little help from either presidents or parties to remain in office.[26]

No president can change the Senate rules that provide great advantages to those who would delay legislation through the filibuster; likewise, informal congressional practices, such as the Senate's reliance on unanimous consent agreements (as presented in Chapter 5) to conduct much of its business, are beyond the executive's control. In addition, there are other key elements of the policy-making context that further restrain executive actions. Aside from a second-term president's ineligibility to run for reelection (thus being labeled a "lame duck"), these include a president's margin of victory in the previous election, the partisan balance of congressional seats, and the president's standing with the public.[27] Regardless of the executive's formal, constitutional powers, much of the president's ability to affect legislation results from the policy-making context, which comprises principally the president's electoral base, his popularity in the country, and the partisan balance within the Congress.[28] Although they do not determine legislative outcomes, these elements do shape the content and scope of executive initiatives, as well as the strategies the president constructs for winning congressional majorities.

Consider, for example, the range of different circumstances faced by presidents from the 1960s to the 1990s as they worked with their first Congresses (see Table 6–1). Lyndon Johnson's prospects differed dramatically from those

TABLE 6-1

Electoral, Partisan, and Popularity Context for Newly Elected Presidents, 1960-2000

President	Year Elected, Percentage of Vote	Initial Party Balance		Favorability after First Year (Percent)
		House	*Senate*	
Kennedy	1960, 49	262D–175R*	64D–36R	79
Johnson	1964, 61	295D–140R	68D–32R	69
Nixon	1968, 43	243D–192R	58D–42R	67
Carter	1976, 50	292D–143R	61D–39R	59
Reagan	1980, 51	243D–192R	46D–54R	49
Bush	1988, 54	260D–175R	55D–45R	75
Clinton	1992, 43	258D–176R†	57D–43R	49
Bush, G. W.	2000, 48	212D–221R‡	50D–50R§	62

*Includes one extra member for Alaska and Hawaii.

†Representative Bernard Sanders (Vt.) elected as Independent.

‡Two Independents elected.

§In June 2001, Senator James Jeffords (R-Vt.) changed to Independent, caucusing with Democrats.

Sources: Vital Statistics on American Politics; Vital Statistics on Congress, 1993–1994, 2001–2002, <www.pollingreport.com>.

of George Bush (in 1989), for example. With overwhelming Democratic majorities in each house and a backlog of social programs, many of which had been fully aired in the Congress, Lyndon Johnson could seek passage of dozens of significant pieces of legislation in the Eighty-ninth Congress (1965–1966), literally changing the role of government in society with Medicare, civil rights bills, federal aid to education, and environmental initiatives, along with other elements that made up his Great Society vision.[29] Moreover, Johnson had enough fiscal flexibility that he could actually produce a balanced budget, albeit with a number of gimmicks, during his last year in office.

In contrast, George H. W. Bush was hemmed in by Democratic majorities in both House and Senate, a more modest electoral victory, and the prospect of annual $200 billion budget deficits for many years to come. As president, Bush could reach agreement with the Democrats on Capitol Hill on major environmental and deficit reduction legislation, but his role was as a partner to an assertive Congress. Indeed, to address rising deficits, the Democrat-controlled Congress framed a package of legislation that essentially forced Bush to accept a modest tax increase, which broke his "no new taxes" election pledge and split the Republican Party.[30]

More generally, Congress's partisan balance and the president's overall political strength shape the executive's capacity to focus legislative attention, both in setting the agenda and in helping to move legislation through the labyrinth of Capitol Hill. Even in difficult circumstances, the president remains a powerful centralizing force in that, first, his agenda items require congressional attention (if not agreement). Second, the president alone commands the position from which authoritative negotiations with legislators can take place. Legislating in the decentralized context of the U.S. Congress necessarily includes focusing attention and deal making, and only the president can serve as both chief focuser and key deal-maker.

The initial years of the Carter and Reagan presidencies illustrate the differences in focusing and deal-making skills. Carter sent a large number of proposals to Capitol Hill, 60 percent with accompanying messages that "suggested in each case that they were of the *highest priority* to the administration."[31] If everything is important, nothing is, and the president found himself lacking the political capital (to say nothing of the political skills) to make the deals essential to passing many of his true priorities, most notably comprehensive energy legislation. Conversely, the Reagan administration's focus on its 1981 tax cut proposals represented a textbook example of direction, only to be followed by a combination of firmness and flexibility in negotiations with members of Congress that outflanked as savvy a legislative veteran as Ways and Means Committee chair Dan Rostenkowski (D-Ill.), even though Democrats retained formal control of the House.

Legislating: Presidential Tools in a Retail Politics Era

My vote cannot be bought, but it can be rented.

Representative John Breaux (D-La.), 1981

I don't have bottom lines. You can't afford them in this business. I mean,
we deal with the possible. That's what we have to be guided by: What can
we get? What can you do? And as long as it's better than what
we have, that's the bottom line.

Senator John Breaux (D-La.), 1994

Despite the rise in congressional partisanship since the 1980s, most major legislative initiatives require "cross-partisan" majorities.[32] Given the narrow Republican margins of recent Congresses, major legislative victories ordinarily require constructing majorities across party lines. Although there may not be extensive bipartisan cooperation, some legislators from the opposing party ordinarily join with the bulk of the president's partisans to forge a temporary majority. Cross-party majorities have long been important; for example, Northern, moderate Republicans would sometimes join liberal Democrats in the 1950s and 1960s to provide the margin of victory for urban initiatives. In 1961, for example, a handful of Republicans gave the Kennedy administration and Speaker Sam Rayburn their crucial victory in expanding the House Rules Committee, thus wresting control from the Conservative Coalition.

Twenty years later, in 1981, it was crucial for Ronald Reagan to negotiate with Representative John Breaux about Louisiana's oil and gas interests as he sought to push through spending cuts. It was not essential that Breaux buy into the entire Reagan program, but the president could "rent" the congressman for a few important votes in return for protecting a handful of key Louisiana interests. More than a decade later, President Bill Clinton worked closely with the opposition Republican Speaker and the Republican Party to enact the North American Free Trade Agreement (NAFTA), over the objections of many members of his own party. Likewise, in 2001, when President George W. Bush sought to regain "fast track" negotiation authority on free trade issues (see Chapter 3 and Chapter 10), he pulled together numerous bargains — although in this instance, he addressed broad concerns of interest groups rather than a specific legislator's concerns. Thus, "the Administration turned to protectionism to realize both its political and policy aims, [as President] Bush curried favor with steel-state lawmakers — and voters — by imposing tariffs on imported steel. He secured support among Western senators by slapping tariffs on Canadian lumber. And he caved in to farm-state legislators on massive subsidies for agriculture."[33] As one observer noted of President Bush's single-vote, fast track victory in the House, "What's happening on Capitol Hill is not pretty" in that the Congress demanded "restrictions on Vietnamese catfish, Caribbean and African clothing, and shoes from Bolivia and Peru — precisely the countries that might benefit most from open markets."[34] In short, the president can usually win the close votes, but the policy costs are often substantial.

As a rule, presidents can neither dictate the final content of legislation nor bargain fecklessly for votes to produce congressional majorities. Often they must attach their support to items already on the legislative agenda, and only when victory is within shouting distance in the Congress can they affect the outcome through bargaining with individual representatives and senators or with the interests that support those legislators. Presidents possess their greatest advantages on such close votes, when they can pressure, bargain with, and cajole fence-sitting lawmakers. Even so, presidents may have to give up a lot to achieve a victory.

The Presidential Record

Political scientists and pundits have long attempted to measure rates of presidential success in winning congressional support for their proposals. On occasion, as with the outpouring of legislation in 1964–1966 under Lyndon Johnson, the evidence of presidential impact is overwhelming. Most of the time, however, the results are mixed and often depend on how success is measured. Until 1975, *Congressional Quarterly* generated a so-called box score of presidential success, but this measure was flawed and ultimately discontinued.[35] Subsequently, scholars have relied both on other broad measures, such as overall success rates, and more specific indicators, such as the key votes for a given Congress. In addition, many scholars have either constructed their own sets of important votes and attempts at presidential influence or relied on historical evidence that indicates those issues on which presidents sought to influence outcomes.[36]

As recent scholarship on the core idea of presidential influence illustrates, all-encompassing measures of success rates rarely provide much insight into overall presidential influence.[37] This is illustrated by two examples of *Congressional Quarterly's* scoring of presidential success rates: In 1981, Ronald Reagan achieved 82 percent support on issues on which he took a position; in 1994, Bill Clinton obtained an 86 percent rating.[38] No sensible analysis of these two presidents and these two years would have found Clinton's record better than Reagan's. Indeed, Clinton not only lost his major initiative, health care reform, but found himself stymied by Senate Republicans for much of 1994 in that many major bills never even came to a vote. Moreover, in his sixth year as president (1998), with a Congress controlled by the opposing party, Bill Clinton achieved a 51 percent success rate on legislation on which he took a position. Ronald Reagan and Richard Nixon, in similar circumstances, won 56 percent and 60 percent of the time, respectively.[39]

Perhaps the greatest problem in pinning down presidential influence is the task of disentangling context from presidential impact. The recent Republican presidents who faced Democratic congressional majorities — Nixon, Ford, Reagan, and Bush — won 61.5 percent of the votes on which they took a position; Democrats from Kennedy to Clinton (1993–1994) won 81.5 percent, a margin of 20 percent over the Republicans. Were Democratic presidents more skillful? Hardly, but they did enjoy large party majorities in both the House and Senate.

It is more useful to view congressional contexts as offering presidents varying options as they pursue their legislative agendas. Should their lists be long or should they be short, emphasizing only a few key issues? Peterson notes, "large agendas invite problems," yet "as LBJ powerfully demonstrated, extremely ambitious, diverse, and sizable programmatic agendas can be guided through the legislative labyrinth."[40]

In the end, a skillful president can offer centralized guidance for a coherent set of proposals, but the congressional context of committees, individual entrepreneurs, and wavering support by some party leaders renders questionable any consistent attempts at strong executive leadership. Moreover, in the post–Twenty-second Amendment era, second-term presidents face especially difficult circumstances because they only have about six years of governing power, rather than an indefinite time frame. In his second term, faced with Republican majorities in Congress, tight budget limitations, and the memories of a spotty first-term record, President Clinton proved no more willing or able than his predecessors to place a formidable policy agenda before the Congress. Indeed, relations between the Congress and the president may well be defined not by current executive initiatives but by the budgetary constraints imposed by decades of past spending decisions, such as the funding of the interstate highway system and the adoption of Medicare.

BUDGETARY POLITICS: CENTRALIZATION THROUGH CONSTRAINT

> *When Congress consents to the Executive making the budget it will have surrendered the most important part of a representative government.*
>
> Former Speaker of the House Joseph Cannon, 1919

One of the president's most significant powers in setting the national policy agenda has been the capacity to propose an annual budget.[41] The Congress, of course, retains the power of the purse — the appropriations authority — but the president and executive budgetary staff provide both the overarching thrust of proposed spending (for example, by proposing new programs) and the myriad details of where federal monies will be spent. As federal responsibilities and spending increased from the 1930s through the early 1970s, executive budget officials came to play an important role in shaping policy initiatives, large and small, old and new.[42] The president and Congress generally agreed on the expansion of executive authority as the scope and complexity of public policy grew steadily. Budget scholar Howard Shuman concludes that "in almost every case the delegation [of congressional authority] resulted in the aggrandizement of the executive at the expense of the Congress, but *this was done willingly, even joyously, and had few narrow or partisan or siege-mentality overtones.*"[43]

By the late 1960s, however, the Congress and the president had begun to engage in budget wars, as spending levels and priorities began to be vigorously contested. Party leaders and increasing numbers of backbench legislators wanted to exercise some control over spending, and Republican President Richard M. Nixon had sought to gain more control over spending levels and priorities through the use of the veto and his willingness to impound funds (refuse to spend them) that the Congress had appropriated. As a Democratically controlled Congress grew frustrated with both an aggressive Republican president and its own incapacity to control overall levels of spending, the stage was set for major reform of the budget process. And, as luck would have it, the Congress confronted a president who had been grievously wounded by the Watergate affair.

In the spring of 1974, Congress enacted the Congressional Budget and Impoundment Control Act; President Nixon would resign less than two months later. Although originally meant as an attack on executive power over the budget, the 1974 legislation also sought to rationalize budgetary policy making (to control overall expenditures and increase capacities to set priorities) and to strengthen the budget-related capacities of the Congress. By both accident and design, the reforms have paradoxically led to members' greater participation in budgetary politics and, simultaneously, to increased centralization of the ultimate budget decisions.

By setting a supposedly firm timetable for action and by requiring the Congress to address total levels of spending early in the process, the 1974 budget act sought to allow Congress greater control over the levels and composition of federal spending. To accomplish these goals, the Congress needed more resources and some organizational changes; thus, both houses created budget committees, and the nonpartisan Congressional Budget Office (CBO) was established. CBO provides the legislative branch with an independent capacity to analyze the mountains of budget-related data and to make the projections for future revenue and spending patterns that are the heart of contemporary fiscal politics. The new committees increased the number of legislators who played a major role in budgetary politics; the well-respected CBO offered leaders, committees, and even individual members the opportunity to pose alternative budget scenarios to those offered by the executive branch's OMB. In a sense, budgetary politics became more open and democratic in the aftermath of the 1974 reforms. Various factions ranging from conservative Republicans to the generally liberal Congressional Black Caucus could propose their own budgetary priorities, even if they had little chance of winning congressional approval.[44]

In fact, the adoption of the budget reforms, especially when combined with the major tax cuts of 1981, conspired to "fiscalize" congressional politics during the 1980s.[45] With annual deficits escalating, budgetary restraints required that key legislators — budget committee members and party leaders, in particular — consider overall patterns of spending. Political scientist Ken Shepsle concludes, "The most significant consequence of the Budget Act has been that Congress has had little time to consider anything else. . . . The fiscalization of politics has diminished the stature of standing committees, encouraged members to become generalists rather than specialists, ceded political advantage to those in party leadership positions, and put a premium on coordination among policy areas."[46]

Throughout the 1980s, the memberships of the House and Senate played minor roles in reaching budget deals, but they could — and sometimes did — upset their leaders' applecarts by defeating the entire package. Indeed, as top legislators and presidential envoys met to negotiate, both sides had to bear in mind their constituents. Congressional leaders knew they had to convince majorities of their followers to approve their actions, whereas the president's constituents were the voters whom he would eventually face. Thus, for chief executives and congressional leaders alike, there remain real limits to the exercise of centralized power.

Among legislators, this was brought home forcefully in 1985, when junior Republican senators and conservative Democrats forced the issue of deficit reduction after top-level "budget summitry" broke down. The Congress agreed to a reduction package proposed by Senators Phil Gramm (R-Tex.), Warren Rudman (R-N.H.), and Ernest Hollings (D-S.C.), which they attached to a "must-pass" bill to raise the debt ceiling (without which the federal government would be forced to shut down).[47] To oversimplify a most complicated set of maneuvers, congressional leaders realized that the Gramm-Rudman-Hollings (GRH) formula of annual, automatic cuts in the absence of real deficit reduction would obtain majority support in both houses. After some modifications, the proposal became law and thus framed subsequent budgetary politics. With GRH, the centralized powers of congressional leaders had been severely limited by insurgent budget-cutters.

Despite some judicial setbacks and legislative modifications, the GRH principle of holding down spending through automatic cuts in the absence of legislation remained dominant for several years. Then, in 1990, President Bush reluctantly agreed to provisions in the Budget Enforcement Act that contradicted his "no new taxes" pledge of the 1988 campaign. After much partisan jousting, in which the Bush administration made further modest concessions on tax increases, the Budget Enforcement Act was passed, only a few days before the 1990 elections and with relatively little Republican support. In the House, for example, only 47 of 173 minority members voted for the bill. The highly centralized, highly political negotiations did produce some real deficit reduction and thus reduced the need for invoking GRH, but it also resulted in significant political damage to President Bush.

The 1990s generally remained an era of budget summits between the administration and top congressional leaders. Even as deficits temporarily gave way to surpluses in the late 1990s, budgets remained highly conflictual, as Republican leaders with their narrow majorities confronted the Clinton administration. As former Clinton Chief of Staff Leon Panetta (who had previously served as House Budget Committee chair) observed:

[It] is the threat of failure that drives the process. Presidents' budgets rarely are acceptable to the Congress. Congressional budgets are rarely acceptable to the president. Rather than resolve those differences, the budget process is driven to the edge of a cliff late in the congressional session. There is a threat of a potential shutdown [as occurred in late 1995/early 1996], and that ultimately forces a final deal.[48]

Although budget surpluses briefly altered some budget contentiousness, by 2002–2003 deficits had returned with a vengeance, and Congress continued to pass budgets and spending measures in large, omnibus packages, which made it very difficult for legislators to oppose.[49] Some legislators perceive the return of deficits as a renewed opportunity to reduce the size and spending of the federal government. As Representative Sue Myrick (R-N.C.) stated, "Anything that will help us stop spending money, I'm in favor of. . . . This place is set up to spend money; you know it's just the nature of the beast. And we've tried to say, hey, we don't have to spend so much of it. And if there's a deficit, that may help us." Still, experience from the Reagan and Bush years has demonstrated that large deficits over a prolonged period of time usually lead to economic hardships, which may well be a far more serious consequence than minimizing federal spending.

POLICY, POWER, AND DIVIDED GOVERNMENT

Between 1969 and 2004, divided partisan control of the national government has been the rule, not the exception, with only Jimmy Carter (1977–1980), Bill Clinton (1993–1994), and George W. Bush (part of 2001, 2003–2004) serving while their fellow partisans controlled the Congress. Politicians and journalists have often assumed that divided government produced legislative *gridlock,* a pejorative term linked to the apparent inefficiencies and incoherence of Congress.

To be sure, divided government can lead to deadlock, as the mid-1990s battles between a Republican Congress (especially in the House) and Democratic President Bill Clinton demonstrated. But, since 1990, congressional scholars have examined the paired concepts of divided government and legislative gridlock with some care, and their conclusions have clarified the role of divided control of the Congress and the presidency.

Political scientist David Mayhew opened the discussion here by demonstrating that divided government has not prevented the federal government from enacting major legislation on important public policy topics.[50] Divided government, particularly since the early 1980s, has required congressional negotiation with the White House, whether on budget issues, clean air, or Social Security reform. Negotiation encourages centralization in that only a handful of leaders can effectively represent the legislature, especially as they confront the White House and the executive branch. More generally, Mayhew has raised systematic questions about the nature of American policy making, a process that has become increasingly centered in the presidency.[51]

Despite the growth of the so-called imperial presidency in the 1960s and early 1970s, the president remains enmeshed in a system of shared powers, even in foreign and military affairs, where chief executives retain wider latitude.[52] From time to time, certain presidents may take advantage of circumstances (such as party majorities and crises) to extend their influence, but congressional reaction is rarely long in coming, as legislative leaders seek to assert their institutional prerogatives. Although Lyndon Johnson pushed the Eighty-ninth Congress mercilessly to pass Democratic domestic programs and to support the growing American involvement in Vietnam, he correctly recognized that his window of opportunity for great change would probably close with the 1966 election.[53] Richard Nixon, operating without Republican majorities in either chamber, recognized the need for extraordinary administrative actions, such as impounding huge amounts of appropriated funds, placing key loyalists in departmental slots, and encouraging clandestine operations, that would bypass normal congressional participation in many policy decisions.

In surveying presidential-congressional relations, Charles Jones concludes, "understanding the production of laws requires analysis of law-making" and that the "system is now, *and always has been,* one of 'separated institutions sharing powers' as Neustadt puts it [originally in 1960]."[54] Indeed, within the context of an extended period of split-party control of government, Jones reformulates Neustadt's observation as "separated institutions competing for shares of power."[55] The 104th Congress, with its Republican majorities, offered renewed support for such a conclusion. Speaker Newt Gingrich clearly succeeded at establishing the policy agenda and, early on, dominated the legislative process. But a bicameral system, with its separation of powers, denies the likelihood of congressional dominance, save through overwhelming majorities. Rather, as John Bader states, congressional leaders must ordinarily strive to maintain "a balance . . . between heavy-handed leadership and fragmenting anarchy"[56] as they struggle against the relatively unified executive branch.

Mayhew's original research on divided government has spawned a vigorous debate over the very nature, even existence, of gridlock and its relationship to divided control of the levers of government. Most notably, scholars have found that divided control may reduce the government's capacity to address a substantial number of potential issues. This reflects the so-called denominator argument, which emphasizes not only the number of major issues decided (the numerator), but also the number of potential major issues (the denominator).[57] And Sarah Binder has noted that gridlock may stem from divisions between the congressional chambers as much as between Capitol Hill and the White House.[58]

In the Republican congressional era (1994–), after a difficult, even disastrous, first year, President Clinton learned to take advantage of the constitutional system and the modest divisions among congressional Republicans to win both political and policy points. If the first Bush and early Clinton administrations were marked by high-profile, comprehensive budget summits in 1990 and 1993, the post-1995 Clinton strategy was to move toward Republican positions on some major issues, such as welfare reform and "saving" Medicare, while articulating a number of modest policy initiatives of his own. In the end, Leon Panetta argues that we should not expect consistent bipartisanship across a wide range of concerns, especially given the partisan dominance of congressional organization in the modern era. He observes that:

> institutional power in both House and Senate resides with the parties [that] rely on activists and interest groups that tend to bunch on the left and right. . . . [Moreover,] the legislative process allows centrist coalitions little power or time to coalesce for action. . . . Once party discipline descends on an issue, it leaves little room for representatives to gather at the center without the risk of angering the party leadership.[59]

Indeed, the highly partisan postreform era in congressional politics may have redefined the nature of presidential-congressional relations, whether control of the government is divided or not. In many ways, George W. Bush has tested the limits of presidential leadership in a period of narrow partisan divisions. Although congressional parties have surely grown stronger and more disciplined since the early 1980s, the structure of Congress, whether in representation (e.g., the different apportionment of the House and Senate) or rules (the Senate filibuster) or the need to reconcile House and Senate legislation into a single bill, works against the easy extension of a centralizing presidential influence. As with so much of American politics, presidential-congressional relations remain part of a continuing experiment in self-government.

CHAPTER BIBLIOGRAPHY

Binder, Sarah. *Stalemate* (Washington, DC: Brookings Institution Press), 2003.

Bond, Jon, and Richard Fleischer, eds. *Polarized Politics: Congress and the President in a Polarized Era.* Washington: CQ Press, 2000.

Mayhew, David R. *Divided We Govern.* Cambridge, MA: Harvard University Press, 1991.

Peterson, Mark A. *Legislating Together.* Cambridge, MA: Harvard University Press, 1990.

Thurber, James, ed. *Rivals for Power,* 2nd ed. Washington, DC: CQ Press, 2002.

NOTES

1. George Edwards, *At the Margins* (New Haven, CT: Yale University Press, 1989), p. 234.

2. This story is well told in former OMB director David Stockman's *The Triumph of Politics* (New York: Harper & Row, 1986).

3. See Richard E. Cohen, *Washington at Work* (New York: Macmillan, 1992), chap. 3, and Gary C. Bryner, *Blue Skies,*

Green Politics (Washington, DC: CQ Press, 1993), pp. 86–93.

4. See Richard E. Neustadt, "Presidency and Legislation: The Growth of Central Clearance," *American Political Science Review* 48 (1954): pp. 641ff, and John Hart, *The Presidential Branch,* 2nd ed. (Chatham, NJ: Chatham House, 1995).

5. James P. Pfiffner, "The President and the Post-Reform Congress," in Roger H. Davidson, ed., *The Postreform Congress* (New York: St. Martin's, 1992), pp. 216–217.

6. Paul Light, *The President's Agenda,* rev. ed. (Baltimore: Johns Hopkins University Press, 1991).

7. Mark Peterson, *Legislating Together* (Cambridge, MA: Harvard University Press, 1990), p. 295; emphasis added.

8. Ibid., p. 295.

9. See Cohen, *Washington at Work,* and Bryner, *Blue Skies, Green Politics.*

10. Bill Keller, "The Radical Presidency of George W. Bush," *New York Times Magazine,* January 26, 2003, p. 28.

11. The growing literature here includes, most notably, Keith Krehbiel's *Pivotal Politics* (Chicago: University of Chicago Press, 1998), and Sarah Binder's *Stalemate* (Washington, DC: Brookings Institution Press, 2003).

12. Richard Neustadt, *Presidential Power* (New York: Wiley, 1960); Charles O. Jones, *The Presidency in a Separated System* (Washington, DC: Brookings Institution, 1994).

13. Pfiffner, "The President and the Post-Reform Congress," p. 233. More generally, see Louis Fisher, *Presidential War Power* (Lawrence: University Press of Kansas, 1995).

14. Richard Watson, *Presidential Vetoes and Public Policy* (Lawrence: University Press of Kansas, 1993), p. 35.

15. See Charles Cameron, *Veto Bargaining: Presidents and the Use of Negative Power* (New York: Cambridge University Press, 2000).

16. Jones, *The Presidency in a Separated System,* p. 181.

17. See Frank R. Baumgartner and Bryan D. Jones, *Agendas and Instability in American Politics* (Chicago: University of Chicago Press, 1993), and Paul R. Schulman, *Large-Side Policy Making* (New York: Elsevier, 1980).

18. See Jeffrey Cohen, "Presidential Rhetoric and the Public Agenda," *American Journal of Political Science* 39 (February 1995): pp. 87–107.

19. See James L. Sundquist, *Politics and Policy* (Washington, DC: Brookings Institution, 1968), and Arthur Schlesinger, Jr., *The Cycles of American History* (Boston: Houghton Mifflin, 1986).

20. Light, *The President's Agenda,* p. 218.

21. Paul C. Light, "Passing Nonincremental Policy: Presidential Influence in Congress, Kennedy to Carter," *Congress and the Presidency* 9 (Winter 1981–1982): p. 78.

22. James Thurber, "Centralization, Devolution, and Turf Protection in the Congressional Budget Process," in Lawrence Dodd and Bruce Oppenheimer, eds., *Congress Reconsidered,* 6th ed. (Washington, DC: CQ Press, 1997), p. 338.

23. E. J. Dionne, "Profile of a Wartime Leader," *Washington Post National Weekly Edition,* February 3–9, 2003, p. 21.

24. Allen Schick, *The Federal Budget* (Washington, DC: Brookings Institution, 1995), p. 58.

25. Krehbiel, *Pivotal Politics,* p. 47.

26. Peterson, *Legislating Together,* pp. 102ff.

27. Somewhat strangely, Peterson labels these elements as "malleable" context (ibid., pp. 118ff), but of the three, only the president's popularity can change between elections and ordinarily not as a direct result of his actions.

28. Jon R. Bond, Richard Fleisher, and B. Dan Wood, "The Marginal and Time-Varying Effect of Public Approval on Presidential Success in Congress," *Journal of Politics* 65 (2003): pp. 92–110.

29. For a recent perspective by a Johnson loyalist, see Joseph Califano, *The Triumph and Tragedy of Lyndon Johnson* (New York: Simon & Schuster, 1991).

30. See Jones, *The Presidency in a Separated System,* pp. 266–268, and Barbara Sinclair, "Governing Unheroically (and Sometimes Unappetizingly): Bush and the 101st Congress," in Colin Campbell and Bert Rockman, eds., *The Bush Presidency: First Appraisals* (Chatham, NJ: Chatham House, 1991), p. 175.

31. Peterson, *Legislating Together,* p. 256; emphasis added.

32. See Jones, *The Presidency in a Separated System.*

33. Paul Magnusson,, "Bush: What Price Fast-Track?" *Business Week,* June 3, 2002, p. 38.

34. Ibid., p. 38.

35. For a discussion of this measure and others, see George Edwards, *At the Margins,* pp. 16ff.

36. See Edwards, *At the Margins;* Jones, *The Presidency in a Separated System,* chap. 7; and Peterson, *Legislating Together,* especially appendix B, which offers an excellent review of quantitative research.

37. See, in particular, "Jon R. Bond, Richard Fleischer, and Glen A. Krutz, "An Overview of the Empirical Findings on Presidential-Congressional Relations," in James A. Thurber, ed., *Rivals for Power* (Boulder, CO: Westview Press, 1996), pp. 103–139, and Nathan Dietz, "Presidential Influence on Congress," in James Thurber, ed., *Rivals for Power: Congressional-Presidential Relations* 2nd ed., (Washington, DC: CQ Press, 2002), pp. 105–139.

38. *Congressional Quarterly Weekly Report,* December 31, 1994, p. 3654.

39. David Hosansky, "Clinton's Biggest Prize Was a Frustrated GOP," *Congressional Quarterly Weekly Report,* January 9, 1999, p. 76.

40. Peterson, *Legislating Together,* pp. 220–221.

41. Since 1921, the Bureau of the Budget (renamed the Office of Management and Budget [OMB] in 1971) has monitored government spending and produced increasingly large compilations of proposed expenditures.

42. Lance T. LeLoup, *Budgetary Politics,* 3rd ed. (Brunswick, OH: Kings' Court, 1986), pp. 6ff.

43. Howard E. Shuman, *Politics and the Budget,* 3rd ed. (Englewood Cliffs, NJ: Prentice Hall, 1992), p. 213; emphasis added.

44. Allen Schick, *Congress and Money* (Washington, DC: Urban Institute Press, 1980), chap. 2.

45. Barbara Sinclair, *Legislators, Leaders, and Lawmaking: The U.S. House of Representatives in the Postreform Era* (Baltimore: Johns Hopkins University Press, 1995), p. 143.

46. Kenneth Shepsle uses this term in "The Changing Textbook Congress," in John E. Chubb and Paul E. Peterson, eds., *Can the Government Govern?* (Washington, DC: Brookings Institution, 1989), pp. 259ff.

47. For more extensive discussion, see Shuman, *Politics and the Budget,* 3rd ed., pp. 286ff.

48. Leon E. Panetta, "Politics of the Federal Budget Process," in Thurber, *Rivals for Power,* p. 205.

49. Among others, see Glenn Krutz, *Hitching a Ride: Omnibus Legislating in the U.S. Congress* (Columbus, OH: Ohio State University Press, 2001).

50. David Mayhew, *Divided We Govern* (New Haven, CT: Yale University Press, 1991).

51. See, for example, Arthur M. Schlesinger, Jr., *The Imperial Presidency* (Boston: Houghton Mifflin, 1973).

52. See Barbara Hinckley, *Less than Meets the Eye* (Chicago: University of Chicago Press, 1995).

53. See Jeff Fishel, *Party and Opposition* (New York: David McKay, 1973), and Sundquist, *Politics and Policy.*

54. Jones, *The Presidency in a Separated System,* p. 207; emphasis added.

55. Ibid., p. 207.

56. John Bader, *Taking the Initiative: Leadership Agendas in Congress and the Contract with America* (Washington, DC: Georgetown University Press, 1996), pp. 222–223.

57. George C. Edwards III, Andrew Barnett, and Jeffery Peake, "The Legislative Impact of Divided Government," *American Journal of Political Science* 41 (April 1997): pp. 545–563; Sarah Binder, "The Dynamics of Legislative Gridlock, 1947–96," *American Political Science Review* 93 (September 1999): pp. 519–533. See also the articles by James Pfiffner ("The President and Congress at the Turn of the Century") and Nathan Deitz ("Presidential Influence on Congress") in Thurber, *Rivals for Power.*

58. Sarah Binder, *Stalemate* (Washington, DC: Brookings Institute Press, 2003).

59. Leon E. Panetta, "The True Balance of Power," *New York Times,* February 2, 1997, p. 11, section 4.

Seven

THE LEGISLATIVE PROCESS
AND THE RULES
OF THE GAME

F rom universities to corporations to legislative bodies, all institutions operate under parallel sets of expectations, one established by formal rules and structures, the other resulting from informal arrangements that have grown up over an extended period of time. Legislatures rely heavily on the different kinds of order that are imposed by formal procedures and implicit understandings. Watching Congress on C-SPAN, one immediately observes the elaborate courtesies that legislators ordinarily extend to each other, even when they are engaged in fierce battles over a particular bill. Courtesy is one of many important, if informal, rules of the game that most members observe, although perhaps less so in the contemporary Congress than thirty or forty years ago. In addition, procedural constraints and time limitations that characterize the way the House does business appear largely absent in the Senate, where debate can be held up simply because one senator does not like another senator's proposal.

The House and the Senate operate under separate sets of formal rules, and each chamber fosters its own so-called folkways[1] — expectations about behavior that influence actions on Capitol Hill. For example, courtesy and hard work are encouraged, and insolence and sloth are discouraged (if not eliminated). Folkways are especially important in Congress, where members are technically equal in that they each can cast a single vote and because members must interact with each other in some way, shape, or form on a daily basis. In such an organization, power relationships are often delicate and unstated, expressed through agreed-upon norms rather than in explicit procedures.

Overall, formal rules play a more important role in the House, whereas norms are more important in the Senate. This makes sense because the larger House must rely on procedures in order to reach decisions in a timely, less-than-chaotic manner. Members of the smaller Senate depend much more on informal agreements reached among all senators.[2]

This chapter first discusses the ways in which formal rules affect the legislative process and then considers the evolution and impact of congressional folkways. Neither chamber can function effectively without a blend of formal and informal strictures, but the mixes of procedures and norms differ greatly on the different sides of the Capitol.

RULES, PROCEDURE, AND THE LEGISLATIVE PROCESS

> *If you let me write procedure and I let you write substance,*
> *I'll screw you every time.*
>
> Representative John Dingell (D–Mich.)

Although the Congress is a thoroughly rule-oriented institution, only a few of its procedures are mandated by the Constitution; these include the requirement that each chamber maintain a journal, that half the membership constitutes a quorum, that tax bills must originate in the House of Representatives, and that the two chambers can override a presidential veto by a two-thirds vote in each body.[3] Notably, the Constitution includes a Speaker of the House but makes no mention of a Majority Leader of the Senate. Beyond these basics and the more expansive constitutional limitations on the entire federal government, the House and Senate have been free to establish their own distinct sets of rules. The House rules currently run to more than seven hundred pages, but the Senate makes do with about one hundred pages.[4]

The point of origin for a public law begins with bill sponsorship. House members and senators each introduce a number of bills throughout the two-year congressional session. In the House, over 7,000 bills are introduced in a session, while the number in the Senate hovers around 3,000; only about 500 bills ever become law — either on their own or as part of a larger legislative package. From the vantage point of individual legislators, introducing bills can allow them to claim credit for addressing an issue that is important to their constituents or perhaps enable them to become a key player on a legislative issue, even if the bill fails to win approval.

After their introduction by individual legislators, bills are referred to committees by the Speaker or the Senate's presiding officer, who consults when necessary with the parliamentarians of the respective chambers. As appointees of the majority party, the parliamentarians work closely with the leadership. In the Democratic House of the 1980s and 1990s, a steadily growing number of bills were referred to multiple committees (almost one in five by the 1991–1992 period).[5] Starting with the 104th Congress, majority Republicans refashioned House committee jurisdictions, which reduced the need for such referrals.[6]

The hurdles to enacting legislation are substantial. First, the bill has to get out of subcommittee and full committee and then garner a majority of votes on the House and Senate floors. On many major issues, a compromise version must be worked out between the two chambers in conference; only then is the bill sent to the president for signature or veto. Because the House floor is so tightly controlled by party leaders and firm rules, representatives have far fewer opportunities to push their own legislation than do senators, who can freely offer their bills as amendments on the Senate floor. In both chambers, laws most frequently flow from bills sponsored by members who hold a committee or subcommittee chair and can thus influence their progress in the legislative process. Overall, lawmaking emphasizes a winnowing of proposals, allowing those to pass that have broad enough support to make it to the president's desk. Sometimes a single party's backing is enough, but usually cross-party coalitions are required.

The House

PATHS OF LEGISLATION   All bills are not created equal, nor do they move along the same path toward final passage. Minor bills appear on the House Consent Calendar and are considered on the first and third Mondays of each month; other legislation can take the shortcut of being considered under a suspension-of-the-rules procedure, which requires a two-thirds affirmative House vote and cannot routinely exceed $100 million in expenditures.[7] Within the Democratic postreform House of the 1980s, more than a third of all legislation was essentially symbolic, commemorating events such as Black History Month and National Peach Week.[8] Although these noncontroversial bills were routinely passed, they did consume a growing amount of legislative resources, and the Republicans essentially eliminated them after winning control of Congress in 1994.

Major legislation moves to the floor from House committees in two ways. Budget and appropriations measures are entitled to a privileged status that allows them to be brought to the floor at almost any time; most other important legislation must go before the Rules Committee to receive a rule that will govern debate and amendments. Given the sheer size of the House, a Rules Committee is necessary to maintain an orderly flow of legislation. Otherwise, the politics of delay could dominate, and chaos might well reign on the House floor. Important legislation, such as budget resolutions and large-scale, or omnibus, spending packages, almost always obtain rules that set out strict constraints on deliberation and waive procedural points of order.[9] Thus, the amount of time for debate and the number and sequence of amendments will often be clearly defined within a rule.

In national service legislation and changes in student loan mechanisms, the relevant bills took different paths in gaining legislative approval (see Figure 7–1). After being introduced at the behest of the administration, both proposals went to the House Education and Labor Committee, but national service proceeded as a stand-alone bill, whereas student aid policy was incorporated into the overall budget bill. The politics of the two pieces of legislation were not dissimilar, despite their distinct routes to passage. Each proposal could have been defeated on its merits, but the student aid changes could also have been derailed within the highly partisan process that culminated in the August 5, 1993, vote to approve the budget package (see Chapter 1).

ORGANIZING HOUSE FLOOR ACTION UNDER DEMOCRATIC CONTROL   Given the ample staff resources of individual members, the proliferation of subcommittees (at least through the 1980s), and the growth of special interest

FIGURE 7-1
Two Regular Order Versions of the Legislative Process

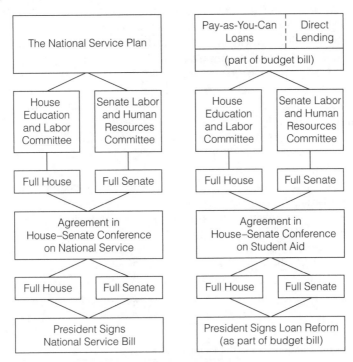

Source: Adapted from Steven Waldman, *The Bill* (New York: Viking, 1995), p. xv.

caucuses, Democratic leaders struggled to control legislation that reached the floor of the postreform House. As Barbara Sinclair summarizes:

> The 1970s reformers, most of them liberal Democrats, were motivated by concerns about both policy and participation. The changes they instituted would . . . produce better . . . policy and provide greater opportunities for the rank and file to participate in the legislative process. By the late 1970s many had concluded that unrestrained participation, particularly on the House floor, hindered rather than facilitated . . . good public policy. And in the more hostile political climate of the 1980s [that is, divided government], the policy costs of unrestrained and uncoordinated legislative activism rose further.[10]

Most troubling to party and committee leaders was a sharp increase in amendments offered on the House floor both by members of committees that processed the legislation and by other backbenchers.[11]

The House Democratic leaders adopted various tactics to regain control of the floor, including an increased reliance on suspension-of-the-rules votes, but the most important procedural changes came in their use of the Rules Committee.[12] This committee dictates both the flow of major, nonprivileged legislation onto the House floor and the procedural limitations that apply once it gets there. Although the Rules Committee had at times past proven to be an obstacle to the Speaker's control of business on the House floor, since the mid-1970s it has become a reliable "arm of the leadership."[13] Given the Speaker's power to appoint (and remove) Rules Committee members, the panel has served the leadership by reporting out rules that structure floor action according to the party leadership's wishes. Moreover, it has resolved disagreements among committees with overlapping jurisdictions as to which bill or combination of bills will be used as the legislation to be considered on the floor.

More importantly, however, the Rules Committee sets time limits for floor debate and establishes which amendments, if any, can be offered. As floor action grew more partisan during the 1980s, Democratic leaders relied heavily on restrictive rules to maintain control of the legislative process, as well as to structure substantive decision making to favor their own policy positions (see Table 7–1). Although some of these rules simply imposed a deadline for amendments, in the 103rd Congress, 45 of 104 rules "barred all amendments [closed rules] or allowed only specific proposals" that the Democratic leader-

TABLE 7-1
Restrictions on Amendments in the Democratic House, 1977–1994

Congress	Open Rules	Restrictive Rules	Percent Restrictive
95th (1977–1978)	179	32	15
96th (1979–1980)	161	53	25
97th (1981–1982)	90	30	25
98th (1983–1984)	105	50	32
99th (1985–1986)	65	50	43
100th (1987–1988)	66	57	46
101st (1989–1990)	47	57	55
102nd (1991–1992)	37	72	66
103rd (1993–1994)	31	73	70

Source: Congressional Quarterly Weekly Report, November 19, 1994, p. 3321.

Restrictions on Amendments in the Republican House, 1995–2002

Congress	Open Rules	Restrictive Rules	Percent Restrictive
104th (1995–1996)	83	59	42
105th (1997–1998)	74	66	47
106th (1999–2000)	91	88	49
107th (2001–2002)	40	67	63

Source: Congressional Quarterly Weekly Report, November 19, 1994, p. 3321; data for 1995–2002 compiled by Donald Wolfensberger, Senior Fellow, Woodrow Wilson International Center for Scholars; see also his paper "The House Rules Committee Under Republican Majorities: Continuity and Change" (presented at the Northeastern Political Science Meetings, November 2002).

ship approved.[14] Only thirty-one rules were open to any amendment from the floor. Some rules even extended the Democrats' procedural control of the House deep into substantive concerns. The Rules Committee employed two specific types of rules that directly affected policy results:

1. The king-of-the-hill rule, first devised in 1982, waived various precedents and procedures in allowing a series of votes on several major policy amendments, each offered as an entire substitute an original proposal. This rule "gave ultimate victory to the last one approved, even if one of the earlier options had gotten more 'yea' votes."[15]

2. The self-executing rule "stipulates a two-for-one procedure: adoption of the rule simultaneously enacts another measure, amendment, or both."[16] Long employed for technical purposes in considering Senate legislation, in the 1980s this ploy was used to enact policies without requiring a direct vote on the issue.

Through these procedures the Democratic leadership could use the Rules Committee to provide members with the chance to vote in favor of policies they knew would not become law (the initial king-of-the-hill substitutes) and to approve policies without requiring a recorded vote (self-executing rules).

In sum, within a majoritarian institution, the majority-party Democratic members invested in their leadership, the Rules Committee included, the power to structure legislation so that it would have the best chance of winning, often in a highly partisan vote. The only recourse available to Republicans and dissident Democrats was to defeat the rule on the House floor; on occasion this occurred, but ordinarily the Democratic leadership could hold its troops together on the procedural vote to approve the rule. With little effect and growing frustration, the Republican minority of the postreform era argued that the Democratic leadership acted unfairly in constructing rules that restricted the introduction of potentially embarrassing amendments and manipulated the voting process through king-of-the-hill and self-executing procedures.

One additional consequence of the Democrats' practices was to foster sentiments among the minority Republicans that they had little stake in maintaining comity and civility within the chamber. The Democrats' reliance on formal rules may well have undermined the informal bonds that had allowed cross-party cooperation in the House.

RULES AND PROCEDURES IN THE REPUBLICAN ERA   After forty years in the House minority, Republicans pledged that they would not rely on House procedures to dominate the legislative process. Rather, bills would come to the floor with fewer restrictions on amending activity, and the body would be given a chance for up-or-down votes on amendments offered by members of both the majority and the minority. Running counter to this promise was the hectic schedule of the first year of Republican control, 1995, when consideration of the Contract with America required voting three hundred times in ninety-three days.

Early on, the Republican leadership demonstrated how a well-disciplined majority could dominate the House. When push came to shove during the session's initial one hundred days, Speaker Gingrich could call up his party majority to support him on both procedures and substance (see Chapter 5 for a more extended discussion). At the same time, the emphasis on speed demonstrated graphically that any benefits of legislative efficiency came accompanied by a set of costs in deliberation.[17] With the partisan shoe on the other foot, Democratic Minority Leader Richard Gephardt (D-Mo.) complained that the Republicans' intense focus on one hundred days time frame "caused all of them to jerk stuff through the procedure much faster than it should have been. There hasn't been enough committee considerations or floor consideration."[18]

Whether the Republicans held to their promise of opening up the House is subject to debate. Unsurprisingly, the Republican House rules committee claimed that their data (somewhat different from that shown in Table 7–1) showed that 65 percent of all rules for floor amendments were open (or mostly so) in the first year of the 104th Congress, compared to 44 percent in the 103rd.

Democrats complained that, although rules might have been more open, the Republican leadership enforced tight time restrictions on legislation that served the same purpose — to restrict debate and amending activity. One study concluded that the Republicans did follow through on their promise of greater openness in that, compared to the 103rd Congress, there was more debate, more amendments were offered, and more amendments passed in the first, highly partisan, session of the 104th Congress.[19] Inevitably, as the Democrats did before them, Republicans relied on a substantial number of restrictive rules, as well as adopting self-executing rules to adopt substantive policies without a separate vote. The Republican majority did eschew the king-of-the-hill rule and overall did bring a measure of greater openness to the House floor, even in the raucous, exhausting first months of the 104th Congress.

After the Contract with America sprint, the House slowed down substantially. In the end, the House voted more, held longer sessions, but passed less legislation, although the latter observation is deceptive, given the decline in symbolic commemorative bills. As Table 7–2 illustrates, the first session of the 104th Congress (1995) was an aberration, and from 1996 to 1998 the Republican House looks a lot like the Democratic House of the early 1990s. However, starting in 1999 and continuing through 2002, there has been an increase in the number of days and hours in session, an increase in the number of bills introduced, and an increase in the number of roll-call votes taken. This rise in overall workload may have been a function of the declining economy and greater national security threats; it remains to be seen if this workload is sustained in the 108th Congress.

TABLE 7–2
Congress by the Numbers, 1991–2002

	102nd Congress		103rd Congress		104th Congress		105th Congress		106th Congress		107th Congress	
	1991	1992	1993	1994	1995	1996	1997	1998	1999	2000	2001	2002
Days in Session												
House	154	123	142	123	168	122	132	119	137	135	142	123
Senate	158	129	153	138	211	132	153	143	162	141	173	149
Time in Session (Hours)												
House	939	857	982	905	1,525	919	1,004	999	1,125	1,054	922	772
Senate	1,201	1,091	1,270	1,244	1,839	1,037	1,093	1,095	1,184	1,018	1,236	1,043
Average Hours/Day												
House	6.1	7.0	6.9	7.4	9.1	7.5	7.6	8.4	8.2	7.8	6.5	6.3
Senate	7.6	8.5	8.3	9.0	8.7	7.9	7.1	7.7	7.3	7.2	7.1	7.0
Bills/Resolutions Introduced												
House	5,057	2,714	4,543	2,104	3,430	1,899	3,662	2,253	4,241	2,701	4,318	2,711
Senate	2,701	1,544	2,178	999	1,801	860	1,829	1,321	2,352	1,546	2,203	1,563
Recorded Votes												
House	444	488	615	507	885	455	640	547	611	603	512	483
Senate	280	270	395	329	613	306	298	314	374	298	380	253
Public Laws												
Enacted	243	347	210	255	88	245	153	241	170	410	136	195
Vetoes	3	10	0	0	9	6	13*	6*	5	7†	0	0

*Does not include line-item vetoes.
†Includes pocket vetoes.

Sources: *Congressional Quarterly Weekly Report*, January 9, 1999, p. 85; *Vital Statistics on Congress 1997–1998*, pp. 147–148, PL105-55, 1997; *Congressional Roll Call 2001*, p. 5; Final Senate Calendar 2002; Calendar of the House of Representatives, 2002; resume of Congressional Activity; *Congressional Record*, December 16, 2002, D1193.

The Senate

Unlike the House, the Senate has far fewer formal rules, largely attributable to its smaller size (one hundred members). Because senators have longer terms in office, and only one-third of the Senate is ever up for reelection at the same time, it does not face the same time pressures as the House to produce legislation. Senators have a formal right to speak on the Senate floor, and this power confers their rights to object to consideration of any bill brought to the Senate floor.[20] Therefore, the Senate must essentially operate on a unanimous consent basis, which gives tremendous leverage to a single senator in negotiating the conditions of debate.

In many ways unanimous consent agreements resemble House rules, but they are hatched in very different ways. As opposed to the domination of the House process by partisan majorities in the chamber and the Rules Committee, Senate leaders must satisfy all of their interested colleagues from both parties in crafting a set of conditions for debating and amending legislation. Unanimous consent means precisely that: *All* senators must acquiesce to the provisions of the agreement. As with House rules, unanimous consent agreements can be complex, but the complexity tends to serve both the Senate as a whole and specific members rather than advancing the interests of the majority party.

Moreover, a senator may use his or her right of speech to extend debate on a bill or an amendment indefinitely, a tactic commonly known as the filibuster. In the absence of formal rules that structures debate, limit amendments, and impose time limits, the Senate is more governed by informal interactions and negotiation than the House of Representatives.

CONGRESSIONAL FOLKWAYS: THE INFORMAL RULES OF THE GAME

Looking back to the 1950s, the "textbook Congress" era seems positively quaint. Speaker Sam Rayburn could sincerely counsel incoming House members to "get along, go along." And Senate Majority Leader Lyndon Johnson would give each new senator a copy of journalist William S. White's *Citadel,* with its glorification of the chamber's "Inner Club," where "Senate types" of legislators informally dominated the institution. To be sure, Rayburn's advice was generally sound, and White's description roughly accurate. For all their formal leadership and committee structures, both bodies harbored well-accepted sets of norms — informal rules of the game — that governed the behavior of most, if not all, members.

In contrast, the Congress of the 1990s and 2000s has become a thoroughly contentious place. No contemporary Speaker could — or would — deliver Rayburn's fatherly advice, and there is no club of insider senators that can dominate their chamber. Social ties in both House and Senate have weakened substantially since the 1950s, in part because more and more congressional actions are conducted in public by legislators whose workloads have increased steadily and who have spent rising amounts of time back in their districts. More generally, members of Congress may well reflect the declining levels of trust and civility within the public at large.[21]

The decline of comity scarcely means its elimination.[22] Viewers of C-SPAN can still observe the elaborate formalities and courtesies of the legislative process. But these niceties are often more perfunctory and forced than they were a generation or two ago. The social fabric that holds together congressional life has been frayed, sometimes to the breaking point. Although the partisan, often acidic, nature of debate has reduced civility in the postreform House, this chamber has never relied completely on informal ties to maintain order. The Senate, however, is a different story, with the lack of comity and the growth of partisanship combining to increase individual rancor and reduce the institution's capacity for deliberation.

The Senate of the 1950s: The Old Club Ties

In his classic study of the Senate, published in 1960, political scientist Donald Matthews approvingly quoted a senator as observing that each member "of the Senate has as much power as he has the sense to use. For this very reason he has to be careful to use it properly or else he will incur the wrath of his colleagues."[23] Such restraint typified the unspoken limits imposed by the "folkways" that Matthews discovered in his research.

Six important norms governed Senate behavior, according to Matthews:[24]

▶ *Apprenticeship*, which included performing menial tasks (such as presiding over floor debate on routine matters), speaking only occasionally on the floor, and generally deferring to senior senators.

▶ *Legislative work*, which emphasized doing the unglamorous tasks that fill up most days, as opposed to seeking publicity for one's actions and statements.

▶ *Specialization*, which meant focusing virtually all of one's efforts on work within two or three of the ten-plus subcommittees and committees that a member was assigned to.

▶ *Courtesy*, which "permitted competitors to cooperate"[25] by discouraging public, personal attacks, especially in floor debate, and encouraging elaborate compliments between senators of all political stripes (for example, "My good friend, the most distinguished senator from _____, has made an excellent point, but I must offer an alternative perspective . . .").

▶ *Institutional patriotism*, which translated into a willingness to defend the Senate, with a strong emotional commitment to the body and its members.

▶ *Reciprocity,* which was perhaps the single most important folkway, in that the bargaining among senators depended on the unstated premise that no individual would take advantage of the practice of performing mutual favors on a host of issues and procedures.

One effect of general adherence to the Senate's folkways was to reinforce the decentralized power of the committee system, where the norm of seniority, a well-established element of reciprocity, had been elevated to a governing principle for both parties in advancing members toward committee chairman-ships. Relying on seniority meant that consecutive service on a committee was virtually the sole criterion for selecting a chair. This encouraged senators to build careers on given panels and defend the related programs and jurisdic-tions (the turf) against all challenges. At the core of the Senate, according to both supporters (such as White) and critics (such as Senator Joseph Clark, [D-Pa.]), was an "Inner Club" of senators who, along with the party leaders, pulled together the committee-based structure that dominated the legislative process.[26] This was a tidy state of affairs for a relatively conservative, Southern-dominated Senate that had a limited policy agenda.

Given their informality, norms are always susceptible to erosion, and the Senate was beginning to change, however imperceptibly, in the 1950s. Although the large, liberal Democratic "class of 1958" would increase pressure on some of the norms, such as apprenticeship, it was Lyndon Johnson who initiated the slide toward individualism. In a bid to strengthen his own posi-tion, as minority leader in 1953, Johnson instituted a committee assignment rule that guaranteed every Democratic senator a seat on at least one major committee. He continued this practice as majority leader (1955–1960), and Republican leaders followed suit. The "Johnson rule" thus enhanced the indi-vidual standing of all incoming senators while simultaneously placing each in the debt of the party leadership. Although this practice did not demolish the apprenticeship norm, it did increase the expectations that every senator had something to contribute, even during their initial months of service.

Norm Change and the Individualistic Senate

In two distinct but related ways, power within the Senate changed dramat-ically between the late 1950s and the early 1980s. First, liberal and mostly non-Southern Democrats rose to occupy key committee positions.[27] Second, the Senate became more thoroughly individualistic as various institutional norms evolved or, in the case of apprenticeship, simply disappeared. As the public role of the media and interest groups in the legislative process intensified throughout the 1970s, senators faced more pressure to appear attentive and active on a wider range of issues than ever before.[28] This external force eroded the incentives for senators to stay quiet in their early years in the Senate; they simply did not have the time to wait in the background. All one hundred sena-tors were expected to participate in the process, and there was little time for learning the ropes through years of committee experience.

By 1984, Rohde and his colleagues noted "the egalitarian trend that opened up the Senate and shared power more widely among its members still holds sway."[29] Moreover, they observed a decline in the other general benefit norms, as an increasing workload and greater ideological divisions had begun to undermine some of the traditional Senate comity. The Senate that John McCain (R-Ariz.) entered in 1986 was much more hospitable to the cultivation of a reputation as a maverick than was the Senate of 1958, when the iconoclastic William Proxmire (D-Wis.) was first elected. Senator McCain shares many of Proxmire's traits; he goes his own way and does not seem to care whom he offends in the process. The juxtaposition of behavior and norms is, of course, one of the problems in assessing the importance of informal rules of the game. Sooner or later, if there are lots of violations of norms, we are justified in asking if the folkways have any effect in restraining behavior.

Still, the fact remained that the procedures that govern the Senate reinforced some degree of cooperation and comity among senators because each senator could retaliate against any other at any time by blocking legislation. And the dominant core of senators in the 1980s had been socialized under the norm-based structure of the 1960s and 1970s Senate. It was not until around 1996, when many older, moderate senators retired, that the character of the Senate completed its transformation away from a collegial and informally governed body to a partisan and increasingly less cooperative place.[30] This change becomes a major problem for the Senate, given its absence of formal tools that would allow the majority party to dominate the process, as in the House. The Senate thus has little capacity to replace "norms" with a different system of self-governance.

Obstructionism and the Partisan Impulse in the Contemporary Senate

Given its informality and reliance on cordial, respectful relations among its members, the Senate is fractured by declining reciprocity and courtesy. Tending to the well-being of the entire chamber does not offer many rewards. Rather, as congressional scholar Barbara Sinclair bleakly reports, "Asked their prescription for being an effective senator, several staffers (not attached to senators particularly known for pushing their powers to the limit) responded that *the senator who does not care if he is liked can be very effective.*" There is perhaps no better indicator of how much the Senate has changed.[31]

The Senate has always provided great leeway to its members, and its processes have emphasized lengthy deliberation rather than speedy action. Indeed, the filibuster is probably the best-known single element of Senate procedure, as much as a result of Jimmy Stewart's performance in *Mr. Smith Goes to Washington* as of the speeches of LaFollette, the record-setting effort of Senator Strom Thurmond (R-S.C., more than twenty-four hours straight), or a well-organized Southern opposition to civil rights legislation in the 1950s and early 1960s.

Filibusters have become much more common in the contemporary chamber, as both individual members and organized factions have used the tactic to
bring the chamber's business to a halt over minor issues and even for matters
of convenience (such as a scheduling dispute). Despite the procedural importance of filibusters, their frequent use and even more frequent threatened use
demonstrate a pernicious side of the increasingly individualistic Senate. Sinclair concludes that the Senate has created this situation "*not by changing its
rules,* but by being *unwilling and unable* to prevent senators from fully
exploiting the power those rules grant to each of them."[32]

Majority leaders have had an increasingly difficult job managing senatorial
behavior and forcing senators to conduct filibusters according to the strictest
definition. Typically a filibuster requires senators to be on their feet the entire
time that they are talking in opposition to the pending business on the floor.
But in today's busy political world, most senators no longer have the time to
do that, so they merely threaten a filibuster and speak for a few hours on the
floor. Leaders are forced to accommodate these senators. As a consequence, in
the absence of real costs to mounting a filibuster, senators have come to view
this tactic as just one more tool to get what they want. A majority leader who
tried to penalize a senator for engaging in a filibuster might very well face the
wrath of all the other senators in his or her party, and such opposition might
threaten the majority leader's position.

Again, we get the kind of Senate that the senators give us. Especially when
combined with the frustrations inherent in addressing tough issues within a
chamber that is so difficult to lead, it is no wonder that such noted senators as
Nancy Kassebaum (R-Kans.), Warren Rudman (R-N.H.), David Boren
(D-Okla.), Bill Bradley (D-N.J.), and Sam Nunn (D-Ga.) decided voluntarily to
leave the body. It is thus ironic that the increasing overlay of partisanship (see
Chapter 5) in the Senate has done little to curb rampant individualism.

In the Senate of 2001–2002, with a slim majority of essentially one vote,
the incentives for individual senators to protect their own interests were never
stronger. On any vote, a single senator could be pivotal, which gave each
legislator enhanced power above and beyond the formally recognized privileges on the Senate floor. The combination of (a) partisan behavior, (b) individualism, (c) the filibuster,[33] and (d) a slim majority has left the Senate in
search of a "stable and satisfying role" in American politics.[34] The 108th Congress promises to bring more of the same emphasis on individual senators.
With a 51-49 margin, the Republican Senate majority is so slim that two or
three senators can still play a pivotal role on any given vote.

The House Is Not a Home

Given its size and the related need for organization, informal rules of the
game have never been quite as important in the House as in the Senate.
Nonetheless, until the partisan era of the 1990s, norms remained significant in
this fragmented body. The Rayburn-era House (late 1930s–1961) resembled

the clubbish Senate in many ways. Apprenticeships were long, specialization was expected, and virtually all members assumed that courtesy and reciprocity would govern their relations.

Today, the steady infusion of new members into the House — especially after the Democratic landslides of 1958, 1964, and 1974 and the widespread Republican victories of 1966, 1978, 1980, and 1994 — has prompted a reevaluation of legislative folkways,[35] and all evidence points to a substantial "decline in comity" in the House.[36] Although the data are sketchy, the trend is clear: Fewer than half the junior members completely accept the bedrock norms of courtesy and reciprocity. In addition, almost all of these legislators reject the notions of apprenticeship and institutional loyalty.

Much of the influence of norms in governing members' behavior was due to the skewed length of Democratic majority control of the House. Despite their long-term majority status (1955–1994), Democratic leaders did not necessarily dominate the legislative process; only in 1965–1966 did their large numbers (290-plus) allow them to control the floor and consistently overwhelm the Conservative Coalition. In the early 1970s, the party began to splinter, and the House became more structurally fragmented in committees; exercising leadership thus turned into a difficult one-vote-at-a-time process. In the 1980s, as it grew more unified and partisan, the Democratic caucus gave its leaders enhanced powers to push party-based initiatives. When the Republicans won control of the House in 1994, they took party governance several steps further. Former Speaker Newt Gingrich (R-Ga.) bypassed seniority in making committee assignments and awarding committee positions, which effectively reduced the incentive for apprenticeship and replaced it with an incentive for party loyalty above all.

The partisan differences between the Democrats and Republicans in the 1990s were compounded by the Republican opposition to President Clinton. The rhetoric and rancor of the policy debate spilled over to personal interactions: The days when Democrat and Republican members could play basketball together, or dine together in the House dining room, were largely over. The decreasing margin of majority votes for the Republicans in the 1999–2002 period led to even less comity. With narrow margins, highly partisan messages and procedures, and a Republican president in the White House, partisanship in the House continues to outstrip the desire for less conflict and more cordial relations between members of opposing parties.

RULES, NORMS, AND THE LEGISLATIVE ARENA

Structurally, the legislative process has become more complex over the past forty years in that it has moved from generally closed and informal sets of interactions between legislators to a more open but more formal environment. The parties have asserted strong control over committees and legislators in the House, discouraging individual influence, while the Senate has become more dominated by individualism infused with strong partisan policy positions. These developments have affected the possibilities for congressional integration and coherence in distinct ways, with the majoritarian House often facing a Senate that is hard-pressed to act quickly and effectively.

The trajectory of change in the House is curvilinear. It has moved from the seniority-dominated system of the 1950s to a period of democratization of the committee and subcommittee structure in the 1970s to a post-1980 era in which the parties have wrested a great deal of control over the policy agenda from individual members and committees. This pattern also follows the careers of many of the current senior members of the House, especially the Democrats. The "new apprenticeship" of the 1970s and 1980s encouraged members to take on key policy roles in caucuses, party task forces, and subcommittees very early in their careers.[37] Twenty years later, these same members were reaping the benefits of seniority and formal committee powers. So even though the process has ostensibly opened up, it may well take substantially longer term experience to become a major force in lawmaking, regardless of the norms governing activity. In his article on congressional careers, John Hibbing demonstrates that House members who reach a certain level of seniority are the most effective and efficient legislators and carry the majority of the workload of the House.[38] By 1994, when Democrats lost control of the House, most of the reformers of the 1970s were in fact sitting as committee and subcommittee chairs and exercising all the formal powers associated with those positions.

When the Republicans gained control of the House, they faced a different situation because their majority included seventy-three new members, and they did not have the deep bench of senior members from which to select their committee and subcommittee chairs. Consequently, the Republican Party in the House relied heavily on junior members not only to cast important votes but also to sit on key committees, chair important subcommittees, and head major task forces.[39] Subsequently, ten years after gaining control of the House, the Republican Party has in place a number of legislators who have finally accrued enough experience in majority legislating that a slow shift toward committee independence is beginning to show itself. The party is still well in control, but individual GOP legislators, like their Democratic counterparts before them, have realized that seniority brings influence and power, and they continue to seek ways of exercising that power in the modern House of Representatives. Nevertheless, Republicans continue to enforce term limits on committee chairs, though they voted in January 2003 to lift the prior term limits on the Speaker of the House — another small blow to committee power.

The Senate, in contrast, has not seen as big a shift in the pendulum of power between parties, committees, and individual legislators. If anything, the increasingly public nature of Senate proceedings has exacerbated its worst tendencies toward individualism at the expense of collective action. Senators increasingly try to bypass committees through attempts to legislate from the Senate floor. Ironically, they are not more successful in this endeavor, as their amendments usually fail on the floor. Still, entertaining individual motions and amendments chews up increasing amounts of the Senate's legislative time. Without effective institutional mechanisms of control, the legislative process itself in the Senate has become less efficient, which is no mean feat given its historically low levels of efficiency.

On a Capitol Hill that discourages comity and cooperation and rewards the promotion of individualism, generating the succession of majorities necessary to pass important legislation has grown more and more difficult. Given both new and continuing legislative challenges, one might predict that the House and especially the Senate will ultimately have to contract the diffusion of power points within and between the chambers in order to meet the legislative responsibilities of the federal government, as well as the expectations of the public.

CHAPTER BIBLIOGRAPHY

Binder, Sarah A. *Stalemate: Causes and Consequences of Legislative Gridlock.* Washington, DC: Brookings Institution Press, 2003.

Oleszek, Walter. *Congressional Procedures and the Policy Process,* 5th ed. Washington: CQ Press, 2000.

NOTES

1. Donald Matthews first employed the "folkways" notion in his groundbreaking *U.S. Senators and Their World* (New York: Vintage, 1960).

2. See Ross K. Baker, *House and Senate,* 2nd ed. (New York: Norton, 1995), pp. 71–73.

3. Steven S. Smith, *The American Congress* (Boston: Houghton Mifflin, 1995), pp. 25–26.

4. Ibid., p. 43.

5. Gary Young and Joseph Cooper, "Multiple Referral and the Transformation of House Decision Making," in Lawrence Dodd and Bruce I. Oppenheimer, eds., *Congress Reconsidered,* 5th ed. (Washington, DC: CQ Press, 1993), p. 214.

6. The Speaker can refer a bill to multiple committees, but he or she designates a lead committee and sets deadlines (see Chapter 8).

7. Roger Davidson and Walter Oleszek, *Congress and Its Members,* 4th ed. (Washington, DC: CQ Press, 1994), pp. 330–331.

8. Roger Davidson, "The Emergence of the Postreform Congress," in Roger Davidson, ed., *The Postreform Congress* (New York: St. Martin's, 1992), p. 17.

9. Allen Schick, *The Federal Budget* (Washington, DC: Brookings Institution, 1995), p. 79.

10. Barbara Sinclair, "House Majority Leadership in an Era of Legislative Constraint," in Davidson, *The Postreform Congress,* p. 92. More generally, see Barbara Sinclair, *Unorthodox Lawmaking* (Washington, DC: CQ Press 1997).

11. For a detailed analysis, see Steven S. Smith, *Call to Order* (Washington, DC: Brookings Institution, 1989).

12. Where not otherwise noted, the following discussion is drawn from Walter Oleszek, *Congressional Procedures and the Policy Process,* 3rd ed. (Washington, DC: CQ Press, 1989), pp. 119 ff. Suspension of the rules allows bills to be considered in a expedited manner, subject to passage by a two-thirds vote.

13. See, in particular, Bruce I. Oppenheimer, "The Rules Committee: New Arm of Leadership in a Decentralized House," in Lawrence Dodd and Bruce I. Oppenheimer, eds., *Congress Reconsidered* (New York: Praeger, 1977), pp. 96–116.

14. Pat Towell, "GOP's Drive for a More Open House . . . Reflects Pragmatism and Resentment," *Congressional Quarterly Weekly Report,* November 19, 1994, p. 3321.

15. Towell, "GOP's Drive for a More Open House," p. 3320.

16. Oleszek, *Congressional Procedures and the Policy Process,* p. 129.

17. Kristin Kanthak and Elizabeth M. Martin, "House Republicans and Restrictive Rules: A New Regime?" (paper presented at the American Political Science Association meetings, San Francisco, August 29–September 1, 1996), pp. 4–7.

18. Richard Gephardt quoted in Donna Cassatta, *Congressional Quarterly Weekly Report,* April 8, 1995, p. 990.

19. Kanthak and Martin, "House Republicans and Restrictive Rules," pp. 4–7.

20. Floyd M. Riddick and Alan S. Frumin, *Riddick's Senate Procedure,* (Washington DC: Government Printing Office, 1992), pp. 1092–1097.

21. Eric Uslaner, *The Decline of Comity in Congress* (Ann Arbor: University of Michigan Press, 1994), esp. chap. 5.

22. See, for example, Judd Choate "Changing Perspectives on Congressional Norms" (paper presented at American Political Science Association meeting, San Francisco, August 29–September 1, 1996).

23. Quoted in Donald Matthews, *U.S. Senators and Their World,* p. 101. Matthews discusses at length the men in the Senate, and this quote makes the assumption of gender. The fact is that the Senate of the 1950s was a white male institution, as it has always been. Senator Margaret Chase Smith (R-Maine) was the single exception in the 1950s.

24. Ibid., pp. 92ff.

25. Matthews, *U.S. Senators and Their World,* p. 99.

26. See Joseph S. Clark, *Congress: The Sapless Branch* (New York: Harper & Row, 1964).

27. See Ripley, *Power in the Senate;* David W. Rohde, Norman J. Ornstein, and Robert L. Peabody, "Political Change and the U.S. Senate, 1957–1974," in Glenn Parker, ed., *Studies of Congress* (Washington, DC: CQ Press, 1985), pp. 147–188, and Barbara Sinclair, *The Transformation of the U.S. Senate* (Baltimore: Johns Hopkins University Press, 1989).

28. Sinclair, *The Transformation of the U.S. Senate.*

29. Rohde, Ornstein, and Peabody, "Political Change and the Senate," p. 183.

30. For a collection of speeches by some of these retired senators, see Norman J. Ornstein, ed., *Lessons and Legacies: Farewell Addresses from the Senate* (New York: Perseus Publishing, 1997).

31. Sinclair, *The Transformation of the U.S. Senate,* p. 204; emphasis added.

32. Ibid., p. 125; emphasis added.

33. Sarah Binder and Steven S. Smith, in *Politics or Principle: Filibustering in the United States Senate* (Washington, DC: Brookings Institution, 1997), conclude

that filibusters have generally served partisan purposes, not those of principled advocates.

34. Norman J. Ornstein, Robert L. Peabody, and David W. Rohde, "The U.S. Senate: Toward the 21st Century," in Dodd and Oppenheimer, eds. *Congress Reconsidered,* 6th ed., (Washington, DC: CQ Press, 1997), p. 27. See also Robert Dreyfuss, "Mississippi Waltz," *American Prospect* (March–April, 1999), pp. 18–25.

35. The data here come from Burdett Loomis, *The New American Politician* (New York: Basic Books, 1988), p. 48, and Herbert Asher, "The Learning of Legislative Norms," *American Political Science Review* 67 (June 1973): p. 503.

36. See Uslaner, *The Decline of Comity in Congress,* chap. 2.

37. Christopher J. Deering, "The New Apprenticeship: Strategies of Effectiveness for New Members of the House" (paper presented at the American Political Science Association meeting, August 30–September 2, 1984).

38. John R. Hibbing, "Contours of the Modern Congressional Career," *American Political Science Review* 85 (June 1991): pp. 405–428.

39. See Linda Killian, *The Freshmen* (New York: Westview Press, 1998).

Eight

CONGRESSIONAL COMMITTEES

The House sits, not for serious discussion, but to sanction the conclusions of its Committees as rapidly as possible. It legislates in its committee-rooms; not by the determination of majorities, but by the resolutions of its specially-commissioned minorities [the committees]; so that it is not far from the truth to say that Congress in session is Congress on public exhibition, whilst Congress in its committee-rooms is Congress at work.

Woodrow Wilson, 1885

The future of the committee [system] is seriously in doubt.

Representative John Boehner (R-Ohio), 1995

Wilson's words, most notably in the last two lines, have been quoted ad infinitum, and, like Tip O'Neill's dictum that "all politics is local," Wilson's phrase has become a cliché. Yet its essence remains true.[1] The Congress, especially the House, performs the vast majority of its work within the confines of its committee rooms. Despite the enhanced powers of contemporary party leaders and the independence of individual members, committee decisions and committee leadership dictate much of the pace and content of congressional legislation. At the same time, former Republican Conference Chair Boehner articulates a position that, while extreme, reflects the attitudes of many legislators who feel strongly that party majorities should be able to work their will. Since 1995, the decentralizing influence of committees has come under intense pressure from a relatively unified Republican Party in the House and to a lesser degree in the Senate.

Committees remain important and powerful because their existence makes such good sense, both for individual legislators and for the Congress as a whole. Acting on their own, 435 House members or 100 senators cannot reasonably be expected to hammer out coherent legislation across the entire spectrum of issues on each year's congressional agenda. Like most large organizations, the Congress has profited from a division of labor among smaller work groups. Committees specialize in particular policy areas ranging from the myriad issues taken up by the broadly inclusive Commerce Committee to the relatively narrow focus of the Small Business Committee. Committees are designed to serve their parent chambers, which has meant continuing changes over the years in the number, membership levels, and jurisdictions of the units. In 1995, for example, the House's Republican majority endorsed its leadership's proposal to eliminate three committees, to alter the jurisdictions of others, and to limit the number of subcommittees to five per committee. In the 104th Congress, the District of Columbia, the Post Office and Civil Service, and the Merchant Marine and Fisheries Committees all ceased to exist, and their responsibilities were farmed out to other panels (see Table 8–1). In the Senate, on the other hand, the Republican majority initially proposed no major changes (see Table 8–2) but subsequently embraced some modest restraints on committee chairs.

Viewing committees as efficient sharers of information allows one to see how decentralization can benefit the Congress as a whole.[2] Given an annual budget and a federal government that regulates everything from trucking to tuna, congressional decentralization through the committee system allows lawmakers to specialize and make informed decisions on a wide range of complex, often conflicting proposals. In fact, by sharing information across committees, Congress as a whole may produce a relatively coherent, consistent set of policies. In short, committees and subcommittees can and do serve the Congress *as*

TABLE 8-1
Standing Committees, 103rd, 104th, and 108th Congresses

House of Representatives		
103rd Congress (1993-1994) *(22 Committees)*	*104th Congress (1995-1996)* *(19 Committees)*	*108th Congress (2003-2004)* *(19 Committees)*
Agriculture	Agriculture	Agriculture
Appropriations	Appropriations	Appropriations
Armed Services	National Security	Armed Services
Banking, Finance, and Urban Affairs	Banking and Financial Services	Financial Services
Budget	Budget	Budget
District of Columbia	—	—
Education and Labor	Education and the Workforce	Education and the Workforce
Energy and Commerce	Commerce	Energy and Commerce
Foreign Affairs	International Relations	International Relations
Government Operations	Government Reform and Oversight	Government Reform
House Administration	Oversight	House Administration
Judiciary	Judiciary	Judiciary
Merchant Marine and Fisheries	—	
Natural Resources	Resources	Resources
Post Office and Civil Service	—	—
Public Works and Transportation	Transportation and Infrastructure	Transportation and Infrastructure
Rules	Rules	Rules
Science, Space, and Technology	Science	Science
Small Business	Small Business	Small Business
Standards of Official Conduct	Standards of Official Conduct	Standards of Official Conduct
Veterans' Affairs	Veterans' Affairs	Veterans' Affairs
Ways and Means	Ways and Means	Ways and Means

Sources: Politics in America, 1994 and *1996; Congressional Quarterly Weekly Report,* February 1, 1997, pp. 310–316; the U.S. House of Representatives and Senate Web sites <www.house.gov> and <www.senate.gov>, see the committee membership lists.

TABLE 8-2
Partisan Membership on Senate Committees

	Senate (17 Committees)				
	103rd Congress	*104th Congress*	*107th Congress Jan-June 2001*	*107th Congress July 2001- Dec 2002*	*108th Congress*
Agriculture, Nutrition, and Forestry	10D/8R	9R/8D	10R/10D	11D/10R	11R/10D
Appropriations	16D/13R	15R/13D	14R/14D	15D/14R	15R/14D
Armed Services	12D/10R	11R/10D	12R/12D	13D/12R	13D/12D
Banking, Housing, and Urban Affairs	11D/8R	9R/7D	10R/10D	11D/10R	11R/10D
Budget	12D/9R	12R/10D	11R/11D	12D/11R	12R/12D
Commerce, Science, and Transportation	11D/9R	10R/9D	11R/11D	12D/11R	12R/11D
Energy and Natural Resources	11D/9R	11R/7D	11R/11D	12D/11R	12R/11D
Environment and Public Works	10D/7R	9R/7D	9R/9D	10D/9R	10R/9D
Finance	11D/9R	11R/9D	10R/10D	11D/10R	11R/10D
Foreign Relations	11D/9R	10R/8D	9R/9D	10D/9R	10R/9D
Governmental Affairs	8D/6R	8R/7D	8R/8D	9D/8R	9R/8D
Health, Education, Labor	10D/7R	9R/7D	10R/10D	11D/10R	11R/10D
Indian Affairs	10D/8R	10R/7D	7R/7D	8D/7R	7R/6D
Judiciary	10D/8R	10R/8D	9R/9D	9D/9R	10R/9D
Rules and Administration	9D/7R	9R/7D	9R/9D	10D/9R	10R/9D
Small Business	12D/10R	10R/9D	9R/9D	10D/9R	10R/9D
Veterans' Affairs	7D/5R	8R/4D	7R/7D	8D/7R	8R/7D

*One Independent is included in the Democratic committee membership for July 2001–December 2002.

Sources: *Politics in America, 1994* and *1996; Congressional Quarterly Weekly Report,* February 1, 1997, pp. 310–316; the U.S. House of Representatives and Senate Web sites <www.house.gov> and <www.senate.gov>, see the committee membership lists.

a whole by providing specialized information to the chamber at large. At the same time, though, the very decentralization of the committee system allows for *particular* interests to be well represented on very specific subjects in which the stakes are high (and the visibility of committee actions is low). This dispersion of power and information serves both the whole Congress and its individual members, especially in the House of Representatives, where committee-based decentralization shapes how most bills advance and what comes out of legislative process.

Nevertheless, a fragmented committee system can and does serve more individualistic ends. Members often seek committee seats to serve their constituents' interests. Thus, in the House most Merchant Marine and Fisheries members traditionally came from coastal areas, whereas the House Agriculture Committee's members have had rural constituencies.[3] In the Senate, members can sit on more than one major committee, so the membership tends to be more dispersed. However, as in the House, most members of the Agriculture Committee have major farm constituencies in their states, and most of the members of the Energy Committee come from the West, where the federal government controls a great portion of the lands.

The Agriculture Committees in the House and the Senate provide good examples of how committee membership can dominate an entire policy area for decades. In the House, the Agriculture subcommittee responsible for tobacco policy has fought successfully to retain favored treatment for its crop in the face of a constant stream of attacks since the mid-1960s. As John R. Wright notes, "The agricultural price support system [for tobacco] remains solidly entrenched and virtually unchanged after more than twenty years of attack."[4] And no wonder, given the subcommittee's membership over the past thirty years (see Table 8–3). Despite the growing number of subcommittee members

TABLE 8–3

Membership on House Agriculture Committee Subcommittees Dealing with Tobacco Issues (Chairs Appear in Boldface)

Subcommittee on Tobacco, 1973	Subcommittee on Tobacco and Peanuts, 1983	Subcommittee on Specialty Crops and Natural Resources, 1993	Subcommittee on Risk Management and Specialty Crops, 1999	Subcommittee on Specialty Crops and Foreign Agriculture Programs, 2003
Stubblefield, D-Ky.	**Rose, D-N.C.**	**Rose, D-N.C.**	**Ewing, R-Ill.**	**Jenkins, R-Tenn.**
Jones, D-N.C.	Jones, D-N.C.	Baesler, D-Ky.	Barrett, R-Nebr.	Everett, R-Ala.
Mathis, D-Ga.	Hatcher, D-Ga.	Bishop, D-Ga.	Smith, R-Mich.	Combest, R-Tex.
Rose, D-N.C.	Thomas, D-Ga.	Brown, D-Calif.	Everett, R-Ala.	Gutknecht, R-Minn.
Litton, D-Mo.	Whitley, D-N.C.	Condit, D-Calif.	Lucas, R-Okla.	Hayes, R-N.C.
Mizell, R-N.C.	Tallon, D-S.C.	Clayton, D-N.C.	Chambliss, R-Ga.	Rehberg, R-Mont.
Wampler, R-Va.	English, D-Okla.	Thurman, D-Fla.	LaHood, R-Ill.	Rogers, R-Ala.
Madigan, R-Ill.	Stenholm, D-Tex.	Minge, D-Minn.	Moran, R-Kans.	Nunes, R-Calif.
Young, R-S.C.	Hopkins, R-Ky.	Inslee, D-Wash.	Thune, R-S.D.	McIntyre, D-N.C.
	Roberts, R-Kans.	Pomeroy, D-N.D.	Jenkins, R-Tenn.	Etheridge, D-N.C.
	Skeen, R-N.M.	English, D-Okla.	Gutknecht, R-Minn.	Hill, D-Ind.
	Franklin, R-Miss.	Stenholm, D-Tex.	Riley, R-Ala.	Scott, D-Ga.
		Peterson, D-Minn.	Walden, R-Oreg.	Marshall, D-Ga.
		Lewis, R-Fla.	Simpson, R-Ind.	Thompson, D-Miss.
		Emerson, R-Mo.	Ose, R-Calif.	Alexander, D-La.
		Doolittle, R-Calif.	Hayes, R-N.C.	
		Kingston, R-Ga.	Fletcher, R-Ky.	
		Goodlatte, R-Va.	Condit, D-Calif.	
		Dickey, R-Ark.	Brown, D-Calif.	
		Pombo, R-Calif.	Dooley, D-Calif.	
			Hilliard, D-Ala.	
			Pomeroy, D-N.D.	
			Bishop, D-N.D.	
			Goode, D-Va.	
			McIntyre, D-N.C.	
			Stabenow, D-Mich.	
			Etheridge, D-N.C.	
			John, D-La.	
			Boswell, D-Iowa	
			Lucas, D-Ky.	
			Thompson, D-Calif.	

Sources: Almanac of American Politics, 1974; Politics in America, 1984 and *1994;* Web site of the House Agriculture committee, <www.agriculture.house.gov.>.

and the expansion of their jurisdiction, the number of legislators from tobacco-growing states sitting on the subcommittee is far out of proportion to their overall numbers in the Congress. In 1973, with a single minority-party exception, all subcommittee members came from the South or border states. Ten years later, there was a bit more variation, but this region continued to dominate. By 1993, after some committee reshuffling,[5] the subcommittee on tobacco had ceased to exist as a separate entity, but the Specialty Crops subcommittee that handled tobacco policies was chaired by North Carolina Representative Charlie Rose who used his considerable power as chair to protect tobacco. With the Republican takeover in 1995, tobacco interests remained well protected in the Agriculture Committee. Moreover, Virginia Representative Thomas Bliley, an ardent defender of the tobacco industry, became chairman of the Commerce Committee, which had been actively antismoking under Democratic control. When a major overhaul of agriculture policy was enacted in the 107th Congress, Southerners (Texans) served as both chair and ranking member of the full Agriculture Committee, and North Carolina, Kentucky, and Tennessee had more members on the Specialty Crops subcommittee than ever before.

Richard Fenno's simple statement that "we get the kind of Congress that the members give us"[6] meshes seamlessly with his equally straightforward assertion that committees differ one from another.[7] Their environments (including the range of their interests and the scope of their policies) differ, as do the motivations of their members. Members construct the kind of committee system they want, and they seek positions on these committees based on their districts' interests (such as agriculture), their own policy aims (such as those concerning science and technology), or a desire for power within the institution (such as a seat on the House Appropriations Committee or Senate Finance Committee). Some committees are designed to monitor the members themselves, such as the House Standards of Official Conduct panel. In fact, chairing this committee proved dangerous to the political survival of moderate Republican Nancy Johnson (R-Conn.), who presided over the highly publicized investigation (1995–1997) of Speaker Gingrich. Perceptions that she was acting in a partisan manner allowed her 1996 Democratic challenger to come close to pulling a major upset. In the end, Representative Johnson won reelection and succeeded in producing a committee decision (reprimand and a $300,000 judgment) that won broad acceptance by the House. Interestingly, that a committee could reprimand a sitting Speaker testifies to the continuing independence of committees, even in times of strong partisanship.

COMMITTEES OVER TIME

From the first days of the Republic, both the House and the Senate have used committees to process and draft legislation. Early on, most of these were ad hoc bodies that reported back to their chambers on the specific bills. By 1810, however, the 142-member House had organized ten standing committees, including familiar panels such as those on Interstate and Foreign Commerce and Ways and Means. Increasingly, legislation began its journey toward passage within committees, rather than following from an initial floor discussion, in which the House would constitute itself into the committee of the whole and conduct less formal consideration of the issue at hand.[8] The Senate followed suit, and by 1820 it too had established a system of standing committees.[9] The existence of standing committees produced greater continuity from one Congress to the next, both in terms of organizational stability and members' ability to gain expertise on particular subject matters over time. Between the early 1800s and the onset of the Civil War, committees slowly became integral to the legislative process, even though most key decisions were made on the floor. The number of standing committees grew steadily (see Figure 8–1), but their memberships changed substantially from Congress to Congress.

Ironically, the expanding numbers of congressional committees in the era between 1862 and 1919 did *not* lead to increased fragmentation. Rather,

FIGURE 8-1
Number of Congressional Standing Committees, 1789-2000

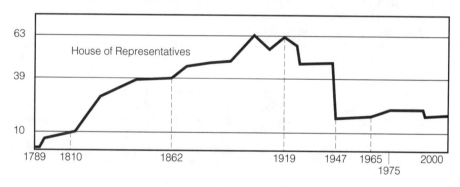

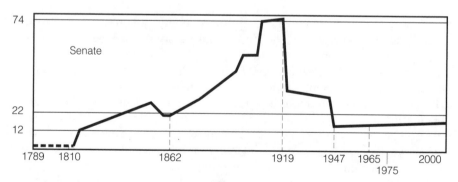

Sources: Adapted from Steven S. Smith and Christopher Deering, *Committees in Congress,* 2nd ed. (Washington, DC: Congressional Quarterly Press, 1990), p. 25, and Norman J. Ornstein, Thomas E. Mann, and Michael J. Malbin, eds., *Vital Statistics on Congress: 1997–1998* (Washington, DC: American Enterprise Institute/Congressional Quarterly), pp. 120–121.

committees most often served the purposes of both chambers' party leaders, who controlled appointments and the capacity to move legislation on the floor. Nonetheless, committees became increasingly important elements of the legislative process, and their memberships grew more stable as lawmakers constructed careers inside the Congress — careers that were often based on expertise accumulated in specialized committees and subcommittees. In large part, such stability grew from the reliance on committee-based seniority in determining which veteran legislators would serve on given committees in each new Congress, to the extent that "by the turn of the century, [seniority] had become such an 'iron-clad formula' that in both House and Senate party leaders' real discretion in committee assignments was limited primarily to new members."[10]

Although Representative Joseph Cannon (R-Ill.) would challenge the seniority basis for appointment during his speakership (1903–1911), the House's 1910 revolt against him and its decision to reduce the Speaker's powers dictated that seniority would prevail on committee assignments; in turn, this meant that both committees and their chairs would become increasingly powerful over the next fifty years. Roger Davidson and Walter Oleszek explain the workings and impact of a committee-based seniority system:

> The majority party member with the most years of consecutive service on a committee *automatically* became its chairman. *There were no other qualifications,* such as ability or party loyalty. As a result, committee chairmen owed little or nothing to party leaders and much less to presidents. This automatic selection process produced experienced, independent chairmen, but many members chafed under a system that concentrated authority in so few hands . . . [and] promoted the competent and incompetent alike. . . . [Moreover,] the system promoted members from "safe" one-party areas — especially conservative southern Democrats and midwestern Republicans — who could ignore party policies or national sentiments.[11]

Not only did the chambers accept the seniority system, they also steadily consolidated committee jurisdictions during the 1915–1965 period. The Legislative Reorganization Act of 1946 sharply reduced the number of committees in both House and Senate, to nineteen and fifteen, respectively (see Figure 8–1). Thus, most committee jurisdictions expanded tremendously, and the chairmen became even more powerful, leading the Congress into a relatively brief, but important, period of committee government (roughly 1947–1970).[12]

The generally conservative nature of the Congress and the modest goals of the Eisenhower administration (1953–1961) coexisted smoothly under the decentralized nature of committee government. Committee chairpeople, drawn disproportionately from the states of the old Confederacy, generally represented the sentiments of the southern Democrat–Republican Conservative Coalition that dominated the Congress. The presence of a pair of legendary congressional party leaders — Speaker Sam Rayburn (D-Tex.) and Senate

Majority Leader Lyndon Johnson (D-Tex.) — did little to reduce the committee chairs' dominance. Both Rayburn and Johnson would consult closely with them, and neither pushed a legislative agenda that was unacceptable to the committee barons. Eventually, large numbers of new members, most notably the herd of young, activist Democrats who arrived after the 1958 elections, would begin to restrict the power of committee chairs. But through the 1950s, congressional decision making was dominated by an informal oligarchy of senior party and committee leaders, along with a few other key legislators.

At the very apex of their independent power, committee chairs generally agreed on a modest agenda and an incremental approach to policy making. Within their individual committee domains, they might well be considered masters of their own turf, but in the 1950s most chairpeople acted more like brokers, largely content with making minor adjustments to the status quo.[13]

The Squeeze Play: Leaders and Members versus Committee Chairs in the House

The combination of full-committee decentralization and leadership oligarchy served to benefit chairs, like-minded party leaders, and various entrenched interest groups that profited from the predictability of the actions within their areas of concern. For policy activists and impatient rank-and-file legislators, especially majority party Democrats, government by strong committee was unresponsive and frustrating. Little change came immediately in the wake of the 1958 elections, even though Democratic majorities widened in both chambers.[14]

From 1959 though 1975, committees and their chairs faced dual threats to their independent influence — simultaneous efforts by party leaders to centralize their own authority and by junior members to win power by having more responsibilities delegated to subcommittees. By the mid-1970s, these movements had significantly weakened the authority of full committees and their chairs.[15] Nevertheless, the Congress, especially the House, continued to rely on its standing committees as fundamental building blocks for most of its actions.

In the twenty years after 1965, congressional reform reared its head in four special House initiatives, three similar Senate attempts, and two joint efforts.[16] In the House, making committees more responsive was a primary objective. But responsive to whom? Democratic Party leaders wanted more control in moving legislation through the House, backbench members of both parties wanted more responsibility and greater impact on the legislative process, and Republicans sought an effective voice on the legislative process. Between 1971 and 1975, the House acted consistently to reduce the authority and discretion of its full-committee chairs. The initial beneficiaries were clearly the junior Democrats, who gained both as individuals (and potential subcommittee chairs) and as members of the majority party caucus, which gained substantial authority. Democratic Party leaders also obtained a great deal of potential power, which they slowly began to exercise during the late 1970s.

Some key House changes came from reforms passed by the entire chamber, but the most profound developments emerged from the Democratic caucus, which effectively controlled the organization of the body. The two most important elements of reform focused on subcommittee rights and responsibilities and on the selection of committee chairs (and those of Appropriations Committee subcommittees). By 1974, the following limitations had been imposed on full committees and their chairs:

SUBCOMMITTEE REFORMS

Democrats could hold only one legislative subcommittee chair.

Subcommittee chairs could select one professional staff member for their panel.

A "Subcommittee Bill of Rights" guaranteed referral of legislation to subcommittees; bidding for subcommittee seats, which protects junior members; and fixed jurisdictions for subcommittees.

DEMOCRATIC CAUCUS/LEADERSHIP REFORMS

Automatic secret-ballot caucus votes would be held on the appointment of all committee chairs and Appropriations Committee subcommittee chairs at the beginning of each new Congress.

The Steering and Policy Committee was created and given committee appointment powers (stripped from Democratic membership of Ways and Means).

The Speaker would nominate Democratic members of the Rules Committee and also had the right to remove these members.

Despite the significant changes of the 1970s in subcommittee powers and authority (at least in the House) and the proliferation of these subunits, decentralization has not continued unabated. Indeed, the number of subcommittees has steadily declined, and both chambers moved toward consolidation in the 104th Congress (see Table 8–4). Republican adjustments in 1995 followed and

TABLE 8–4
Number of House and Senate Subcommittees, Selected Congresses, 1955–2003

	84th ('55–'56)	90th ('67–'68)	94th ('75–'76)	100th ('87–'88)	104th ('95–'96)	105th ('97–'98)	106th ('99–'00)	107th ('01–'02)	108th ('03–'04)
House subcommittees	99	154	172	160	86	88	89	87	88
Senate subcommittees	105	126	174	93	70	68	68	68	68

Sources: Vital Statistics on Congress: 1993–1994; Congressional Quarterly's Players, Politics, and Turf of the 104th Congress, special issue of *Congressional Quarterly,* March 25, 1995; *Politics in America: The 105th Congress, 1998* (Washington, DC: CQ Press, 1997), pp. 1607–1625; <www.capweb.net>, for the 106th–108th Congresses; the U.S. House and Senate Web sites, <www.clerk.house.gov> and <www.senate.gov>.

strengthened the Democratic movement toward committee consolidation in the previous ten years. In the end, large numbers of subcommittees with highly specialized jurisdictions proved unwieldy for the parent chambers and for party leaders who struggled to provide coherent legislative decision making.

Although the powers of full committees and their chairs were limited in the 1970s, subcommittees did not become dominant. Rather, particularly in the House, they emerged as important units, whose decisions often set the agenda for subsequent full-committee and floor actions. Subcommittees have proven most significant on relatively routine, low profile issues, where their specialized knowledge often helps to define problems and prospective legislative solutions. More controversial policies and more highly visible actions, such as health care reform or gun control proposals, move the locus of decision making to the full committee or to the House and Senate floors. In addition, chairs of House subcommittees are responsible to the party caucuses of their respective full committees, much as committee chairs must win approval of the party caucus as a whole, so individual chairs remain beholden to their party peers. To an extent, they must follow their colleagues' preferences, in order to lead them.[17]

Preserving the Status Quo Structure in Senate Committees

The Senate proved far more resistant to the forces of decentralization that swept the House in 1973 and 1974. This absence of substantial revision of committee structure and rules stemmed in large part from the Senate's individualism. Because senators could go to the floor and offer amendments at any time, chairs had to negotiate with the members of their committees, whether from the majority or minority party. Senators had more power in committees relative to their House counterparts, so their desire to overthrow or circumvent their chairs was less intense; thus no real changes were made in their party caucuses. Subcommittees in the Senate, with the exception of the Appropriations and Education Committees, never acquired the power to "mark up" draft bills, vote on them, and then send them up to the full committee. The full committee constituted the Senate venue for markup activity. Absent that key agenda-setting power, subcommittees mostly provided forums for hearings and policy discussion, rather than policy action. Senate subcommittee chairs often make reputations for themselves in certain policy areas, even when they cannot dominate the crafting of policy outcomes. In general, conflict has occurred less frequently between subcommittee chairs and full committee chairs in the Senate than in the House. Senators also hold multiple committee assignments, so that if they disagree with a chair of one of their committees, they can turn their attention to another, or the Senate floor, in attempting to influence policy.

Despite committees' lesser importance in the Senate, their dominance on the Senate floor still remains fairly strong. In other words, when a committee reports a bill to the full Senate, its members can be relatively certain that their bill will remain intact. Even though senators frequently offer amendments to bills from committees that they do not sit on, only 30 percent of these amendments ever pass.[18] And senators certainly realize that if committees were constantly overruled or overturned on the Senate floor, their own committee-based power would diminish. Overall, and in partial contrast to the House, the seniority rule remains alive and well in the Senate in determining committee chairmanships, even when the majority party may not want to grant the position to a particular senator.

Such was the case, over the past two decades, in the committee-related shifts of recently retired Senator Jesse Helms (R-N.C.). Helms concurrently held seats on the Agriculture and Foreign Relations committees, rising by seniority to chair the Agriculture panel when the Republicans controlled the Senate from 1981 to 1987. Helms could serve North Carolina tobacco interests from this position, and his promise to retain it despite a chance to become chair of Foreign Relations helped him win a tight reelection campaign in 1984. Still, the highly visible Foreign Relations committee offered great possibilities for the conservative Helms, who chose to serve as that panel's ranking minority member in 1987, after the Republicans lost their Senate majority. Typically, when the chamber switches majority control, the former chairman of a committee becomes its highest ranking minority member. Senator Richard Lugar (R-Ind.) had served as Foreign Relations chair in 1985–1986, and he challenged the more-senior Helms's right to the ranking position. Despite the Republican caucus's general agreement as to Lugar's effectiveness as chairman, Helms won the ranking position on a 24–17 vote (of all Republican senators). Many moderate Republicans supported Helms, not because they favored either his conservative, even obstructionist, brand of politics, but because they endorsed the seniority principle. By forcing his colleagues to reaffirm the importance of seniority, Senator Helms succeeded in maintaining powerful positions on two important committees, despite the fact that his ideological and policy positions were much more conservative than those of his party colleagues. Helms assumed the chairmanship of Foreign Relations in 1995 and held that position until the Senate switched control in 2001. After Helms retired in 2002, his old competitor, Richard Lugar, became chair of the Foreign Relations Committee in 2003 as its most senior majority member.

The Republican Era: Reforming Committees and Controlling Them in the House and Senate

Like the postreform Democrats, Republicans saw a need to limit the autonomy of committees. Unlike the Democrats, however, the House GOP did not engage in a pincer movement that squeezed committee chairs between strengthened subcommittees and stronger party leaders. Rather, under the initial direction of Speaker Gingrich, the Republicans sought to tilt the balance of power toward the party leadership and away from the committees/subcommittees. Despite some retrenchments after the 104th Congress, the Republican leadership, acting with the consent of the party's rank and file, succeeded at restraining the independent power of committees more than at any time since the 1910–1920 era. In short, "committee leaders have been put on effective notice that they are expected to be servants of the party."[19] Although the Republican majority would pass a set of committee-oriented reforms (see below), the most important initial indications of the party leadership's ascendance came with the appointment of committee chairs in the 104th Congress. Speaker Gingrich and the top leadership "simply asserted the right to choose committee chairs"[20] and in three instances ignored seniority to select chairs for the important Appropriations, Commerce, and Judiciary panels who would aggressively and effectively carry out the Republican agenda. Moreover, all committee chairs knew that they owed their appointment to the Speaker. Both in the rush of the hundred-day whirlwind consideration of the Contract with America in 1995 and during the remainder of the 104th Congress, Speaker Gingrich, Majority Leader Dick Armey (R-Tex.), and the rest of the leadership could legitimately consider the committee chairs as their agents as they moved bills on to the agenda and through the legislative process.

Specifically, the Republicans adopted various significant alterations in committee operations:[21]

▶ Reduce committee staff by one-third and consolidate control of staff under full committee chair.

▶ Limit full committee and subcommittee chairs to six-year terms.

▶ Allow full committee chairs to appoint subcommittee chairs and to control subcommittee staffing and budgets at the full committee level.[22]

▶ Limit most committees to five subcommittees.

▶ Allow members to chair only one full committee or subcommittee.

▶ Permit members to serve on only two full committees and four subcommittees, with exceptions granted by full party conference (Republicans) or caucus (Democrats).

▶ Abolish proxy voting in committee and so-called rolling quorums (when votes are "held open" for absent members to cast their votes).

▶ Reconfigure the committee system by eliminating the District of Columbia, Merchant Marine and Fisheries, and Post Office and Civil Service Committees and by shifting some committee jurisdictions, including a reduction in scope of Commerce Committee responsibilities.

▶ Require that, with few exceptions, committee meetings be open to the public and subject to broadcast, if requested.

Although the limitations on subcommittees and the full-committee control of staff did enhance the power of chairs, most of the other changes have weakened committees. For example, no longer can chairpersons dominate committee decisions by controlling the proxy votes of their partisan colleagues, a tactic often employed in the past by Democrats. And term limits for chairs ensure that Republican committee leaders cannot gain undue advantage from extended tenure — either by building up debts or by shaping expectations about future rewards. In addition, the Republican leadership has often employed party task forces — whose business is conducted in private — to move important legislation. Committees and their chairs thus face the threat of an alternative venue for the development of legislation.[23] Without question, the party–committee balance of power has shifted in the House, as Republican leaders have accomplished much of what their Democratic counterparts would have liked to have done. That is, they now exercise greater control over the potentially autonomous committee units. In the postreform Congress the Democratic caucus and the Republican conference alike have chosen to limit the clout of even the strongest, most assertive committee chairs, who must respond to their own committee members, the party leadership, the party caucus, and the wishes of the House as a whole, as expressed through a majority of the 435 members.

When the GOP regained its Senate majority in 1994, committee changes were far less noticeable, but the new cohort of freshman Republican senators pressed hard for a more unified majority party, as well as more party control over committee chairs and assignments. The partisan overlay that dramatically affected the role of House committees had its own impact in the Senate. As Senate membership has changed from a Democratic to a Republican majority, from older to younger legislators, from moderate partisans to more intense ones, the role of committee chairs as promoters of partisan policies came under increased scrutiny. The "young guns versus older moderates" conflict came to the forefront on the vote for a balanced budget amendment in 1995. As the vote approached, virtually all Republicans and a substantial number of Democrats combined to produce sixty-six votes, one shy of the two-thirds majority necessary to approve submitting a constitutional amendment to the states. Only one Republican, veteran Appropriations Chairman Mark Hatfield (R-Ore.), opposed the proposal, but he would not alter his long-held opposition to a constitutional amendment.

After the amendment lost by a one-vote margin,[24] several junior Republican senators literally marched down to the majority leader's office and requested a party caucus for the express purpose of disciplining Senator Hatfield and possibly stripping him of his chairmanship. The leading proponents of retribution, such as Senators Rick Santorum (R-Pa.) and Connie Mack (R-Fla.), had served in the House and felt strongly about enforcing partisan discipline. At the very least these senators wanted to send a message to Senator Hatfield and other moderate chairs (e.g., Rhode Island's John Chaffee) that such party defections would not be easily accepted. Although Hatfield escaped sanctions, Majority Leader Dole did respond to the young guns by appointing a Leadership Working Group, well populated by former House members with ties to Speaker Gingrich, to explore the relationships between the body of Senate Republicans, their party leaders, and the committees and chairs.[25] In the end, Senate Republicans adopted a set of modified working-group proposals that included six-year term limits for committee chairmen and minor party leaders, the adoption of a party agenda at the start of a new Congress (by a three-fourths vote), secret ballot selection of committee chairmen by committee members and subsequent ratification of the choice by the Republican Conference, and a limitation on members to a single full or subcommittee chairmanship, except on Appropriations. All of these provisions went into effect as of the 105th Congress in January 1997.

Although Senate Republicans did feel many of the same pressures for partisan control as did their House colleagues, once they returned to the majority their responses were in keeping with the normal, evolutionary nature of change in the upper house. Senate party leaders neither sought nor won any significant new weapons in their efforts to limit the individualism that continues to characterize their chamber. Partisanship has certainly increased in the Senate, but not to the point at which it can overcome the individualism, only partly based in committees, that remains the core characteristic of that body.

The election of 2000 and subsequent events in 2001 highlight the limitations of the power of the majority party over the committee system in the Senate. The Senate stood tied at fifty Republicans and fifty Democrats in January 2001, the beginning of the 107th Congress. Despite the fact that the vice president was a Republican and thus gave the Republicans a majority by virtue of his ability to be the fifty-first vote, the Senate Democrats successfully argued that every committee should be evenly divided between the parties because in fact the Republicans did not have a numerical majority. Minority Leader Daschle basically threatened to filibuster the resolution that officially organized the Senate if the Republicans did not agree to parity in committee assignments. The leaders reached an agreement whereby the Republicans would chair each committee but the number of senators from each party would be equal (see Table 8–2). Things changed for committees when Republican Senator James Jeffords announced his switch to Independent in May 2001, and voted with the Democrats to give them a de facto 51-49 majority. It took a month, but at the end of June 2001, the leaders worked out a new arrangement whereby the Democrats gained the chairmanship and an additional seat on each committee (see Table 8–2).

DIFFERENT COMMITTEES AND THEIR VALUE TO MEMBERS

In that the bulk of legislative work takes place within committees, obtaining good committee assignments is crucial to most legislators.[26] But what constitutes a "good" assignment? This depends on members' motivations. To be sure, virtually all want to be reelected, so the first thought of many newcomers is to gain committee slots that will help them win reelection.[27] Many committees can benefit legislators from virtually any district. The more powerful the committee, the more this is true. The committees that write tax laws and control appropriations certainly contribute to their members' reelection successes, but much more important are their roles in fulfilling two other goals of legislators: to influence policy and obtain power within the House and Senate.[28]

Although many veteran legislators who enjoy seniority and key committee positions are able to exercise more internal power and affect a wider range of policies than their less senior colleagues, most representatives and senators can use their committee service to pursue multiple goals. Comparing three cohorts of new House members, Smith and Deering found a mix of motivations for seeking committee seats, especially on panels offering power and prestige. In both chambers, however, committees generally serve the members' interests. The jurisdictional fragmentation of the committees allows lawmakers, especially representatives, to find assignments that serve their particular mix of goals.[29]

Historically, junior members have waited a term or two before moving to the House's "power" committees of Rules, Appropriations, and Ways and Means. In the 104th Congress, however, given the large number of slots that opened up for Republicans, first-termers won six seats on Appropriations, three on Ways and Means, and most remarkably, one on Rules, where insiders and the leadership dominate.[30] In addition, three first-term Republicans won appointments as subcommittee chairs. In the Senate, the Finance Committee, Armed Services, and Appropriations Committees are the most sought after committee seats. In the 104th, there was not the same amount of rapid ascension among first-year senators as in the House because the number of Senate committee slots did not open up to the same extent when the Republicans assumed majority control.

The Republican House leadership continued to reward the 104th freshmen in the committee appointments for the 105th Congress, where sixteen of the remaining fifty-nine (27 percent) have received seats on one of the traditional power committees: Rules, Appropriations, and Ways and Means.[31] Such a pattern is important for two reasons. In historical context, no post–World War II class has ever occupied more than fifteen power committee slots at one time. This augurs well for the long-term influence of these members. Second, many of these members do not come from safe constituencies. Indeed, of the four who won power committee seats in the 105th Congress, none won reelection in 1996 with more than 52 percent of the vote. Republican leaders anticipated that such marginal-seat legislators would benefit from these appointments, but that they would not abandon the party on tough votes to cut spending. In a ideologically homogeneous party, one GOP staffer noted that while "Democrats historically have rewarded their loyal members, Republicans are much more of a team."[32] In sum, Republicans have confidence that their electorally endangered colleagues will not fall prey to the temptation to vote for more spending (or for smaller cuts) than their leaders desire.

Beyond the motivations of their members, committees also reflect a range of environments such as the visibility of their actions or the partisanship of their decision making. Holding high-profile hearings on health care reform, for example, differs substantially from writing regulations for purchasing military equipment. Various legislators and their committee roles illustrate these differences among committees. Representative John Murtha (D-Pa.), a veteran legislator with a talent for cutting deals and avoiding publicity, was perfectly placed on the low-profile but very powerful Appropriations Committee, where he served as a key subcommittee chair. On the other hand, former Senator Jesse Helms (R-N.C.), with his desire for the spotlight, enjoyed his role first as ranking member and then as chairman of the highly visible Foreign Relations Committee. Combining a penchant for publicity and an extensive issue agenda, for sixteen years Representative Henry Waxman (D-Calif.) operated effectively as an Energy and Commerce subcommittee chair, where he successfully pursued a host of initiatives on health and environment issues.

THE CONTINGENT NATURE OF COMMITTEE POWER

Committees are advantaged by their positive capacity, within a large and diverse Congress, to write detailed legislation on hundreds of separate, often complex, topics. Committees possess the tactical advantages of great informational resources, the ability to block legislation desired by other lawmakers, and the capacity to shape conference committee agreements at the end of the legislative process.[33] This monopoly over information, along with its bill-crafting role (which the party leadership protects on the floor), gives committee members power over policy. In the Senate, committee power is lessened in that individual senators can offer floor amendments to any bill, especially those from committees that they do not sit on. Still, in both chambers, the best way to influence policy in a specific issue area is to win a seat on the committee of jurisdiction. In short, committees remain important in framing most legislation.

Committees differ over time, and their profile can change with emerging public policy agendas or new leadership. An active, high-profile chair can energize a committee and bring it greater public notice and prestige, while an older or more reticent chair can diminish a committee's clout. For example, when Dan Rostenkowski (D-Ill.) ran the House Ways and Means Committee in the 1980s and early 1990s it was a committee to be reckoned with in the House and in negotiations with the president. But under the leadership of Bill Archer (R-Tex.) from 1995 to 2000, the Ways and Means committee was largely reduced to a rubber stamp for the party leadership and Speaker Gingrich. Part of that reduction in power stemmed from the term limits imposed on committee chairs, which prevented them from building extended power relationships with either their own committee members or other committee chairs. Chairman Archer retired from the House in 2000, both because he had to relinquish his committee chairmanship and because the committee itself had lost much of its independent clout.

The following case follows the path of two committee chairs and one subcommittee chair in the House Energy and Commerce Committee over a period of twenty years. It illustrates the extent to which individual House members can take advantage of their committee power and under what circumstances party leaders can take that power away.

Committee Power and Entrepreneurship: The Case of the House Energy and Commerce Committee

After the sudden death of Representative John Dingell, Sr., in 1955, his son and namesake won the special election for his seat and has served ever since, building seniority on the Energy and Commerce Committee (the Energy label was dropped in 1995) and becoming chairman in 1981 after thirteen terms of service. As chair, John Dingell, Jr. (D-Mich.), expanded the committee's already extensive jurisdiction, which touched on most important domestic issues.[34] Supported by a large, talented staff that reflected the chair's instinct for the jugular, Dingell influenced governmental approaches to dozens, even hundreds, of issues ranging from health care to university research procedures. At the same time, he protected his basic constituencies in his Detroit district and within the entire auto industry. This has meant that he has fought relentlessly on its behalf against clean air legislation, remarking unapologetically, "That's what I'm sent here to do."[35]

During the 1980s, Representative Dingell and his committee labored fruitlessly to modify clean air legislation, failing in part because the Energy and Commerce Committee was split over various provisions of an extremely complex bill.[36] In particular, as head of the full committee, Dingell had to contend with Representative Henry Waxman (D-Calif.), who chaired the subcommittee on health and the environment and who represented a Los Angeles district that suffered greatly from auto emissions. The smart and politically savvy Waxman, who challenged a more senior member to win his chairmanship, has been both a worthy adversary and an often valuable ally for Dingell throughout his almost thirty years on the committee.

Even more important than the intracommittee politics of the 1980s was the unqualified opposition of President Ronald Reagan to any new law regulating air quality. Richard Cohen bluntly recounts:

> The end of the Reagan era meant that lawmakers could no longer posture on clean-air legislation. . . . The key change . . . happened at the White House: Nixon and Carter supported clean-air laws and legislation went through. Reagan opposed it so nothing happened. With the [1988] election . . . of George Bush, the self-proclaimed "environmental president," the gridlock of divided government would no longer be an excuse for inaction.[37]

For John Dingell and Henry Waxman, President Bush's (senior) potential cooperation meant that they could finally legislate, if they could first find common ground between their own positions and then with the president's approach.

Understanding that indefinite delay was no longer possible, and unsure of his ability to control results either within his committee or on the House floor, Dingell sought to forge an alliance with his subcommittee adversary (on clean air legislation, at least). Waxman had begun to rework the Bush administration's proposed bill in his subcommittee and had made some progress by late 1989, when Dingell joined the discussions. Within a few days, the unlikely duo announced an agreement on the difficult issue of tailpipe emissions, as well as several related items. Dingell had placed his trust in Waxman, and vice versa; these two skilled legislators could then join together to work on behalf of the bill, even as their own constituents expressed reservations about the unexpected alliance.

Although it would take several months for the full committee to agree on a bill and more than year for clean air legislation to win final congressional approval, the Dingell–Waxman deal held firm; committee member Representative Phil Sharp (D-Ind.) observed that the agreement "allowed the process to go forward dramatically and . . . made it clear that we were going to move forward on a bill."[38] In sum, neither the full-committee chair nor the subcommittee chair felt assured of victory, so they reached a compromise agreement, forged in private, that they hoped would serve as a basis for building an entire bill that could survive intact on the House floor and through the remainder of the legislative process. They more or less succeeded. At least as important for the principals, Waxman won a substantial number of policy points, and Dingell, in the words of one legislator, "prevailed on issues important to him *and he kept control of the committee.*"[39] Even for a strong committee chair like John Dingell, power remained contingent on the support of his committee members and the ability to win majorities on the House floor.

Thomas Bliley and the Commerce Committee

The Republican era in the House brought with it no old-line committee chairmen, like John Dingell, who had accumulated knowledge, turf, staff, and power over an extended congressional career. In fact, no House Republican in the 104th Congress had ever served in the majority. Dingell's successor as Commerce Committee chair, Thomas Bliley (R-Va.), illustrated both the similarities and differences between how Democrats and Republicans have operated in the postreform House. First elected in 1980 (at age 48) and a natty dresser, complete with bow tie, Bliley consistently reflected his Virginia roots as an aggressive defender of the tobacco industry. Still, fourteen years of service on Commerce, with its wide jurisdictional range, did expose him to many pressing national issues. In particular, his work on the Health/Environment and Telecommunications subcommittees gave him important experience in crucial policy areas.

Standing second in seniority on the Commerce Committee, Representative Bliley would have played an important role in health and telecommunications legislation in the 104th Congress, but Speaker Gingrich elevated him to the panel's chairmanship with firm expectations that he would mesh the committee's work with the Republican agenda. Bliley observed: "The Speaker made it very clear from the outset that he looks to the chairmen of the committees, and that the chairman runs his or her committee."[40] In other words, committees were to serve as the agents of the party leadership, and indirectly the Republican members at large.

Bliley discovered that — no matter how well he ran his committee — there were unspoken but real limits to the freedom granted by the Speaker. On telecommunications deregulation, the central issue for Commerce in the 104th Congress, the chairman initially succeeded in leading the committee to adopt a bill that generally favored the long distance side of the industry at the expense of the regional Bell companies. As one participant noted, "He was in clear command without being dictatorial," and the committee voted in favor of the Bliley package by an overwhelming 38-5 margin in May 1995.[41] Given the huge stakes involved in deregulation, the regional Bells, with their strong local presence across the country, appealed to the House leadership to revise the legislation. Less than two months after the lopsided Commerce vote, Bliley capitulated to Speaker Gingrich and other leaders in adding "refinements" to the committee's bill. In fact, the Republican leadership dictated major new provisions in the telecommunications package that benefited the regional Bells. In a meeting with executives of the long distance companies, Bliley "appeared to be reading from a script," stating "he did so because he was under instructions by the leadership. . . ."[42] The apparently powerful chairman had become a messenger for the party leadership.

In the end, this was but a single chapter in the long, complex story of telecommunications reform, but it dramatically illustrates the essential relationship between party leadership and committees in the early days of the Republican era. Representative Bliley owed his chairmanship to Speaker Gingrich, both in general (the creation of a Republican majority) and in particular (the bypassing of a more senior committee member). The chairman was in no position to protest the leadership's desire for substantial policy changes in telecommunications policy. Still, the passage of the complex piece of legislation, which included far more than telephone deregulation issues, stood as a victory for Chairman Bliley, who helped win the support of Representative Dingell by not forcing too much deregulation, too soon, on consumers (e.g., a three-year delay in freeing large cable systems from some regulatory rules). In the 105th and 106th Congresses, Bliley gained more leeway in setting the Commerce Committee's agenda, in part due to the narrowing Republican majority in the House. Given the broad reach of Commerce's jurisdiction, Bliley could push more of his own priority items through the legislative process.

Ultimately the same reforms within the House GOP that allowed Bliley to jump the line to become chair cost him the chairmanship in 2000. The limit of six years as a chair meant that Bliley had to give up the post after the 2000 elections. It is unclear which was worse — losing control of the majority and hence the committee chairs, as with John Dingell, or losing the chair even when your party still controlled the House. One telling piece of evidence is that John Dingell remains in the House, and even won a hard-fought, post-redistricting primary in 2002. In contrast Bliley, after twenty years in the House, decided to retire in 2000 (just as Bill Archer had done) rather than return to being one more senior House member.

The Last Element of Committee Power:
Conference Committees between the House and Senate

All committee chairs have one last chance to shape policy outcomes even after a bill has passed the full House or Senate. Most, though not all, major legislation requires a conference committee, which is an interchamber committee composed of representatives from both the House and Senate who meet to iron out the differences in the versions of the bills passed by the two chambers. The ability of standing committees to influence the outcomes of conference committees has been labeled "ex post veto" power.[43] By virtue of their members' potentially influential participation in conference committee decisions near the end of the legislative process, committees can exercise substantial power, especially when their original proposals are modified on the floor of the House or Senate. The conferees may choose not to lobby hard against such changes; rather, they might support a version of the legislation closer to the committee's original proposition. The full House or Senate can only vote a conference report up or down; thus, committee members can often have the last word in terms of the shape of a given piece of legislation. Of course, this power is hardly absolute. One of the chambers may reject the conference version or, on major legislation, there may be conferees from several committees, which negates any advantage a single panel might enjoy.[44]

Prior to 1994, most conference committees consisted of the committee chair and ranking member, as well as subcommittee chairs from each chamber. The party leaders would appoint the conferees, but typically they relied heavily on the advice of the chair and ranking member as to whom to appoint. The average number of conferees from the House hovers around twenty-five, and the Senate usually sends twelve members to a conference.[45] For very large omnibus or multi-committee bills, the number of conferees can exceed one hundred members from the House and Senate combined.

Traditionally, conferees from each chamber choose to vigorously defend their chamber's version of the legislation at hand. After 1994 in the House and 1996 in the Senate, party leaders in both chambers took advantage of their power to appoint conferees to put themselves or their lieutenants on conference committees; in some instances, they could drastically rewrite major portions of bills that had already passed both the House and Senate. Because a conference report (the final version of the bill that gets sent to the president) contains a multitude of provisions, it is nearly impossible to amend on the floor without unraveling the entire bill. The party leaders relied on having enough members with a stake in passing a bill to maintain support for the conference report; they would accept the conferees' negotiations and send the bill to the president. Members have often complained about their lack of influence at this stage. Indeed, on the 1996 telecommunications bill, most House members, even Republicans, argued that they were being shut out of the negotiations.[46]

One hotly contested conference occurred during the deliberation of the 2002 Farm Bill. In October 2001 the House Agriculture Committee, chaired by Larry Combest (R-Tex.), passed a major overhaul of agriculture policy that reinstated subsidies and crop support payments. The Senate Agriculture Committee, under the leadership of Tom Harkin (D-Iowa), passed a much different version of the bill in February 2002. In both the House and Senate, attempts at amending the bill on the floor largely failed to change the committee-reported language. And the Senate bill cost almost $9 billion more than its House counterpart.[47] In addition, the Senate bill was generally more liberal because it reflected the work of Democratic majorities in committee and on the floor. It thus included specific provisions designed to promote environmental conservation, increase funds for food stamps and rural development, and cap the amount of financial subsidies that individual farmers could receive at a much lower number than did the House bill. After two months of negotiation, primarily between the two Agriculture committees, and the intervention of Senate Majority Leader Tom Daschle (D-S.D.) and President George W. Bush, the two chambers essentially split the difference on most of their provisions. Because President Bush weighed in, the Republican House conferees were relegated to a being a third party in the negotiations, acceding to the wishes of the White House. In May 2002, the president signed a final version of the bill that included: (1) subsidies for sugar, corn, grain, wheat, wool, peanuts; (2) payments to small farmers if their crop prices fell below a set level; (3) a subsidy for the dairy industry; and (4) increased funds for the food stamp program.[48] In this major piece of legislation, the conference process generally preserved the influence of the Agriculture committees in both chambers over farm and rural policy.

HOUSE AND SENATE COMMITTEES IN A PARTISAN ERA

In assessing the roles of committees and committee chairs in the contemporary House and Senate, it is perhaps most important to recognize that committee leaders increasingly act either as or with party leaders. The willingness and capacity to act effectively with the party leadership has grown more significant for members seeking prestige committee appointments. Political scientists Lawrence Evans and Walter Oleszek, close students of congressional reform, argue that the post-1994 shifts in committee structure and practice have reflected partisan rationales. They conclude: "The personal power agendas of Republican committee leaders were dominated by rank-and-file Republicans who wanted to center power in the leadership and the Republican Conference as a whole. . . . [Thus,] throughout the mid-1990s, key decisions on major bills were made in private by Republican leaders rather than openly, with minority party participation, in the primary committees of jurisdiction."[49]

Since the fall of Newt Gingrich in 1998, Republican chairs have recovered some of their autonomy, as their party leadership's control of the House became more tenuous. Although some Republicans sought to ensure that chairs would support the leadership on virtually all votes, Speaker Hastert argued that some real cross-party alliances would be necessary between chairs and ranking members.[50] More importantly, the chairpersons who were put in place by Gingrich have relinquished their chairs because of the six-year term limit. This limitation precluded any Republican from developing the kind of tenure that Representative Dingell used to his advantage. Moreover, there is a new group of Republican committee chairs who have had time to build experience and electoral safety since 1994, and thus can act more independently of the party leadership than their predecessors. This freedom is tempered somewhat by the election of a Republican president; the Republican party leaders and committee chairs now take direction from their president in a way that contrasts with their freedom during the Clinton years.

In the Senate, the 108th Congress produced a set of younger and older senators committee chairs, resulting in a group with varied experience as committee leaders. Moreover, the committee chairs may be empowered because the new majority leader, Bill Frist (R-Tenn.), has not risen through the ranks of the party caucus and does not have the same kind of internal Senate party clout wielded by his predecessor, Trent Lott. The wild card in committee–party relations in the Senate may very well be President Bush, who played a major, behind-the-scenes role in promoting Frist to majority leader. President Bush will expect Senate Republicans to back his agenda, and he will expect majority leader Frist to try to enforce party unity in the committees and on the floor.

Overall, committee and party leaders will continue to view the legislative process from different perspectives. Committee chairs desire a degree of autonomy; party leaders want greater control and coordination. It is unlikely that such a fundamental division will be easily bridged, especially in an era of declining resources and difficult, often painful, decisions directed at programs and favored constituencies. As congressional scholar Steven Smith concludes, "The *direction* of change over the last two decades or so — toward less autonomous committees and a less committee-oriented process — must not be confused with the *degree* of change."[51] Although committee power has been diminished by the assignment process, bill referrals, and the growing importance of omnibus legislative packages, committees continue to represent the source of most legislation. Indeed, the very size of the congressional policy agenda requires that committees retain substantial power, and House and Senate members continue to have a strong motivation to use their committees to shape policy outcomes.

CHAPTER BIBLIOGRAPHY

Cohen, Richard E. *Rostenkowski: The Pursuit of Power and the End of the Old Politics*. Chicago: Ivan Dee Publishers, 1999.

Evans, C. Lawrence. *Leadership in Committee: A Comparative Analysis of Leadership Behavior in the U.S. Senate*. Ann Arbor: University of Michigan Press, 1991.

Maltzman, Forrest. *Competing Principals: Committees, Parties, and the Organization of Congress*. Ann Arbor: University of Michigan Press, 1997.

Schickler, Eric. *Disjointed Pluralism: Institutional Innovation and the Development of the U.S. Congress*. Princeton, NJ: Princeton University Press, 2001.

NOTES

1. Woodrow Wilson, *Congressional Government* (Baltimore: Johns Hopkins University Press, 1981 [original publication date, 1885]), p. 69.

2. Keith Krehbiel, *Information and Legislative Organization* (Ann Arbor: University of Michigan Press, 1990).

3. Theodore J. Lowi, "How the Farmers Get What They Want," *Reporter,* September 14, 1964, pp. 34–37; William Browne, *Cultivating Constituents* (Lawrence: University Press of Kansas, 1995); John Mark Hansen, *Gaining Access* (Chicago: University of Chicago Press, 1991).

4. John R. Wright, "PAC Contributions and Voting on Tobacco Policy in the U.S. Congress, 1981–2000" (paper presented at the Midwest Political Science Association Meetings, April 2002).

5. As of the 103rd Congress (1993–1994), committees were limited to six subcommittees. The Agriculture Committee chose to eliminate all crop-specific committees, replacing them with three umbrella panels that dealt with general farm commodities, livestock, and specialty crops, respectively. More generally on the politics of jurisdiction, see David C. King, *Turf Wars* (Chicago: University of Chicago Press, 1997).

6. Richard F. Fenno, Jr., "If, as Ralph Nader Says, Congress Is the 'Broken Branch,' How Come We Love Our Congressmen So Much?" in Norman Ornstein, ed., *Congress in Change* (New York: Praeger, 1975), p. 287.

7. Richard F. Fenno, Jr., *Congressmen in Committees* (Boston: Little, Brown, 1973).

8. Smith and Deering, *Committees in Congress,* 2nd ed., p. 26. The House ordinarily dissolves into the committee of the whole to conduct its legislative business under lenient rules that allow for the more efficient conduct of business. Decisions made in the committee of the whole are formalized in subsequent passage through the House.

9. Elaine K. Swift, *The Making of an American Senate* (Ann Arbor: University of Michigan Press, 1996).

10. Smith and Deering, *Committees in Congress,* 2nd ed., p. 35.

11. Roger Davidson and Walter Oleszek, *Congress and Its Members,* 4th ed. (Washington, DC: CQ Press, 1994), p. 207; emphasis added.

12. See Smith and Deering, *Committees in Congress,* 2nd ed., pp. 38ff. Why, one might ask, did many committee chairs allow their positions to be eliminated,

especially in the House? Many chaired panels with modest jurisdictions, and the 1946 act provided benefits to those who were displaced and to those who had anticipated becoming chairs. Committees were granted several staff members, and their powers to oversee the executive branch were enhanced. In practice, committee chairs controlled many of these resources and opportunities, and consolidation of the number of committees worked hand in hand with the rise in resources to empower the chairs as individuals and as a group.

13. Ibid., p. 45. More generally, see William S. White, *Citadel: The Story of the U.S. Senate* (New York: Harper & Row, 1956); Clem Miller, *Member of the House* (New York: Scribner's 1962); and various articles by Ralph K. Huitt, several contained in Huitt and Robert L. Peabody, eds., *Congress: Two Decades of Analysis* (New York: Harper & Row, 1969).

14. For a detailed account of the obstacles to shifts in power, see James Sundquist, *Politics and Policy* (Washington, DC: Brookings Institution, 1968).

15. For an excellent contemporaneous examination of these changes, see Norman Ornstein, "Causes and Consequences of Congressional Change: Subcommittee Reforms in the House of Representatives, 1970–73," in Ornstein, ed., *Congress in Change*, (New York: Praeger, 1975), pp. 88–114.

16. Smith and Deering, *Committees in Congress*, 2nd ed., p. 47. See also, among others, Roger Davidson and Walter Oleszek, *Congress Against Itself* (Bloomington: Indiana University Press, 1977), and various works by Leroy N. Riselbach, including, most recently, *Congressional Reform: The Changing Modern Congress* (Washington, DC: CQ Press, 1994), which contains a comprehensive list of congressional reform efforts from 1970–1993.

17. The classic study here is John Manley's analysis of Ways and Means Committee chairman Representative Wilbur Mills (D-Ark.): "Wilbur Mills: A Study of Congressional Influence," *American Political Science Review* 63 (1969): pp. 442–464.

18. Steven Smith. *Call to Order* (Washington, DC: Brookings Institution Press, 1989).

19. Steven S. Smith, quoted in David S. Cloud, "Shakeup Time," *Congressional Quarterly's Players, Politics, and Turf of the 104th Congress,* supplement to *Congressional Quarterly Weekly Report,* March 25, 1995, p. 9. More generally, see Christopher Deering and Steven Smith, *Committees in Congress*, 3rd ed. (Washington, DC: CQ Press, 1997).

20. John H. Aldrich and David W. Rohde, "Conditional Party Government Revisited: Majority Party Leadership and the Committee System in the 104th Congress," *Extension of Remarks/Legislative Studies Newsletter,* December 1995, p. 5.

21. Some of these were incorporated into the Rules of the House, which are adopted at the start of each congress; others were adopted internally as practices of the Republican Conference. For a more extensive discussion, see Lawrence Evans and Walter Oleszek, *Congress under Fire* (Boston: Houghton Mifflin, 1997), pp. 91–101.

22. This set of practices effectively reversed the "Subcommittee Bill of Rights," adopted by the Democrats in 1973.

23. See Steven S. Smith and Eric D. Lawrence, "Party Control in The Republican Congress," in Lawrence C. Dodd and Bruce I. Oppenheimer, eds., *Congress Reconsidered,* 6th ed. (Washington: CQ Press, 1997), pp. 177–178.

24. The final vote was 65-35, with Majority Leader Bob Dole voting with the minority so that he would have the standing, as a member of the losing side, to move for reconsideration of the amendment if he could later find another supporter. This did not happen.

25. Evans and Oleszek, *Congress under Fire,* p. 155.

26. Kenneth Shepsle, *The Giant Jigsaw Puzzle* (Chicago: University of Chicago Press, 1978).

27. The classic statement here comes from David Mayhew, *Congress: The Electoral Connection* (Cambridge, MA: Harvard University Press, 1974).

28. Fenno, *Congressman in Committees,* p. 1.

29. See Smith and Deering, *Committees in Congress,* 2nd ed., p. 110.

30. In the 103rd Congress, in comparison, two Democratic freshmen won Appropriations slots and one was grudgingly accepted by Representation Dan Rostenkowski (D-Ill.) for Ways and Means.

31. See Tim Barnett and Burdett Loomis, "The 104th Congress: Of Classes and Cannon Fodder," *Extension of Remarks/ Legislative Studies Newsletter,* January 1997, p. 14.

32. Richard E. Cohen, "Congressional Committee Custom Bites the Dust," *National Journal,* November 30, 1996, p. 2604.

33. For a more extensive discussion of positive and negative power, see Steven S. Smith, *The American Congress* (Boston: St. Martin's, 1999), 2nd ed., pp. 223ff.

34. Republicans substantially cut back the jurisdiction of the Commerce Committee, in part as a rebuke to Dingell's success in expanding it during his fourteen years as chair.

35. Quoted in Phil Duncan, ed., *Politics in America 1994* (Washington, DC: CQ Press, 1993), p. 802.

36. This account relies on Richard E. Cohen, *Washington at Work* (New York: Macmillan, 1992), and Gary C. Bryner, *Blue Skies, Green Politics* (Washington, DC: CQ Press, 1993).

37. Cohen, *Washington at Work,* pp. 43–44.

38. Quoted in Cohen, *Washington at Work,* p. 77.

39. Representative Tom Tauke (R-Iowa), quoted in Cohen, *Washington at Work,* p. 171; emphasis in original.

40. Quoted in Kirk Victor, "Mr. Smooth," *National Journal,* July 8, 1995, p. 1758.

41. Victor, "Mr. Smooth," p. 1759.

42. Kirk Victor, "How Bliley's Bell Was Rung," *National Journal,* July 22, 1995, p. 1892.

43. See Kenneth Shepsle and Barry Weingast, "The Institutional Foundations of Committee Power," *American Political Science Review* 81 (March 1987): pp. 85–104.

44. On conferences generally, see Lawrence Longley and Walter Olezsek, *Bicameral Politics* (New Haven, CT: Yale University Press, 1989).

45. Walter J. Oleszek, *Congressional Procedures and the Policy Process,* 5th ed. (Washington DC: CQ Press, 2002), p. 254.

46. Dan Carey, "Overhaul Comes Down to Issue of Broadcast Ownership," *Congressional Quarterly Weekly Report,* December 16, 1995, p. 3796.

47. Gebe Martinez, "Farm Bill Conference Forecast: Long and Stormy," *Congressional*

Quarterly Weekly Report, February 16, 2002, p. 469–476.

48. Gebe Martinez, "Provisions of the Farm Bill", *Congressional Quarterly Weekly Report,* June 1, 2002, pp. 1475–1484.

49. Evans and Oleszek, *Congress under Fire,* p. 157.

50. Karen Foerstal, "From Panel Ratios to Paychecks: Parties Tackle the Nuts and Bolts of Working Together on the Hill," *Congressional Quarterly Weekly Report,* November 28, 1998, p. 3218; Jim VandeHei, "Back to the Future: Hastert Tries to Return House to Michel Era," *Roll Call,* February 22, 1999.

51. Steven B. Smith, *The American Congress,* 2nd ed. (Boston: Houghton Mifflin, 1999), p. 235; emphasis in original.

Nine

THE INDIVIDUAL ENTERPRISE

I n September 1997, Dennis Moore was a defense attorney in the affluent Kansas City suburb of Lenexa. A month later he decided to run in
Kansas's Third Congressional District and hired his first campaign
staffer, a young fund-raiser. By early 1998, a campaign manager came on
board. The Moore enterprise grew steadily through the first half of the year,
with a scheduler and a field director in place by June. A professional press secretary followed in September, along with dozens of volunteers. During the
year, Moore also hired a polling firm, a Washington, DC, fund-raiser, media
consultants, a direct mail specialist, and an opposition research analyst. With a
million dollars in funding, plus significant Democratic Party and labor union
assistance, Moore created a substantial campaign organization that helped him
defeat incumbent Republican Vince Snowbarger in the November 1998 general
election.[1]

Moore's organizational tasks had just begun, however. In the basement of
his suburban home, his campaign morphed into the beginnings of a full-blown
congressional enterprise. He immediately hired a veteran administrative assistant, a loyal district director, and a young woman from the campaign who
would become his scheduler. By early January, when Moore moved into his
cramped, hidden three-room office suite in the fifth floor "attic" of the Cannon
House Office Building, he had almost an entire staff in place, including his former campaign manager, who had become his press secretary.

Back in the district, Moore opened three offices, with staffers doing casework, along with a few interns. Nor was the new congressman ignoring the
political side of his operation; his campaign continued to operate, raising
funds for what would surely be an expensive reelection campaign in 2000. The
Moore enterprise — reduced to a couple of aides in the days after his election
victory — numbered more than twenty individuals by January 15, 1999.

Two major elements made up the Moore enterprise. First were the personal office resources available to every member of the House, which included
at that time more than $1 million in salaries and benefits for Moore and his
staff, along with the ability to send franked mail and an allowance of more
than $150,000 for travel, telephones, computers, rent on district offices, and
other, miscellaneous expenses.[2] The campaign organization represented a sec-

ond distinct part of the enterprise; it would provide Moore with political expenses throughout his term of office, as well as raise funds for the 2000 campaign. More senior members often enjoy an additional source of resources for their enterprise — committee or leadership staffers. As a first-term member, Moore himself would not benefit, but many veteran legislators can take advantage of such assets.

Making Moore's — or any legislator's — enterprise all the more formidable was its overall flexibility. Even with strict adherence to the formal rules prohibiting campaign work on government time, staffers could fulfill their job obligations and perform political work. Campaign funds could cover a wide variety of political expenditures during the 1999–2000 period. Office staff could go off the payroll to work on the campaign. Two elements of the enterprise remained clear: Representative Moore was in charge, a chief executive officer so to speak, and the organization had one major "product" to push — Dennis Moore as U.S. representative, policymaker, service provider, and candidate for reelection, all in a district where he had won his initial election by a mere four percentage points. Moore's enterprise helped him win reelection, first in 2000 and again in 2002, despite his district's status as one of the two most Republican-leaning seats in the country held by a Democrat. His victory margins remained narrow (three percent), but the incumbent's enterprise provided him with a distinct edge.

THE LEGISLATOR AS ENTERPRISE

Nothing captures the fragmentation of congressional politics better or contributes to it more than the husbanding of resources in 535 separate congressional enterprises.[3] The enterprise notion is extremely useful in understanding the actions of individual legislators within the context of the Congress as a whole. To put it simply, House members and, even more so, senators must allow others to act for them; there is so much to do and so little time. Thus, staffers negotiate agreements, answer letters, feel out allies, return constituents' calls, and perform a thousand other tasks. On occasion, staffers may act on their own, but ordinarily their actions follow the dictates — however general — of their bosses, who historically have had the absolute power to hire and fire their congressional employees.[4]

The idea of an enterprise *purposefully* blurs the distinction between members of Congress and those who work on their behalf. In the end, the legislators will gain the accolades for the actions of the staffers, whose careers will rise or fall with their bosses' fortunes. Using this idea, we can examine a legislature filled with enterprises — a hallmark of the post-1960 Congress. As Robert Salisbury and Kenneth Shepsle conclude, "The result of the actions and interactions of one hundred senatorial enterprises . . . generates a quite different institution than the one of a century ago, or even a few decades ago, consisting of individual senators acting more or less alone."[5] If enterprises provide more structure to Senate individualism, they exert even more influence on the larger House, where 435 separate legislators have come to possess enough resources to insert themselves into policy making and constituency affairs in dozens of ways.

Since World War II, congressional resources have grown steadily and profoundly (Figure 9–1). Personal office and committee staff numbers have risen sharply, as have the number of special interest caucuses, the budgets of legislative support agencies,[6] and campaign expenditures. In short, senators and representatives control adequate resources to pursue multiple, individually defined goals, which range from winning reelection to influencing policy decisions to running for higher office.

Congressional enterprises for veteran legislators often become multimillion-dollar small businesses that must maintain themselves as they seek to promote their members' interests. Despite some variation, most enterprises look roughly like the one depicted in Figure 9–2. At the heart of the miniconglomerate is the

FIGURE 9–1
Growth in Congressional Staff, 1891-2000

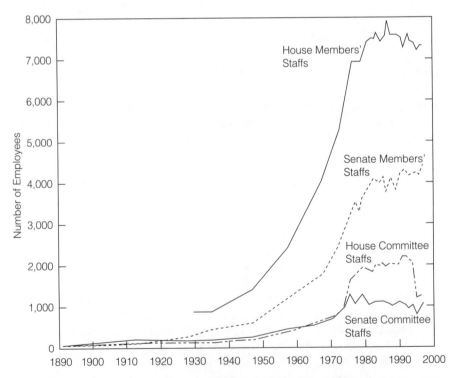

Source: Norman J. Ornstein, Thomas Mann, and Michael Malbin, eds., *Vital Statistics on Congress, 1997–1998* (Washington, DC: CQ Press, 1997).

FIGURE 9–2
The Congressional Enterprise

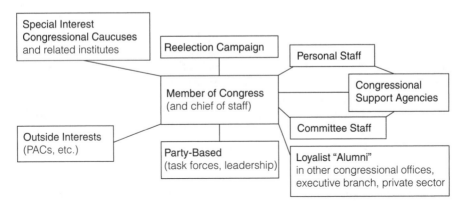

legislator, often in tandem with his or her top aide — usually the chief of staff. Around this essential nucleus each legislator builds a unique combination of contributing components. Although some senior members may construct their organizations from all the building blocks, most emphasize a few key elements, always including the personal office.

The Personal Office

Except for a handful of lawmakers such as top party leaders or committee chairs, the personal office lies at the heart of each legislator's congressional enterprise. In the House, even the most junior minority party representative is entitled to exactly the same personal office allowances as the most senior majority party member: up to eighteen staffers and an overall budget of approximately $1.5 million.[7] Thus, Representative Rahm Emanuel (D-Ill.), elected to his first term in 2002, can purchase the same basic personal office resources (staff, travel, communications, computers, etc.) as those purchased by his fellow member from Illinois, Speaker Dennis Hastert, who has served in the House since 1987. In the Senate, office budgets are determined by state population size; therefore, senators from large states typically have much larger enterprises than their colleagues from small states.

Although there is some variation in structure and work assignments, the cast of characters in most congressional offices is roughly the same. It includes a chief of staff responsible for overseeing the entire operation; several legislative aides, with one often designated as a legislative director; a personal secretary; an office manager; a press secretary; caseworkers (in Washington and in the home district); a top district aide; and other district staff. Senate offices are larger and more likely to encourage specialization, but the basic configuration is similar.

Variation also occurs in *what* legislators do with their office staff and other resources — and *where* they do it. Two major generalizations hold true here. First, there are some tasks that virtually all legislators must attend to: answering constituent mail, pursuing "cases" (often regarding bureaucratic snafus) that constituents bring to their attention, seeking new benefits and protecting existing ones for local interests, and maintaining at least minimal knowledge about major legislation under consideration. Much of this work reflects the service and allocation responsiveness that make up a good part of representation.

Beyond these essential tasks and routine office maintenance such as personnel and scheduling, the personal office can be constructed to serve the specific interests of a particular legislator. Thus, the second generalization: Members of Congress have tremendous discretion over how they use their basic resources. A marginal-seat congressman may establish several district offices to deliver the best possible constituency service; he may use substantial amounts of franked mail and send out the maximum number of newsletters each year, all the while making do with a couple of legislative assistants. Conversely, a member who considers herself relatively safe, having consistently won 65 percent of the vote in reelection contests, might hire six or seven legislative aides to assist in achieving her own policy goals.

An ambitious House member might well want to hire a top-notch press secretary in anticipation of running for a Senate seat, whereas a junior senator might hope to use a couple of legislative aides to research and write a bill to correct a modest but real policy snarl. All House offices receive almost identical resources,[8] but given the great differences among state populations, Senate operations vary considerably. (See Table 9–1.)

TABLE 9–1
Average 2000 Salaries for Staff Positions, House and Senate

Washington Positions	House	Senate*
Chief of Staff	$97,615	$116,573
Legislative Director	61,075	91,438
Press Secretary/Communications Director	45,301	65,362
Office Manager	44,009	57,330
Scheduler	41,068	44,273
Legislative Assistant	36,500	48,276
Systems Administrator	30,205	39,612
Legislative Correspondent	26,745	25,226
Staff Assistant	23,849	22,504
State/District Positions		
State/District Director	$62,152	$73,872
State/District Scheduler	34,143	34,205
Caseworker/Constituent Services Rep.	31,341	29,980
State/District Staff Assistant	24,959	24,454

*Senate figures are for 1999, most recent year with published comparable data.

Source: 1999 Senate Staff Employment and *2000 House Staff Employment* (Washington, DC: Congressional Management Foundation).

In 1995, the Congress placed itself under the Fair Labor Standards Act and adopted the Congressional Accountability Act, both of which imposed some modest limitations on staff hiring and working conditions. Overall, however, staff serve at the pleasure of the legislator and remain part of the overall enterprise.

In sum, the annual personal office resources can be used, within broad limits, to pursue legislators' individual goals. Offices tend to look roughly the same, but this is largely because of a general similarity in members' goals — to win reelection (and perhaps advance to higher office), to produce good public policy, and to exercise power within the Congress. Their considerable resources allow members a base from which to act effectively as individuals; in particular, they can establish strong constituency ties that make it very difficult for them to be effectively challenged for reelection. Given the resources that allow 535 legislators to play to their constituencies and to operate with such flexibility, the personal office contributes greatly to the centrifugal tendencies of the Congress. Along with the control of their individual votes in committee and on the floor, personal office resources represent a key source of individual power for any legislator. These resources can also be used to build coalitions and seek consensus; even the most isolated and iconoclastic members need cooperation from their legislative peers if they are to act effectively in passing legislation.

Committees and Subcommittees

There are strict limits on personal office resources, particularly on the numbers and salaries of staff. Whatever the member's goals might be, if a congressional enterprise is to grow it must lay claim to other assets. Since the 1970s, the Congress has been generous in complementing the resources available to all its members, especially for those in the majority party, who, by dint of their status, chair all committees and subcommittees. Holding a committee or subcommittee chair in the House or Senate gives members a separate but connected source of public visibility and exposure. Members can use these positions to advance policy goals through hearings and bill markups or they can use the investigative arm of committees to conduct oversight of the executive branch. Either way, members incorporate their committee power into their larger personal enterprise.

As Figure 9–1 illustrates, committee-based staff in the House tripled in the 1970s, and committee budgets grew even faster. If the committee system of the 1950s and early 1960s had remained intact, this change would simply have meant more resources under the control of a handful of powerful full-committee chairs. As noted in Chapter 8, however, subcommittees proliferated in the 1970s, and their chairs came to control substantial resources and power. Not only did total committee staff in the House grow from 461 to 1,600 between 1970 and 1990, but the subcommittee allocation of staff grew from 23.2 percent (107) of total committee staff in 1970 to 45.2 percent (723) twenty years later.[9]

In 1970, only one in four subcommittee chairs controlled their own staff, an average of four aides. By 1989, almost half the subcommittee chairs had such control, and the average staff size stood at ten. These figures understate the actual control of staff by subcommittee chairs in the pre-1995 era, however. Although various full-committee chairs may have formally controlled hiring, their subcommittee chairs often chose their own aides.

In short, many members of the majority party in the House greatly expanded their enterprises in the wake of subcommittee changes of the 1970s. Minority staffing on committees and subcommittees has not increased nearly as much as for the majority — a constant irritant for Republicans during the long period of Democratic control. Republicans long requested a third of all committee staff, only to be continually rebuffed.

In the 104th Congress, the majority Republicans moved immediately to bolster the power of full committees by placing the responsibility for hiring staff with committee chairs and by limiting to five the number of subcommittees permitted for most committees. In addition, committee staff numbers were cut by one-third, as Republicans made good on their promise to trim staffing levels (see Figure 9–1). Overall, the individual enterprises of many members — most notably Democrats and subcommittee chairs — were substantially reduced, while Republican committee chairs came to control a much greater proportion of available resources. In an admittedly extreme example, former Energy and Commerce Committee Chair Representative John Dingell (D-Mich.) was not able to keep Republicans from slashing his committee staff from almost one hundred aides to about twenty.[10]

On the Senate side, subcommittee staff numbers have not grown nearly as fast as in the House, nor are subcommittee aides as important to individual enterprises, given the much larger personal staffs that most senators command. In addition, about a third of majority party senators chair full committees and thus control their considerable resources. Even so, with the relatively small number of senators, committee staff play major roles in developing policies, and Senate staff are ordinarily much more aggressive in their efforts on behalf of their bosses.[11] Given senators' larger numbers of committee assignments and attendant responsibilities, it makes sense that staff members take on great responsibilities in the Senate. Indeed, many top Senate aides function as entrepreneurs who operate to further the influence of their own bosses.[12] Such reliance serves to extend the reach of individual senators, as they designate knowledgeable, skilled, and unelected staffers to act in their stead.

Enterprise and Influence: Two Illustrations

It is one thing to generalize that legislative enterprises allow representatives and senators to exert independent influence and quite another to demonstrate how such influence is exerted. Both Senator John McCain (R-Ariz.) and Representative Henry Waxman (D-Calif.) have proven themselves as masters at using their enterprises to affect policies beyond their obvious and immediate interests. McCain, of course, is a familiar figure from his 2000 presidential campaign and high-profile attempts to reform the campaign finance system. Waxman, too, is well known, but more so among the realm of congressional junkies and policy wonks. Still, his policy impact over the past thirty years may outweigh even that of the highly visible McCain.

JOHN MCCAIN: THE MODERN MAVERICK   After the 2000 presidential campaign and the 2002 passage of the McCain–Feingold campaign reform legislation, John McCain has become perhaps the best known U.S. senator. Such notoriety allows him to gain attention for his policy ideas; for his often quirky, nonpartisan critiques of American politics; and for his increasingly frequent attacks on pork barrel spending.

Despite representing a small state, McCain benefits from having a fair number of personal office staff members, which he supplements with those he receives as the chair of the Senate Commerce committee. Thus, when the space shuttle *Columbia* crashed, McCain could use his committee-based enterprise to hold hearings on the space program and address an important issue in a timely way. At the same time, his committee membership and subcommittee chairmanship on Armed Services give him a platform to address issues related to war on Iraq.

These committee and personal staff resources merely complement McCain's highly visible, media-friendly approach to politics and policy making, in which he depends on the press to air his criticisms and new ideas. In addition, McCain's enterprise has directly assisted a wide range of Republican candidates. In the 2001–2002 election cycle, McCain (who was not up for reelection) raised almost $4.8 million and spent almost $4.9 through his personal campaign committee. These funds, which dwarf his Senate resources, allowed him to travel, make contributions to other candidates, and appear at various candidates' fund-raisers. Moreover, his leadership PAC ("Straight Talk America") raised and spent $2.7 million, with expenditures going for such items as extensive air travel, thousands of dollars in cell phone charges, $18,000 of "promotional materials" from Bag It, a D.C. firm, and on and on.[13]

Aside from McCain's official Senate sources, which allowed him to employ dozens of staffers across his committees and personal office, his campaign and PAC receipts meant that he could raise and spend $7.5 million during two years that he was not running for office. To be sure, Senator McCain would receive a good deal of media attention simply of his charismatic style, but his D.C.-based enterprise has helped him extend his reach throughout the Republican Party and beyond on a systematic basis.

HENRY WAXMAN: POLITICS, POLICY, AND PERSISTENCE   For sixteen years (1979–1994), Representative Henry Waxman chaired a key House Energy and Commerce subcommittee, from which he had a platform to engage in extensive "policy entrepreneurship" activities on health and the environment. Waxman, who has long cultivated a highly expert and loyal staff, both in committee and in his personal office, developed a range of expertise across any number of health issues and helped rewrite the extension of clean air standards. Combining a powerful subcommittee chairmanship with substantial staff and his own energetic, persistent efforts to expand health and environmental coverage, Waxman personified the aggressive, tough-minded liberal who sought results rather than stardom. Not only did he involve himself in political campaigns, through his well-oiled, Hollywood-based organization, but he also fought his own committee chairman (John Dingell) in a lengthy battle over clean air standards (see Chapter 8).

As interesting and important as Waxman's activism was prior to 1994, it has become all the more important in the decade since Democrats lost their House majority. In particular, Waxman has proven how important a single member's enterprise can be in the years since 1997, when he became the ranking minority member on the Government Reform Committee. Ironically, Waxman benefited mightily from the committee's well-staffed and thorough investigation into Bill Clinton. Chairman Dan Burton (R-Ind.) bulked up his committee with dozens of new hires, and in the process Waxman obtained substantial new staff resources, given the two-to-one allocation ratio that the Republicans had agreed to. As ranking member, Waxman found himself with thirty to forty staffers whom he could direct as he chose. Both Burton and Waxman used their committee position to bolster their individual power.

Waxman did little to counter Burton's prosecution of Clinton; after all, the White House had plenty of resources to address his complaints. So he created a minority staff operation that could provide research to fellow House members (and potential challengers) as well as establishing a policy organization that could challenge both majority House Republicans and (later) President Bush over myriad issues. A visit to the Governmental Reform Committee's minority Web site (http://www.house.gov/reform/min/) is highly instructive. There, one finds investigations into Vice President Cheney's energy connections, an analysis of Enron's demise, research into tobacco regulation, and analyses of nursing home abuse. Of course, most committees, subcommittees, and even members have Web sites that address any number of issues, but the Government Reform site, in combination with Waxman's personal site, offers more than a glimpse into the workings of a legislator who has strived to change policies for more than a quarter of a century.

Special Interest Caucuses

Much as House members have taken advantage of expanding subcommittee resources, so too have they enlarged their enterprises by advancing to leadership positions in a host of special interest caucuses. By the mid-1980s, almost 150 such groups had formed, with House organizations outnumbering those in the Senate by a three-to-one margin (ninety-one in the House to thirty-one in the Senate; twenty-five more were bicameral groups).[14] For members, especially junior ones, caucuses have provided opportunities to participate in the policy-making process in various ways, from constituency service, as with the Auto Task Force, to building a policy-based coalition such as the Military Reform Caucus. Resources vary greatly across caucuses, but the strongest groups often command budgets into the hundreds of thousands of dollars and substantial numbers of staff. Some of these groups won House designation as officially sanctioned legislative service organizations (LSOs), which were granted office space and were allowed to receive financial support from members' accounts. Then in 1995, the Republican-controlled House denied funding and office space to the twenty-eight groups that qualified as LSOs.

Even as they lost their financial backing from the House, caucuses continued to prosper. Susan Webb Hammond, the foremost student of these groups, argues that caucuses are significant precisely because the Congress requires "centralization to build majorities from disparate points of view" as well as to reflect the decentralizing pressures of representation.[15] Caucuses play significant roles in both overcoming congressional fragmentation (as in building bridges between committees) and sometimes furthering decentralization, as they represent particular interests like the Mushroom Caucus, the High Altitude Caucus, and the Auto Task Force within the Congress.

On average, representatives belong to about sixteen caucuses, and senators, about fourteen, all in addition to their positions on committees and subcommittees, as well as within their parties. Why would busy legislators want to take on so many obligations?

First, joining most caucuses can be a cost-free task, often requiring little more than agreeing to place one's name on the membership roster; subsequently, a lawmaker can be as active as he or she wants to be. In fact, mere membership in a caucus does have its benefits. Former Representative Bill Richardson (D-N.M.) observed, "If someone writes me on an arts issue, I can write back and say, 'I'm a member of the Congressional Arts Caucus.'"[16]

Second, depending on the caucus, members can obtain different kinds of useful information. For example, *party-based* caucuses, such as the moderate-to-conservative Democratic "Blue Dogs," frame issues from their own perspective. *Personal interest* caucuses offer information on subjects that unite members with similar interests (e.g., the arts, environment). And various *constituency-based* caucuses provide members who represent given national (the Congressional Black Caucus), regional (the Sunbelt Council), state/district (the Suburban Caucus), and industry (the Textile Caucus) interests with organized means to share information and help set the legislative agenda.[17] (See Table 9–2.)

Third, junior members have often found opportunities for action within caucuses that committees or party structures would not have allowed for years. Although many caucuses provide no resources to their leaders, some well-established groups have staffs that complement their leader's regular enterprises. Groups such as the Congressional Black Caucus and its Hispanic counterpart host expensive fund-raising galas (at least $500 per seat) to support outside institutes that complement the inside groupings of members. The

TABLE 9-2
Caucus Establishment, 1959-1996 (By Type)

			Caucus Type				
Time Period	*Party*	*Personal Interest*	*National Constituency*	*Regional*	*State/District*	*Industry*	*Total*
1959–1970	2	1	0	1	0	0	4
1971–1976	5	6	2	5	1	1	20
1977–1980	1	5	3	5	9	15	38
1981–1986	6	25	0	7	10	16	64
1987–1990	2	17	0	7	8	16	50
1991–1996	7	21	1	9	21	17	76
Total	23	75	6	34	49	65	252

Source: Susan W. Hammond, *Congressional Caucuses in National Policy Making* (Baltimore: Johns Hopkins University Press, 1998), Table 3–2, p. 42. Reprinted with permission.

access to such resources makes these caucus leaders important forces within the House, all the more so as the numbers of African American and Hispanic members have grown sharply in the 1990s.

Finally, there can be some tangible benefits for holding a caucus leadership position, as individual donors and PACs seek out those with apparent influence on their specific issue. For example, in 1990 Representative Bud Schuster (R-Pa.), the cochair of the Congressional Truck Caucus, received more than $32,000 in PAC contributions from Ryder, the Teamsters Union, North American Van Lines, and other related groups.[18]

The policy, electoral, and power incentives to join and become active in caucuses are substantial for most legislators, even senators and senior House members. The costs of affiliation are often minimal, usually outweighed by the symbolic benefits of membership. For those who invest time and energy in caucus activity, the returns can be substantial in terms of campaign funds, access to the executive branch, and attention from party leaders.

An apt example of a powerful special interest caucus in both the House and the Senate is the bi-partisan Steel Caucus. Over a third of all senators belong to the Senate Steel Caucus, and 133 members belong to the House Steel Caucus; the members come from both parties and range from liberal to conservative in ideology.[19] The caucus unites these otherwise opposing members in the effort to advocate for policies that are favorable to the steel industry, and their membership in the caucus allows them to advertise their efforts to their constituents in steel producing regions. The power of this caucus derives from its bipartisan status and a membership that comes from a range of medium to large population states that are important in presidential elections (e.g., Pennsylvania and Ohio).

The caucus works closely with both manufacturers and employees in the steel industry. In recent years, this industry has faced renewed and strong economic competition from a greater number of countries that produce and export steel to the United States. In response to the influx of cheaper imported steel, the caucus mobilized its representatives and senators to exert more pressure on the administration. On March 4, 1999, Representative Peter Visclosky (D-Ind.), the vice chair of the House Steel Caucus, introduced the Steel Import Limitation Bill (H.R. 975) with 204 cosponsors. The bill directed "the President to impose quotas, tariff surcharges, or negotiate enforceable voluntary export restraint agreements in order to ensure that the volume of imported steel products . . . during any month does not exceed the average volume of imported steel for the 36 months period preceding July 1997."[20] It passed the Republican-controlled House, which is normally opposed to tariffs on imports, by a vote of 289–141 on March 17, 1999.

In the Senate, Senator Arlen Specter (R-Pa.) and Senator Jay Rockefeller (D-W.V.), the chair and vice chair respectively of the Senate Steel Caucus, introduced a companion measure to the House bill. The Senate took up the House bill on June 18, and Majority Leader Trent Lott immediately filed a cloture motion to thwart a possible filibuster of the bill by free trade advocates (though Lott himself expressed opposition to the bill). A cloture vote was held on the bill on June 22, and it failed by a vote of 42 to 57, with a pro-cloture vote equal to a vote in support of steel import quotas.

Despite the failure of supporters to pass the bill in the Senate, the Steel Caucus still sent a powerful message to President Clinton. In response to the 1999 congressional votes on the steel import quota bill, the Clinton administration subsequently agreed to impose tariffs worth about $410 million on imported steel from South Korea, Brazil, Germany, and Japan.[21] The Steel Caucus has continued to exert strong influence within Congress and the executive branch during the Bush presidency, and, in late 2001, members from the House and Senate caucuses called on the president to impose additional tariffs on imported steel. President Bush responded to their pressure and announced he was imposing 30 percent tariffs on imported steel in order to protect the U.S. steel industry, an action that ran contrary to his otherwise free trade position. The president's response was welcomed by members of the House and Senate Steel Caucus who had been vocal in calling for additional protection against imported steel.[22]

The Steel Caucus is just one illustration of the way that House and Senate members can join together across districts, states, and party lines to achieve policy and reelection goals that they might not otherwise achieve without being a member of the caucus.

Congressional Offices and Political Expenditures

On top of staff and office resources are piled hundreds of thousands of dollars of political expenditures, which the Congress has defined exceptionally broadly. For example, former representative and convicted felon Carroll Hubbard (D-Ky.) paid $3,000 in campaign funds for a portrait of his father. Although the exact political purpose of the painting remains unclear, the congressman enjoyed great freedom in defining political expenditures as he saw fit.[23] One intensive study of campaign financing identifies a wide range of so-called political expenditures that systematically contribute to the overall congressional enterprise of many, though not all, incumbents. These include:[24]

- ▶ A professional campaign staff
- ▶ Substantial entertainment budgets
- ▶ Travel expenses (such as auto leases)
- ▶ Political consultants
- ▶ Lawyers and accountants
- ▶ Civic and political donations
- ▶ A fund-raising apparatus (parties and direct mail)
- ▶ Investments such as certificates of deposit[24] and a building that housed former Representative Steve Neal's (D-N.C.) campaign organization
- ▶ Contributions to civic groups and establishment of college scholarships

With the continuing growth in fund-raising by safe incumbents, the campaign sides of their enterprises have amassed large political slush funds (à la McCain) that they can use to build their political careers at home, through gifts, entertainment, and scholarships, and in the capitol, through large contributions to other members' campaigns or to national party organizations. How far these limits extend was dramatically demonstrated in 2003, when former Representative Gary Condit (D-Calif.), whose career was cut short by an affair with a murdered D.C. intern, distributed most of his $200,000 in excess campaign funds to his two children.[25] He labeled them as consultants on a documentary film, but provided no clear records of any work. Of course, he was already out of office, but there was no formal prohibition on such a maneuver.

Although congressional rules formally require expenditures to have a direct political purpose, almost no enforcement has taken place. Indeed, when contemplating a run against an entrenched incumbent, a challenger not only faces the Herculean task of raising funds to match those of the sitting legislator, but also confronts an established enterprise that has often been constructed over years by substantial spending of both federal funds and privately raised political monies.

To be capable of making political expenditures, one must amass substantial campaign resources, and contemporary legislators have proven most adept at raising these funds. Although academics have debated the ultimate impact of incumbents' spending patterns, there is little debate over the rise in costs since the mid-1970s, when the Federal Election Commission was established and began to publish, and make widely available, accurate figures on receipts and expenditures. As we saw in Chapter 4, the average House candidate's political expenditures have risen from $54,000 in 1974 to $651,000 in 2002, a hefty increase even when taking inflation into account. During the same period, average Senate candidate expenditures have grown from $437,000 to $3,553,000. Crucial here is the fact that many of these funds were expended to perpetuate strong, continuing enterprises — organizations that allow incumbents maximum flexibility in pursuing their individual goals. In 2002, the average House incumbent raised $929,000 and the average sitting senator who sought reelection received $5.6 million.

Both the necessity of raising money (for competitive races) and the benefits of raising money (for relatively safe legislators who can distribute it to others) lead to the establishment of permanent, highly professional campaign finance operations for most sitting legislators. Fund-raising to provide for a large campaign establishment has become a constant preoccupation. Although it is theoretically and legally separate from a House or Senate member's office enterprise, the advantages that come with incumbency in building a personal enterprise directly affect his or her reelection chances.

Additional Enterprise Resources

Legislators' enterprises extend far beyond the structures of personal offices, committees, caucuses, and reelection operations. Many additional resources are available to all, and access to others resides formally or informally with key committee and party leaders.

CONGRESSIONAL SUPPORT AGENCIES   The most democratic resource on Capitol Hill is the Congressional Research Service (CRS), which responds to requests from all members in a reasonably equitable manner. In terms of providing basic information on a wide range of questions (from setting up an office to an economic analysis of the North American Free Trade Agreement), CRS is an invaluable source of timely insights. On more complex questions, which might require extensive staff time (from approximately 800 researchers), CRS is more likely to act quickly and comprehensively on requests from formal leaders within the committee or party hierarchy.

Likewise, the General Accounting Office (GAO) and the Congressional Budget Office (CBO) provide only modest assistance to legislative backbenchers, even though any member can request studies or information.[26] On the other hand, all members of Congress benefit from the independent information generated by these support agencies through reports and testimony. More than any other legislative body in the world, the Congress has sources of information and analysis that are intentionally separate from the executive branch and the federal bureaucracy. All members can use the volumes of information to help form their own policy positions, explain these positions and related votes to their constituents, and resist the entreaties of party leaders and presidents alike.[27]

LEADERSHIP RESOURCES   During the Democratic postreform era in the House (1981–1994) the joke went that any time one wanted to get the attention of a House Democrat and couldn't remember his name, all one had to do was call out "Mr. Chairman," and the legislator would respond; approximately half the 258 Democrats in the 103rd Congress chaired a committee or subcommittee, and almost all Democratic senators were chairs of some committee or subcommittee. Much the same could be said of the House Democratic leadership in recent Congresses. For example, in the 103rd Congress almost half the 256 House Democrats held some kind of formal party leadership position, including 92 who were considered part of the party's whip system. This inclusive leadership structure helped to define the postreform House, but relatively few resources accompany the vast majority of these positions. Only at the top of the ladder do leadership roles confer many resources, for either political party in either chamber.

For these few representatives and senators, though, the benefits are substantial. Serving as a majority or minority leader in the House or Senate typically adds twenty or so staffers to a leader's enterprise. In addition, the four chairs of the respective parties' House and Senate campaign committees enjoy large staffs and travel budgets as they raise funds, recruit candidates, and provide campaign assistance each election cycle. For those legislators who succeed at helping elect (and reelect) their colleagues, the rewards can be great. For example, after chairing the National Republican Senatorial Committee during its successful attempt to retake the Senate in 2002, Bill Frist (R-Tenn.) became a consensus candidate to succeed Trent Lott as majority leader in the wake of Lott's unacceptable statements on segregation. For Representative Tom Davis (R-Va.), the chair (1999–2002) of the Republican National Congressional Committee, his reward for increasing his party's House majority was to be named chair of the Government Reform Committee, which coincidentally (ironically?) addresses issues of campaign finance. In the contemporary Congress, helping the party achieve campaign success, especially in winning majority status, stands as a great help to one's career on Capitol Hill.

For the most part, party-based resources assist in centralizing the power of leaders, but this is not always the case. In 1993, House Democratic Whip David Bonior (D-Mich.) emerged as the leading critic of the North American Free Trade Agreement, a pact that Speaker Tom Foley and President Clinton strongly supported. Bonoir pledged not to use the resources of his office to oppose the treaty, but given the integrated nature of the congressional enterprise, it was difficult for him not to use — directly or indirectly — his party resources, as he fought the policy position of his legislative party and his president.[28] Likewise, Bonoir and Minority Leader Gephardt consistently worked at cross-purposes with President Clinton in subsequent trade battles, including the granting of permanent normalized trade relations to China in 2000.

THE CONGRESSIONAL ENTERPRISE: BLESSING AND CURSE

Of all the changes that have affected the U.S. Congress in the post–World War II era, none has been more striking than the expansion of the individual lawmaker's enterprise. From the moment new members take the oath of office, they each control $1.5 million worth of staff, communications, travel, and research capacities that allow them to commit substantial resources to reelection efforts, drafting legislation, overseeing the bureaucracy, or seeking higher office. Moreover, most of them will raise campaign funds that underwrite an almost limitless array of political purposes. The congressional enterprise helps all lawmakers to claim credit for governmental programs, to take positions on the issues of the day, and to relentlessly advertise their accomplishments. But this is just the minimum enterprise, the stripped-down model that every first-term member gets upon arriving on Capitol Hill (and obtaining the smallest, most distant office from the floor of the House or Senate).

Virtually all senators and many House members enjoy the services of committee staffers, many benefit from caucus positions, and increasing numbers create their own PACs to reward their fellow legislators and advance their own careers. At the heart of every congressional enterprise stands the individual senator or representative, to whom each of their respective staff members, campaign consultants, and fund-raisers owes his or her job. And their collective task is to promote the career and interests of their principal — the House member or senator. Party leaders and committee chairs regularly seek their support, but legislators know that they *can* defy their leaders and retain their seats. When it comes to reelection, party leaders and committee chairs enjoy no control over the average legislator's enterprise. All House members understand that, if reelected, they will retain the core personal staff of their enterprise, to say nothing of the other campaign, committee, and caucus resources they may have accumulated. In short, party leaders must negotiate with 435 representatives and 100 senators, who control their own electoral destinies and have enough resources to affect the policy process when they so desire. For all the decentralizing forces of subcommittees, committees, and incumbency, the heart of congressional fragmentation and individualism lies in the strength and flexibility of the legislator as enterprise.

That acknowledged, many legislators, especially in the House, have chosen more and more to operate as part of a party team. As the legislative process, again more so in the House, has become increasingly centralized and party-dominated, the individual entrepreneur, with his or her own enterprise, has become somewhat more marginalized. Within the House, at least, the highly partisan context of post-reform congressional politics has reduced the benefits — and increased the costs — of independent action.

CHAPTER BIBLIOGRAPHY

Caro, Robert. *The Path to Power.* New York: Knopf, 1982.

Hammond, Susan Webb. *Congressional Caucuses in National Policy Making.*

Baltimore: Johns Hopkins University Press, 1998.

Loomis, Burdett A. *The New American Politician.* New York: Basic Books, 1988.

NOTES

1. See Burdett A. Loomis, "Kansas's Third District: The 'Pros from Dover' Set Up Shop," in James A. Thurber, ed., *The Battle for Congress* (Washington: Brookings Institution Press, 2001), pp. 123–159.

2. For details on congressional offices, see various useful publications from the Congressional Management Foundation, including *Setting Course: A Congressional Management Guide*, various editions (Washington, DC: Congressional Management Foundation).

3. See Robert Salisbury and Kenneth Shepsle, "U.S. Congressman as Enterprise," *Legislative Studies Quarterly* 6 (November 1981): pp. 559–576, and Burdett A. Loomis, "The Congressional Office as a 'Small (?) Business,'" *Publius* 9 (Summer 1979); and Loomis, *The New American Politician* (New York: Basic Books, 1988).

4. An excellent example here is Eric Redman's description of his work on behalf of former Washington Senator Warren Magnuson, who gave Redman and other staff members broad latitude to formulate legislation encouraging doctors to serve in needy areas. See Redman, *The Dance of Legislation* (New York: Touchstone, 1974). In 1995, the Congress adopted the Congressional Accountability Act, which requires it to adhere to almost all federal laws, including those on conditions of employment. This may have some modest effect on the relations between legislators and their staffers, but the essentially personal and political nature of these ties remains.

5. Salisbury and Shepsle, "U.S. Congressman as Enterprise," p. 563.

6. These include the General Accounting Office, the Congressional Research Service, and the Congressional Budget Office.

7. This is an approximate figure, which includes all salaries, benefits, and other expenses. Travel allowances vary considerably depending on distance from Washington.

8. See *Setting Course: A Congressional Management Guide, 108th Congress Edition* (Washington, DC: Congressional Management Foundation, 2003).

9. Data from Steven S. Smith and Christopher J. Deering, *Committees in Congress,* 2nd ed. (Washington, DC: CQ Press, 1990), p. 152.

10. Allen Freedman, "A Survivor Steps into Minority Role," *Congressional Quarterly Weekly Report,* April 8, 1995, p. 989.

11. See Michael J. Malbin, *Unelected Representatives* (New York: Basic Books, 1980).

12. See David Price, "Professionals and 'Enterpreneurs': Staff Orientations and Policy Making on Three Senate Committees," *Journal of Politics* 33 (May 1971): pp. 316–336.

13. From <http:www.OpenSecrets.com>, accessed February 6, 2003.

14. Susan Webb Hammond, "Congressional Caucuses in the Policy Process," in Lawrence C. Dodd and Bruce L. Oppenheimer, eds., *Congress Reconsidered,* 4th ed. (Washington, DC: CQ Press, 1989), p. 355. See also Susan W. Hammond, *Congressional Caucuses in National Policy Making* (Baltimore: John Hopkins University Press, 1998).

15. Susan Webb Hammond, "Congressional Caucuses in the 104th Congress," in Lawrence J. Dodd and Bruce I. Oppenheimer, eds., *Congress Reconsidered,* 6th ed., (Washington, DC: CQ Press, 1997), p. 276. See also Hammond, *Congressional Caucuses in National Policy Making.*

16. Loomis, *The New American Politician,* p. 150.

17. Hammond, "Congressional Caucuses in the 104th Congress," pp. 278ff.

18. David Segal, "Caucus Crazy," *Washington Monthly* (May 1994): p. 23. Representative Schuster was the ranking Republican on the Public Works and Transportation Committee, which also made him a target for such contributions. Caucus positions can and do pull together various parts of a member's enterprise — in this instance his committee position and campaign. Schuster's leverage grew further when he became committee chair in the 1995–2000 period.

19. Floor Statement by Senator Arlen Specter (R-Pa.), Congressional Record, February 28, 2002, p. 51342.

20. Legislative language (see *Congressional Record,* March 17, 1999, H1349).

21. Joseph Kahn, "Clinton Imposes Tariffs on Steel Imports That Exceed Quota," *New York Times,* February 12, 2000, C2.

22. Chris Rugaber and Angela Swinson, "Congressional Steel Caucus, Industry, and Union Support Bush's Tariff Decision" *International Trade Reporter,* March 7, 2002.

23. Fritz and Morris, *Gold-Plated Politics,* pp. 29–30.

24. Investment income in the 1980s was often truly substantial in that bank CDs paid handsomely. With lower rates of return in the 1990s, some members have invested their excess cash in the stock market.

25. Michael Doyle, "Condit Paid His Children $210k from Political Fund," *Fresno Bee,* February 4, 2003.

26. Another support agency, the Office of Technology Assessment, was defunded and dismantled by the Republican-controlled 104th Congress.

27. At the same time, party and committee leaders can commission studies that will serve to support their own positions. Information can serve both centrifugal and centripetal purposes.

28. Majority Leader Richard Gephardt (D-Mo.) also opposed the pact but took a less publicly aggressive stance. He announced that any actions against NAFTA taken by him would emanate from his personal office, but again the relationships among various parts of the enterprise make such a commitment difficult to monitor.

Ten

THE COMPETITIVE CONGRESS: CENTRIFUGAL FORCES IN A PARTISAN ERA

THE OXYMORONIC CONGRESS: INDIVIDUALISTIC PARTISANSHIP

I n both the House and the Senate, the combining of individualism/ fragmentation with partisanship has made for a Congress that encourages — simultaneously — both centrifugal (decentralizing) and centripetal (centralizing) forces. In the House of Representatives, committees have regained some of the strength that they had surrendered to the Republican Party leadership in 1995, although party leaders retain much of their formal authority. In the Senate, party voting rates have hovered at almost 90 percent on votes that divide the parties, yet an individual senator, such as recently retired Jesse Helms (R-N.C.), can impose lengthy delays on key issues that a clear majority favors, as he did on the ratification of the chemical weapons treaty in 1996–1997. As the so-called postreform Congress of the 1981–1994 period gives way to a series of narrow Republican majorities (1995–2004), both House and Senate are undergoing searches for their own identities.[1] Do we have a Congress in which a majority party sets out a coherent agenda? Or do we have a new phase of governing where presidents emerge as dominant over their own party during unified government, but weakened in a time of divided government? Perhaps, the more things change, the more they remain the same, defined by the checks and balances that have dominated U.S. politics and congressional decision making since the founding.

The Limits of Partisan Policy Making

Whether a unique combination of circumstance and chutzpah or an indication of a sea change in congressional thinking, the House Republicans' capacity to develop a ten-item Contract with America, find near unanimous support for it, and then move all the items through the House in the first ninety-three days of the 104th Congress comprised a remarkable achievement. Despite modest success in winning Senate and/or presidential approval for Contract items, the Republicans demonstrated the potential for issue-based, even ideological, accomplishment by a unified congressional party.

But party unity and ideological zeal count for only so much in a political system that historically has encouraged fragmentation and delay. To be sure, homogeneous parties in the House and Senate have increased partisanship in both chambers, and legislators have been willing — on a conditional, contingent basis — to surrender some powers to their leaders. In the end, however, if elections continue to produce closely divided legislative bodies, homogeneous party memberships and strong leaders will be hard-pressed to overcome the pressures exerted by constituents and organized interests, the traditional sources of centrifugal politics.[2]

For most of the 1990s the Republican-controlled House stayed unified under the leadership of Speaker Newt Gingrich and Whip Tom DeLay. However, after President Clinton's reelection in 1996, the momentum and energy that sparked the Republican Contract with America and their electoral victory faded quite a bit. Then in the beginning of 1998, the Republicans in the House found a new rallying cause in President Clinton's personal scandal involving Monica Lewinsky. The members of the House in particular grabbed onto the charges of perjury launched against the president and marched forward with gusto toward an impeachment proceeding in late summer 1998. The Senate was much more circumspect and quieter on the subject, perhaps knowing that the hard work of deliberation (to convict or acquit) would come to the Senate only if the House voted affirmatively to impeach the president.

Subsequently, after the 2000 election, and reinforced by the 2002 GOP gains, President George W. Bush energized his fellow Republicans in Congress. Not only did Bush dominate defense/security policy in the wake of the September 2001 terrorist attacks, but he also sought to enact an aggressive set of domestic policies, from substantial further tax cuts to Medicare reform to redefining the relationship between church and state.

Across the board, strong partisanship has defined congressional politics in the Republican era. This has been true both under divided government and under unified GOP control of the presidency and Congress. Just as President Bill Clinton proved a lightning rod for often-heated Republican opposition in Congress, so too has President Bush with his tax-cut initiatives, especially in the 2003 legislation that reduced levies on stock dividends. Still, the partisan animosity toward Clinton far surpassed the congressional Democrats' more policy-oriented opposition to President Bush.

THE CONGRESS AND THE CLINTON IMPEACHMENT: OF PARTISANSHIP AND PRINCIPLE

Almost always in the House and often, if in more muted ways, in the Senate, party stood out as the core distinguishing characteristic between Clinton's accusers and his defenders during the 1998 impeachment proceedings. Not that *any* legislator defended the president's actions — especially his sexual relations with an intern, but also his subsequent perjury in a civil case. Rather, party came into play in terms of whether the president had committed an impeachable offense, and subsequently, in the Senate, of whether he was guilty, as charged, to the two impeachment articles.

Drawing heavily on Independent Counsel Kenneth Starr's investigation, his extensive record, and his recommendations, the House majority relied on a highly partisan Judiciary Committee to sort out the charges. Both Republicans and Democrats on the Judiciary Committee reflected the partisan extremes of their respective parties; there was little chance that they would reach some middle ground. Led by conservative (and historically fair-minded) Representative Henry Hyde (R-Ill.), the majority called no witnesses and expeditiously moved toward impeachment in the weeks following the 1998 election.

The partisan context of the impeachment decision was straightforward and reflected the fact that, on various measures, the Congress of the 1990s was highly partisan.[3] This context is well illustrated by a comparison of the House of Representatives in the 93rd Congress (1973–1974) and 104th Congress (1995–1996). The latter House demonstrates much greater ideological compactness than the earlier one (see Figure 10–1). That is, Republicans and Democrats were both more tightly bunched, and more distinct, in the mid-1990s than they were in the period of the Nixon impeachment.[4] Not only were the groupings more compact, fewer House members approached the ideological center of the moment. As political scientist Terry Sullivan concludes, "The middle ground . . . disappears by the 104th Congress. Very few members in either party can bridge the gap between the ideological centers of the two parties. . . . No one scratches anyone's back anymore. Rather, they reserve scratching for the eyes."[5]

As Sullivan implies, congressional partisanship is not just a construct of voting patterns. It also includes an element of hostility than extends both across the aisle within the Congress, especially in the House, and across the branches of government, as with the many Republican members who expressed extensive hostility toward President Clinton. In particular, the consideration of impeachment on the House floor in late 1998 brought out levels of uncivil behavior that exceeded even the breakdown in comity that occurred in the first session of the 104th Congress (1995). Communications scholar Kathleen Hall Jamieson observes that some elements of the House debate were handled with decorum and thoughtful exchanges, but in general the impeachment resolution generated low levels of cooperation and substantial increases in vulgarity and name-calling.[6] Party-based hostilities returned to the House floor, sometimes exceeding the rancor of the tumultuous first few months of 1995.

At the beginning of the House impeachment proceedings, Judiciary Committee chairman Hyde observed that the process would have to be bipartisan, or else it would fail. Yet as the weeks ran on, there was little in the committee's work that was not partisan. Each party in the House has grown more homogeneous, and the Judiciary Committee's composition exaggerated this trend. In

FIGURE 10-1
The Partisan Contest for Impeachment in the House, 93rd and 104th Congresses
(1973-1974 and 1995-1996)

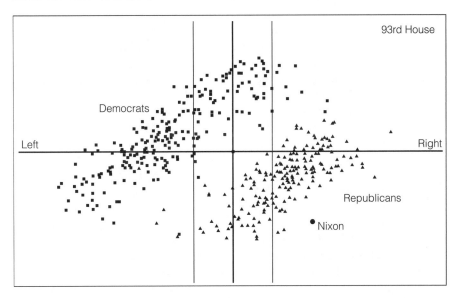

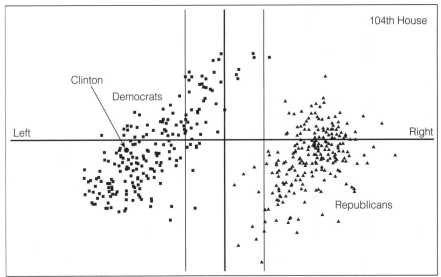

Source: Terry Sullivan, "Impeachment Practice in an Era of Lethal Conflict," *Congress and the Presidency* 25 (Autumn 1998), p. 126. Reprinted with permission.

fact, the committee included virtually no Republican moderates. Rather, its roster was dominated by social conservatives, almost half of whom won their seats in 1994 or 1996.[7] The Republicans who pushed for impeachment viewed political life and President Clinton through an ideological lens that skewed their vision. Without doubt, they could claim to act on principle; they certainly did not act with political acumen, given that opinion polls generally revealed that more than three Americans in five were against impeaching the president.[8] In the end, the Judiciary Committee failed to serve as a forum for any reasoned deliberation.

Nor would the partisanship and the absence of deliberation be any different on the House floor, where debate was limited and the two articles of impeachment (on one count of perjury and one of obstructing justice) were adopted on heavily party-line votes (228-206 and 221-212, respectively). Nevertheless, the House did reject two other articles, including one on abuse of power, which was soundly defeated. In the end, some Republicans broke ranks on these votes, but the key decisions were split along party lines, as only five Democrats voted for impeachment on the two articles that were adopted, while five and twelve Republicans, respectively, voted in opposition.

During all this time, members of the Senate watched and waited for the inevitable: The partisanship of the House debate guaranteed that one or more articles of impeachment would come to the Senate for trial. Most senators were publicly silent on the issue, and privately, many hoped they would not have to use the Senate's time for an impeachment trial that would not result in a conviction. There was simply never any indication that twelve Democratic senators would join all fifty-five Republicans to produce the 67 votes required to convict the president on either count. When faced with the trial, the Senate conducted itself in a manner far different from the House. As Senator Patrick Leahy (D-Vt.) put it, "You know, we didn't ask for this trial. We didn't ask for the President to conduct himself the way he did, and we didn't ask for the House to make a mishmash of this thing. But that's happened and now we have to preserve the Senate and give the country a sense of credibility."[9]

To their credit, most senators felt the need to restore some objectivity to the proceedings that governed their behavior. The Senate itself would be judged by its conduct. To determine the outline of the trial, the entire Senate met as one caucus in the Old Senate Chamber to discuss how the trial would proceed, including issues of witness testimony and the expected length of the proceedings. During this three-hour session, tensions ebbed and flowed, and at one point negotiations threatened to break down. Finally, and dramatically, two senators from different parties and opposite ends of the ideological spectrum, Phil Gramm (R-Tex.) and Edward Kennedy (D-Mass.) took steps to forge an agreement that would produce a brief but fair trial for the President.[10] In the end, some Republican senators even joined with all Democratic senators in voting to acquit the president on both counts. The Senate had proven that the proceedings could be simultaneously partisan and civil, while protecting the right of each senator to decide the merits of the case.

THE STRUGGLE TO GOVERN AND THE LIMITS OF PARTY

If, as John Aldrich and David Rohde contend, the "condition" of party (as measured by the size and unity of the majority, especially in the House) defines congressional politics,[11] why doesn't Congress function more efficiently under majority party control, and especially under a president of the same party? In part the answer is self-evident: That is, we do live in a system of checks and balances, where the president and the courts, to say nothing of the bureaucracy, have their say. Still, some of the limits on parties derive from the nature of congressional politics, both in permanent and transitory ways. Among the permanent limitations are the strength of individual lawmakers, both to win reelection and to use their substantial individual resources to affect the policy process.

In the post-1994 era, however, the greatest limitation on even well-disciplined legislative parties has been the small size of the majorities. The elections of 1994, 1996, 1998, and 2000 produced an average majority of 227 for the Republicans in the House, against 207 Democrats (and one Democrat-leaning Independent). A group of a dozen Republicans could threaten the majority's ability to move legislation. It's no wonder that the 1990s witnessed an *increase* in the number of special interest caucuses within the Congress, even as the Republican leadership sought to discourage their existence and limit their activities.[12] Moreover, even the election of 2002 only managed to give Republicans a 229 to 205 to 1 majority, returning them to their highest majority since the 1994 elections — in other words, it has been nearly a decade and the majority has not managed to greatly expand its numbers.

Two well-established trends indicate that a rough partisan balance is likely to remain for some time. First, the capacity of incumbent House members to win reelection remains one of the cornerstones of Congress in the modern era. After the relatively high turnovers of 1992 and 1994 (see Chapter 4), incumbent survival rates ranged from an average of 94 percent in 1996 to 98 percent in 2002. The price of entry to mount a competitive congressional campaign continues to rise, exceeding $1 million for the 2002 elections. Second, and directly related to the first trend, most House members come from districts that are relatively homogeneous and do not necessarily tend toward being competitive. The number of truly competitive House seats stood at fewer than fifty in 1996 and 1998, and in 2000 and 2002 the actual number may have been as low as twenty. One look at the geography of representation in the House demonstrates the implications of this development (see Figure 10–2).[13] Districts in much of the South, substantial parts of the Midwest, and much of the Mountain West are disproportionately represented by Republicans, often of a very conservative stripe. Conversely, Democrats clearly dominate in the East, on the West Coast, and in some other parts of the Midwest.

Ironically, the small number of competitive races — the remainder of the "vanishing marginals" (see Chapter 4) — has not meant that less money is spent on congressional campaigning. Rather, the national parties have focused their attention and funding on a relatively small number of hotly contested seats.[14] In

FIGURE 10-2
The Geographic Base of Partisanship

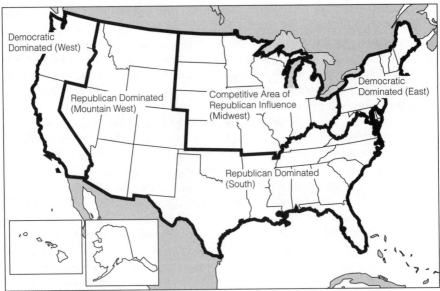

Source: Adapted from *National Journal,* March 29, 1999, p. 751

addition, both parties' congressional leaders in Congress have encouraged their colleagues to send excess campaign funds to the close races. In short, the campaigns for a small number of competitive House seats have become nationally important. Still, no matter how much the parties' congressional campaign committees spend on a handful of close races, a narrow House majority of either party will remain beholden to a myriad of internal factions.

In the Senate, a larger percentage of the seats are competitive, and there is more turnover than in the House, but the margins between the parties remain close. It is highly unlikely that either party in the Senate will win enough seats to hold the supermajority that is necessary to shut down a filibuster. The nature of the Senate is such that even if one party gained seats, each individual senator is a political entity all his or her own, whose power does not derive from the party. Given the structure of the Senate, even perfect party discipline is not sufficient to guarantee a party victory on the floor.

CONGRESS IN A REPUBLICAN ERA: NARROW MAJORITIES AND A GOP PRESIDENT

After the election of 1994, in which Republicans gained control of the Congress for the first time in fifty years, one could only guess at whether a "Republican Era" would occur and what it might look like. After five elections in which Republicans have prevailed in both houses, a new era of consistent, if narrow, Republican majorities has been established. Much of the previous nine chapters has laid out and assessed the postreform Congress, especially in its recent, Republican manifestation. What remains is to sharpen our description of patterns on Capitol Hill in the context of a single party controlling both the legislative and executive branches.

Generalization is no easy chore here. George Bush squeaked into office with the unprecedented Supreme Court decision of December 2000, and for five months he enjoyed slim Republican majorities in both houses of Congress. With the defection of moderate Senator James Jeffords (I-Vt.) in June 2001, Democrats assumed control of the Senate. Then came the 9/11 attacks and the 2002 elections that returned the Senate to Republican hands. This sequence of events means that characterizing the post-2000 Congress is difficult at best. We will examine two policy areas — education and the budget — that illustrate the complicated path that awaits any major legislation in the twenty-first century Congress.

The first example comes from the early months of the Bush administration and demonstrates the agenda-setting power of a recently elected president, even when his margin is extremely thin. Bush had campaigned hard on educational issues, including support for vouchers and increased accountability for K–12 schools. Candidate Bush had learned a few lessons from President Clinton about how to capture an issue that had been traditionally in the hands of the opposite party. When President Bush presented his set of priorities to the 107th Congress, Republicans could hardly challenge their newly elected president, and Democrats had a hard time mounting opposition to an expanded federal role in education.

Despite his agenda-setting advantages, the president discovered that he could not dominate the legislative process. Rather, both dissident Republicans and Democratic opponents found ways to reconfigure the original Bush initiatives. In fact, as he pushed for his preferences in the reauthorizing the Elementary and Secondary Education Act, President Bush found himself working with leaders from both parties, including such liberals as Massachusetts's Kennedy and Representative George Miller (D-Calif.). After both chambers passed separate versions of the education bill in the summer of 2001, a five-month conference took place (extended by 9/11 and its aftermath). Over the course of the debate on education, the Senate changed partisan hands, but the president's initial capacity to set the agenda meant that the reauthorization bill could include potentially far-reaching changes in the balance of power between the federal government and the states. President Bush won a mixed victory; although he and his congressional allies were able to require much higher levels of test-based accountability for K–12 students, they found little support for a broad voucher policy,[15] which was dropped early in the legislative process.

In December 2001, the House and Senate agreed to a K–12 package that promised $22 billion in federal aid as part of a deal that would require annual testing of all elementary students and demonstrated improvement in all schools. With a final vote of 87-10 in the Senate, the bill won overwhelming support, largely because of the bipartisan negotiation that had evolved during almost a year of negotiations.[16] Even if the Senate had not become Democratic in June 2001, the President would still have had to negotiate with key individual Democratic senators because of the ever present threat of a filibuster.

The second example of congressional policy making or, more accurately, the failure of Congress to legislate, is the fiscal year (FY) 2003 budget. The appropriations process has been contentious for the past two decades. The FY 2003 budget was scheduled to go into effect on October 1, 2002 (fiscal years run from October 1 through September 30), but as of January 2003 the Congress had passed only two of the thirteen appropriations bills that would fund governmental operations. Legislators gave up attempting to pass the final eleven bills, and wrote an "omnibus" spending package that grew from $380 billion to more than $397 billion in the weeks before its early February passage. In January 2003, the president won a considerable "victory" by gaining agreements (from the Republican leadership) to restrain spending roughly to levels that the White House had insisted on.[17] But when the final package passed, it had grown by $12 billion, with much of the new spending coming in "earmarked" projects that would benefit particular legislators' states and districts. And this occurred under the guidance of Republican majorities in both the House and Senate.

Such "pork-barrel" spending often constitutes the grease that is required for large spending bills. Representatives and senators all come from particular locales with particular needs; Republicans and Democrats alike take advantage of these packages, even as they decry spending excesses. As a spokesman for Senator Earnest Hollings (D-S.C.) put it, "He fights for the leanest budget possible, but once that budget is set he is unapologetic about getting South Carolina's share."[18] In short, regardless of the partisan context, the politics of distribution remains a powerful force on Capitol Hill. All politics may not be local, but a lot surely is, even in a partisan age.

At the same time, the Republican majority inserted a number of policy changes that seemed to be pork but that may well have more overall impact than a new technology center at Dartmouth or $450,000 for the Bronx Arts Council. Take, for example, the dilution of standards for certifying livestock as "organic." At the behest of a Georgia poultry producer, congressional Republicans inserted a provision that would allow the company to feed its chicken a mix of organic and conventional feed, while retaining the designation "organic" for its chickens.[19] On its face, this provision looked like typical local benefits that all representatives try to secure in appropriations bills. But the organic feed provision changed policy for farmers across the entire nation and was, in effect, much more a policy change than a localized benefit. The ability to put together an immense omnibus spending package provides endless opportunities for all members of Congress to legislate through the appropriations process. And it is the leaders of the majority party that gain the most from an omnibus appropriations bill because they can include local benefits for themselves, fulfill policy desires for powerful interest groups, and obtain the loyalty of their party members by providing benefits for a wide range of districts.

PROSPECTS FOR ONE-PARTY DOMINATION IN CONGRESS OVER THE LONG TERM

Even though parties have grown stronger inside the Congress and as forces within the electoral system, they will not be able to dominate congressional policy making unless one of them produces enough of a majority to survive the influences of small groupings of majority party members who have their own policy preferences. In the 106th and 107th Congresses, for example, moderate Republicans held disproportionate power — not because of their positions or persuasiveness — but due to their capacity to join with Democrats to thwart the leanings of most GOP members. In fact, the region-based homogeneity of the parties, which might conventionally be seen as strengthening them, may serve to reduce their capacity to act effectively in an era of narrow partisan margins. Even if leaders wanted to compromise and deliberate in good faith, their members' constituencies may make such reconciliation difficult, if not impossible. It remains to be seen whether the moderates can retain their influence in moderating the conservative wing of the party in the 108th Congress in light of President Bush's active (and successful) campaigning on behalf of Republican candidates in the 2002 elections. Now that the president again has a Republican majority in the House and Senate, both sides must learn how to relate to each other in the context of unified party government; as Majority Leader Tom DeLay noted, "We are trying to learn how to work with each other."[20] Just as the Democrats and President Clinton learned in 1993–1994, it is often easier said than done.

In the end, a Congress of strong, closely divided parties may be able to act only when they can produce large majorities, regardless of whether the government is formally divided. It may be up to the electorate to provide further direction to a highly partisan yet simultaneously atomistic Congress.[21] The tension between centralization and decentralization remains a defining element of this, our most representative branch.

As with the Congress circa 1900, the contemporary Congress, for all its centralization of power in the House, retains much of its fragmentation. The extreme individualism of the Senate remains the most notable example of the staying power of centrifugal forces on Capitol Hill. Beyond the Senate, however, the unity of House Republicans continues to be tested by divisions on tax cuts, budget deficits, and the appropriate amount of power that should be granted to the federal government in carrying out homeland security. Still, the GOP majority has held firm in pressing for tax cuts and ignoring concerns over increasing federal deficits.

The very nature of representation demands that tensions among individual legislators eat away at strong, centralized party (or presidential) leadership. In the end, presidents and legislative leaders can do little to affect the fates of the lawmakers they seek to lead. On occasion, as in 1995 (or 1964–1966), members provide the votes and cede the authority that makes for strong leadership. But party leaders and presidents rarely capture the Congress for long, as legislators return to Rhode Island, Kansas, or California to renew their personal contracts with the electorate. The very nature of representation — in Hannah Pitkin's words, "acting in the interest of the represented, in a manner responsive to them"[22] — means that the tensions between action and delay, between centralization and decentralization, will continue to define the nature of the contemporary Congress, even in a partisan age.

CHAPTER BIBLIOGRAPHY

Ornstein, Norman. *Lessons and Legacies: Farewell Addresses from the Senate*. Reading, Massachusetts: Addison-Wesley, 1997.

Rosenthal, Alan, Burdett Loomis, John Hibbing, and Karl Kurt.

Republic on Trial. Washington: CQ Press, 2002.

Weisberg, Hebert F., and Samuel C. Patterson, eds. *Great Theater: The American Congress in the 1990s*. New York: Cambridge, 1998.

NOTES

1. Norman J. Ornstein, Robert L. Peabody, and David W. Rohde, "The U.S. Senate: Toward the Twenty-First Century," in Lawrence C. Dodd and Bruce I. Oppenheimer, eds., *Congress Reconsidered*, 6th ed., pp. 390–413. (Washington, DC: CQ Press, 1997): p. 3.

2. See Lawrence C. Dodd and Bruce I. Oppenheimer, "Congress and the Emerging Order: Conditional Party Government or Constructive Partisanship?" in Dodd and Oppenheimer, *Congress Reconsidered*, 6th ed., pp. 390–413.

3. See, for example, the discussion by R. Lawrence Butler, "Conditional Party Government and Its Alternatives: Defining Party Power in the House" (paper presented at Midwest Political Science Association meeting, Chicago, April 15–17, 1999).

4. Terry Sullivan, "Impeachment Practice in the Era of Lethal Conflict," *Congress and the Presidency* 25 (Autumn 1998): pp. 117–129.

5. Ibid., p. 127.

6. Kathleen Hall Jamieson, "Civility in the House of Representatives: The 105th Congress," Annenberg Public Policy Center, University of Pennsylvania, March 1999.

7. Don Carney, "Hyde Staying above Clinton Fray but Tries to Raise Panel Profile," *Congressional Quarterly Weekly Report*, March 7, 1998, p. 564.

8. Alison Mitchell and James Dao, "Impeachment: The Overview; Polls Aside, GOP Stance on Impeachment Hardens," *New York Times*, December 14, 1998, p. A1.

9. Alison Mitchell, "The Trial of a President: The Overview; Senate, in Unanimity, Sets Rules for Trial; Witness Issue Put Off," *New York Times,* January 9, 1999, p. A1.

10. Ibid.

11. John H. Aldrich and David W. Rohde, "Measuring Conditional Party Government," (paper presented at Midwest Political Science Association meetings, April 23–25, 1998, Chicago).

12. Susan Webb Hammond, *Congressional Caucuses in National Policy-Making* (Washington: Brookings Institution, 1997).

13. John Maggs, "Divided We Stand," *National Journal,* March 20, 1999, pp. 748–751.

14. Eliza Newlin Carney, "Winner Take All," *National Journal,* March 20, 1999, pp. 734–740.

15. David Nather, "Broad Support Is Not Guarantee for Bush's Legislative Leadoff," *Congressional Quarterly Weekly Report,* January 27, 2001, pp. 221–223.

16. Adam Clymer and Lizette Alvarez, "Congress Reaches Compromise on Education Bill," *New York Times,* December 12, 2001, p. A1.

17. Joseph J. Schatz, GOP Reluctantly Aligns Spending Plans with White House," *CQ Weekly,* January 11, 2003, pp. 81–82.

18. Clymer and Alvarez, "Congress Reaches Compromise," *New York Times,* December 12, 2001, p. A1.

19. Marian Burros, "Late Addition to Spending Bill Would Dilute Organic Rules," *New York Times,* p. 22A.

20. Carl Hulse, "Congress and the President: One Party, but Divided," *New York Times,* February 23, 2003, p. A19.

21. For an insightful analysis by a veteran political analyst, see Michael Barone, "Life, Liberty, and Property," *National Journal,* February 15, 2003, pp. 502–510.

22. Hannah F. Pitkin, *The Concept of Representation* (Berkeley: University of California Press, 1967).

Useful Web Sites

www.opensecrets.org
    (Center for Responsive Politics)

http://congress.indiana.edu/
    (Center on Congress at Indiana University)

www.congressonlineproject.org
    (Congress Online Project)

www.dccc.org
    (Democratic Congressional Campaign Committee)

www.dscc.org
    (Democratic Senatorial Campaign Committee)

www.dirksencenter.org
    (Dirksen Center on Congress)

www.fec.gov
    (Federal Election Commission)

www.house.gov
    (House Committees)

www.loc.gov
    (Library of Congress)

www.ncec.org
    (National Committee for an Effective Congress)

www.nrcc.org
    (National Republican Congressional Committee)

www.nrsc.org
    (National Republican Senatorial Committee)

www.house.gov
    (U.S. House of Representatives)

www.senate.gov
    (U.S. Senate)

Index